MW00965778

SAP® CRM Middleware Optimization Guide

 PRESS

SAP PRESS is a joint initiative of SAP and Galileo Press. The know-how offered by SAP specialists combined with the expertise of the publishing house Galileo Press offers the reader expert books in the field. SAP PRESS features first-hand information and expert advice, and provides useful skills for professional decision-making.

SAP PRESS offers a variety of books on technical and business related topics for the SAP user. For further information, please visit our website: www.sap-press.com.

Thomas Schneider
SAP Performance Optimization Guide
4th edition, revised and expanded
2006, 522 pp., hardcover
ISBN 978-1-59229-069-7

Thomas Schröder
SAP BW Performance Optimization Guide
2006, 447 pp., hardcover
ISBN 978-1-59229-080-2

Thorsten Wewers, Tim Bolte
mySAP CRM Interaction Center
2006, 261 pp., hardcover
ISBN 978-1-59229-067-3

Föse, Hagemann, Will
SAP NetWeaver AS ABAP — System Administration
3rd edition, revised and expanded
2008, approx. 560 pp., hardcover
ISBN 978-1-59229-174-8

Juliane Bode, Stephan Golze, Thomas Schröder

SAP® CRM Middleware Optimization Guide

Galileo Press

Bonn • Boston

ISBN 978-1-59229-121-2

1st edition 2007

Editor Florian Zimniak
Copy Editor Nancy Etscovitz, UCG, Inc., Boston, MA
Cover Design Nadine Kohl
Layout Design Vera Brauner
Production Iris Warkus
Typesetting Typographie & Computer, Krefeld
Printed and bound in Germany

© 2007 by Galileo Press
SAP PRESS is an imprint of Galileo Press,
Boston, MA, USA
Bonn, Germany

All rights reserved. Neither this publication nor any part of it may be copied or reproduced in any form or by any means or translated into another language, without the prior consent of Galileo Press, Rheinwerkallee 4, 53227 Bonn, Germany.

Galileo Press makes no warranties or representations with respect to the content hereof and specifically disclaims any implied warranties of merchantability or fitness for any particular purpose. Galileo Press assumes no responsibility for any errors that may appear in this publication.

All of the screenshots and graphics reproduced in this book are subject to copyright © SAP AG, Dietmar-Hopp-Allee 16, 69190 Walldorf, Germany.

SAP, the SAP logo, mySAP, mySAP.com, mySAP Business Suite, SAP NetWeaver, SAP R/3, SAP R/2, SAP B2B, SAPtronic, SAPscript, SAP BW, SAP CRM, SAP EarlyWatch, SAP ArchiveLink, SAP GUI, SAP Business Workflow, SAP Business Engineer, SAP Business Navigator, SAP Business Framework, SAP Business Information Warehouse, SAP inter-enterprise solutions, SAP APO, AcceleratedSAP, InterSAP, SAPoffice, SAPfind, SAPfile, SAPtime, SAPmail, SAP-access, SAP-EDI, R/3 Retail, Accelerated HR, Accelerated HiTech, Accelerated Consumer Products, ABAP, ABAP/4, ALE/WEB, BAPI, Business Framework, BW Explorer, Enjoy-SAP, mySAP.com e-business platform, mySAP Enterprise Portals, RIVA, SAPPHIRE, TeamSAP, Webflow and SAP PRESS are registered or unregistered trademarks of SAP AG, Walldorf, Germany.

All other products mentioned in this book are registered or unregistered trademarks of their respective companies.

Contents at a Glance

1   A Journey Through CRM Middleware   25

2   Inbound Processing and Validation   37

3   Outbound Processing   89

4   BDoc Modeling and Storage 135

5   Groupware Integration 155

6   Exchanging Customer-Specific Data 169

7   Introduction to Performance Optimization . 187

8   Inbound Queues 197

9   Replication Model and R&R 235

10 Outbound Queues 269

11 XML in Optimization 297

12 Reorganization 307

13 Performing Optimized Mass Changes 317

14 A Look Ahead 359

A   SAP CRM Middleware at a Glance 369

B   Glossary 375

C   Transactions and Menu Paths 381

D   Coding Examples for Chapter 6 385

E   Analysis Roadmaps 393

F   Authors 399

Contents

Preface 13

Foreword 15

Introduction 17

Part I: Basic Principles of CRM Middleware

1   A Journey Through CRM Middleware 25

1.1   The Journey from R/3 to CRM 25

1.2   The Journey from CRM to R/3 28

1.3   The Journey from CRM to a Mobile Client 30

1.4   The Journey from a Mobile Client to CRM 33

2   Inbound Processing and Validation 37

2.1   BDoc 38

2.2   Flow 40

    2.2.1   Flow Contexts in Inbound Processing and
           Validation 41

    2.2.2   Displaying Flow Definitions 42

    2.2.3   Maintaining Flow Definitions 43

2.3   Inbound Queues 44

    2.3.1   qRFC 45

    2.3.2   QIN Scheduler 51

    2.3.3   The qRFC Monitor for Inbound Queues 56

    2.3.4   Naming Conventions for Inbound Queues 61

2.4   Inbound Adapters 63

    2.4.1   Adapter Framework 63

    2.4.2   Adapter Objects 64

    2.4.3   Mobile Inbound Adapter 73

2.5   Validation 79

2.6   Handling Errors When Processing BDoc Messages 82

    2.6.1   Error Handler 82

    2.6.2   Displaying and Processing Erroneous BDoc
           Messages 83

3   Outbound Processing 89

3.1   Replication Model 90

3.2   Messaging Flow 100

	3.2.1	CSA Queues	101
	3.2.2	Replication Service and Outbound Adapters	102
	3.2.3	Mobile Bridge	104
	3.2.4	Flow Contexts in the Messaging Flow	106
3.3		Synchronization Flow	107
	3.3.1	CDB Service	107
	3.3.2	R&R Service	108
	3.3.3	Mobile Outbound Adapter	122
	3.3.4	Rejection Messages	123
	3.3.5	Flow Contexts in the Synchronization Flow	123
3.4		Outbound Queues	124
	3.4.1	qRFC	125
	3.4.2	QOUT Scheduler	125
	3.4.3	The qRFC Monitor for Outbound Queues	128
	3.4.4	Naming Conventions for Outbound Queues	132

4 BDoc Modeling and Storage 135

4.1	Definition and Structure of BDocs	135
4.2	Data Storage for BDoc Messages	147

5 Groupware Integration 155

5.1	Server-Server Scenario in Groupware Integration	155
5.2	Analyzing Groupware Integration	164

6 Exchanging Customer-Specific Data 169

6.1		Customizations Required in SAP R/3 to Enable the Import of Custom Data	171
6.2		Customizations Required in SAP CRM to Enable the Import of Data from SAP R/3	172
	6.2.1	Creating a CRM Online Table 172	
	6.2.2	Creating the mBDoc Type	174
	6.2.3	Maintaining the Flow	179
	6.2.4	Mapping the BAPI Container into the mBDoc Structure	180
6.3		Loading Data from the R/3 System	183

Part II: Performance Optimization in SAP CRM Middleware

7 Introduction to Performance Optimization 187

8 Inbound Queues 197

8.1	The Number of Inbound Queues Is Too High	199
8.2	The Number of Inbound Queues Is Too Low	208
8.3	Hardware Bottlenecks	209
8.4	Performance Analysis for Processing Single Records	215
8.4.1	Logical Destinations	216
8.4.2	Message Flow Statistics	219
8.4.3	CRM Middleware Trace	228
8.5	Dependencies Between Inbound Queues	231

9 Replication Model and R&R 235

9.1	Basic Principles	236
9.2	Optimizing the Replication Model	239
9.3	Parallelizing the Queues	256
9.4	Optimizing the Access Path	259
9.5	Special Optimization Options in R&R	264
9.6	Mass Changes	265

10 Outbound Queues 269

10.1	System Optimization	274
10.1.1	Optimizing the Disk Subsystem	274
10.1.2	Index Rebuild	275
10.1.3	Buffering qRFC Tables	276
10.1.4	RFC Server Groups	277
10.2	Minimizing the Number of Outbound BDocs	277
10.2.1	Packaged Messages	278
10.2.2	AC Extract	281
10.2.3	Strategies for Using the AC Extract	284
10.2.4	Data Collector	295

11 XML in Optimization 297

11.1	Exchanging Data Between SAP R/3 and SAP CRM via XML	297
11.2	Data Exchange Between the CRM Server and a Mobile Client via XML	300

12 Reorganization 307

12.1	Reorganizing the Middleware	307
12.2	Avoiding Object Links	315

13 Performing Optimized Mass Changes 317

13.1 Optimal Parallelization of the Middleware 318
13.1.1 Key Considerations for the Data 320
13.1.2 Basic CRM System Considerations 324
13.1.3 Summary of the Different Considerations 325
13.2 Organizational Measures 326
13.2.1 Information and Training 327
13.2.2 Final Live Test 328
13.2.3 System Preparations 328
13.2.4 Monitoring 329
13.2.5 Mobile Scenario 329
13.3 System Monitoring and Analysis Roadmap 330
13.3.1 Analyzing the Work Process Occupancy 331
13.3.2 Analyzing the Queue Processing 334
13.3.3 R&R Optimization 337
13.3.4 CPU Bottleneck Analysis 342
13.3.5 BDoc Error Analysis 345
13.4 Immediate Actions When Things Really Go Wrong 347
13.4.1 A Performance Bottleneck Has Occurred
in the CRM 347
13.4.2 Performance Collapse During Inbound
Queue Processing 351
13.4.3 Performance Collapse During Outbound
Queue Processing – "ConnTrans Takes
Forever!" 353
13.4.4 The CommStation Occupies All Work
Processes 358

14 A Look Ahead 359

14.1 Improvements in R&R 359
14.1.1 Effects on the Parallelization Process
Caused by the New Framework 361
14.1.2 Processing Queue Entries in Blocks 362
14.2 BDoc Merge 364
14.3 Changes in the Administration Console 365
14.4 bgRFC 367

| **Appendix** | | .... | **369** |

A	SAP CRM Middleware at a Glance	....	369
	A.1	The Flow	....	369
	A.2	Inbound and Outbound Processing	....	370
	A.3	BDocs	....	371
	A.4	Adapters and Services	....	372
B	Glossary	....	375
C	Transactions and Menu Paths	....	381
D	Coding Examples for Chapter 6	....	385
	D.1	Extracting the Book Data from the R/3 System	....	385
	D.2	Mapping the Extracted Data to the BAPIMTCS Container in SAP R/3	....	388
	D.3	Mapping in SAP CRM	....	389
	D.4	Validating Received Book Data in SAP CRM	....	391
E	Analysis Roadmaps	....	393
	E.1	Checklist	....	393
	E.2	Analysis Roadmaps	....	394
F	Authors	....	399

| Index | .... | 401 |

Preface

SAP Customer Relationship Management (SAP CRM) is a comprehensive solution for effectively maintaining customer relationships, and covers all sales, marketing, and service channels. CRM Middleware enables CRM business processes to be seamlessly integrated with backend logistics processes. In these times of increasingly complex system landscapes containing both SAP and non-SAP components, optimized integration in end-to-end systems is taking on an ever-greater significance. Processes need to work across system boundaries, and data must be kept consistent between several systems.

Middleware is the core of the CRM system; all data streams flow through it and are controlled by it. Therefore, anyone who wants to operate his CRM system at optimized costs and at the highest performance also has to optimize the CRM Middleware.

This book does not only introduce you to the world of CRM Middleware, but also addresses its critical aspects, and provides you with tried-and-tested methods for optimizing your system. You will benefit from the authors' combined experience, which spans a wide range of system optimization services for a variety of customers, including services carried out for customers in the consumer goods and pharmaceutical industries as part of the SAP MaxAttention, SAP Safeguarding, and SAP Premium Support engagements. This firsthand knowledge and experience will enable you to reduce your total cost of ownership (TCO) and achieve a faster return on investment (ROI).

Walldorf, St. Leon-Rot, Germany, July 2007

Dr. Uwe Hommel
Executive Vice President
Active Global Support
SAP AG

Foreword

The idea for this book was first conceived at a meeting where we discussed why we kept encountering customers with difficulties operating their CRM systems. One of our colleagues claimed that it was because the concepts and detailed functions of CRM Middleware were difficult to understand. Another countered this by saying that Middleware was not rocket science. He went on to say that there were simply a few fundamental aspects that had to be taken into account in order for CRM to work smoothly, to which the first colleague replied: "Is there any source that clearly and comprehensively describes how Middleware works and what the central issues are when it comes to CRM optimization? Someone should write a book about that." No sooner said than done. Perhaps it was not as straightforward as that, but the seed for this book was planted then and there.

Some months have passed since that meeting, and "a few" hours have been spent turning this idea into a reality. Our thanks go first and foremost to our families for their understanding and support on all those occasions when we had to retire to our writing duties, or when yet another authors' meeting had to be held.

We would also like to thank our colleagues, who supported us in many different ways.

Particular thanks are due to Thomas Niemtschak for many productive discussions and ideas.

Dr. Barbara Kopff, Dr. Hella Kramer, and Kerstin Klemisch also deserve thanks for their advice and observations, and for being so giving with their free time. Thanks also go to Axel Semling, Dr. Alexander Pilz, and Gabriele Weyerhäuser for their support with the content of the book.

Lastly, we would like to thank Florian Zimniak at Galileo Press for his friendly and constructive collaboration.

Now, it only remains for us to wish you a pleasant read and every success with operating your SAP CRM system.

Juliane Bode   Stephan Golze   Thomas Schröder

Introduction

SAP's Customer Relationship Management application, SAP CRM, is the core of SAP's overall customer care concept. SAP CRM provides a range of CRM functions, such as a web shop (E-Selling) and mobile applications (Field Sales and Field Service), and exchanges data with other systems, such as an R/3 server or groupware server, on an ongoing basis. CRM Middleware is always used for this data exchange, both internal and external, and is therefore the heart of the SAP CRM system.

Just like a human heart, which pumps blood throughout the body and supplies it with oxygen and nutrients, CRM Middleware "pumps" data throughout the CRM system and supplies the individual components with the information they require. If, for whatever reason, the Middleware breaks down or is unavailable, this is just as dangerous for the CRM system as a heart attack is for the human body.

All data flows through and is processed by the Middleware. This applies to each individual change made to the CRM system itself and to changes that are propagated from the backend of the CRM system. If the Middleware is not working, no data can flow through the various CRM components and the system is then unavailable.

Annual adjustments to prices in the R/3 system and the transfer of data from non-SAP systems create large — in some cases, enormous — data quantities that CRM and, necessarily, the Middleware, have to process. With CRM 4.0, the product is now at a level that can handle these data volumes. However, in our past work in SAP's Active Global Support for the CRM area (and for our customers), we have repeatedly observed two phenomena. One is that you cannot run the SAP CRM system optimally and at minimal cost without having a thorough understanding of SAP CRM Middleware and how to monitor it. The other phenomonon is that when a CRM system fails after being successfully rolled out, this is almost always caused by mass changes in the backend.

In this dynamic and globalized world, changes — including those on a very large scale — are common practice in daily life. A restructuring of the field sales force, for example, can be easily planned and executed in R/3 and other ERP systems. However, the implementation of a CRM system and other satellite systems means that the data in question then has to be updated in those systems as well as in R/3.

A change that has been executed in R/3 after all the necessary discussion and planning may come as a complete surprise to the persons responsible for the CRM system. The result is that while the R/3 system was able to process the changes step by step, the unprepared CRM system is flooded with data, the system performance breaks down, and everything comes to a standstill.

This scenario is not a theoretical problem; it is a disaster that we in support see on a regular basis, with both small and large customers. It is also a disaster that is avoidable if the concept of SAP CRM Middleware, the heart of the CRM system, is clearly understood and the relevant parameters are properly set.

Structure of the book

Our experiences in this area motivated us to write this book, which we have divided into two main parts.

Part 1 comprises Chapters 1 through 6, and introduces you to the functionality of SAP CRM Middleware. This part is intended for all project managers, system administrators, consultants, and others who simply want to (or have to) understand how CRM Middleware works in Releases 4.0 and 5.0, and how to monitor it. It focuses on the concept, the design, and the basic structure of CRM Middleware. Part 1 doesn't deal with individual parameters or Customizing settings.

Part 1 starts with **Chapter 1**, which takes the reader on a "journey through CRM Middleware" and introduces the basic terms and concepts. **Chapter 2** looks at how data gets into the CRM system (inbound processing) and how, once it is there, it is checked for correctness. Chapter 3 deals with outbound processing, that is, all the steps required to send data from the CRM system to other systems, such as R/3 or a mobile client. In **Chapter 4**, we look at the central logical objects of middleware, known as BDocs. We show you what BDocs are, how they are designed, and how you can model them. In **Chapter 5**, in order to explain the process of data exchange with other systems, we provide you with an example of how the CRM system can be integrated with a groupware solution. Part 1 ends with **Chapter 6**, which illustrates the procedure for loading data from a non-SAP standard table in R/3 to CRM via an example.

Based on this thorough introduction to CRM Middleware, **Part 2**, which comprises Chapters 7 through 14, addresses what you can do to channel large data quantities through the middleware in an optimized way. On the basis of examples, we describe what measures you can take and what parameters can be modified, and how you can ensure that CRM Middleware processes the data as quickly as possible, without users being adversely affected by a loss of performance. This part also looks at what you can do and what emergency measures you can take when "the horse has already bolted" (i.e., when large data quantities have flowed into the CRM system from a backend system and the CRM system has come to a halt). Although the focus of this book is on optimizing the process of exchanging large data quantities, the measures proposed in this section will also help you to reduce the overall load on your system, as part of a program for optimizing the daily operation of your system.

Part 2 begins with **Chapter 7**, in which we introduce the term mass changes and describe why this kind of change can have serious effects on the overall performance of a CRM system. We also provide some initial insight into the individual parameters that are used in Part 2. In

Chapter 8, we give you tips on how to accelerate the processing of the inbound queue. These recommendations cover a wide range of issues, from optimizing the number of queues to the procedure used for a specific analysis. **Chapter 9** looks at how to optimize the distribution of data to mobile clients. It deals in detail with topics such as the replication model and optimizing replication and realignment. **Chapter 10** explains how you can optimize processing in the outbound queues. Central topics in this chapter include system optimization for high-performance processing, optimizing qRFC, and minimizing queue entries. In **Chapter 11**, we look at XML in a CRM environment. Topics included here are data exchange via XML between an R/3 system and a CRM system, and optimizing data exchange between a CRM server and a mobile client on CRM 4.0. **Chapter 12** describes the measures that are necessary to keep middleware performing at a consistently high level and that therefore need to be carried out on a regular basis. **Chapter 13** closely examines mass changes. Part 2 ends with **Chapter 14**, which provides an outlook on the latest developments and trends that pertain to middleware and performance.

There is also an **Appendix** at the end of the book, which provides you with a technical overview of middleware, a glossary of the main terms, a list of the important Middleware transactions, roadmaps for the procedures referred to in this book, and some code examples.

How to use this book

Although with a topic as complex as CRM Middleware, there must be connections between the individual chapters, we have nonetheless created each chapter as a self-contained unit that deals with one topic in its entirety and can be read in isolation from the other chapters. Where a subtopic of one chapter is the main topic of another chapter, a cross-reference to the main chapter is provided.

Limits of this book

This book deals specifically with how to optimize SAP CRM Middleware. While we do outline general optimization methods where they are relevant, such as hardware tuning, and optimizing and analyzing SQL accesses, a detailed description of these methods exceeds the scope of this book. If you want to know more about these issues,[1] please consult the existing literature and the specific tools and solutions of our hardware partners.

While this book does provide you with well-founded recommendations, its main focus is on explaining the analysis procedure and giving you an understanding of the connections and interactions involved. You should never implement optimization measures "blindly," in other words, without being familiar with the individual case and the specific intended use of your CRM system. Measures that help in one situation may have exactly the opposite effect in another. Also, recommendations that were previously valid can be superseded and thereby rendered obsolete. Therefore, if in doubt, we urge you to always consult other sources, such as the SAP Service Marketplace or the SAP Developer Network (http://sdn.sap.com), and to thoroughly

---

1 To make it easier for you to see how the topics dealt with in the individual chapters fit into the overall framework of CRM Middleware, we use the same diagram conventions as CRM Middleware throughout the book, albeit in a slightly altered form. We also highlight the areas of each diagram that are referred to in the text.

test every intended change to the system before implementing it in the live system.

You will notice various formatting conventions during your reading of this book. These conventions have the following meanings:

Character conventions

▶ We use "quotation marks" for all field values (except numbers) and for terms that are meant figuratively, such as "a journey through CRM Middleware."

▶ **Bold** type is used for menu paths and all other user interface elements. For example: "Click the **Site Attributes** button in the **Object Info:Site** area."

▶ UPPERCASE is used for transaction codes, tables, and field names, and names used in code modules, such as methods and function names.

▶ *Italic* type is used for important terms, file names, file paths, status information, and URLs.

▶ Notes are marked by a corresponding icon in the margin.   **[«]**

▶ Warnings are likewise marked by an icon in the margin.   **[!]**

▶ Examples appear on a shaded background

To make it easier for you to see how the topics dealt with in the individual chapters fit into the overall framework of CRM Middleware, we use the same diagram conventions as CRM Middleware throughout the book, albeit in a slightly altered form. We also highlight the areas of each diagram that are referred to in the text.

Part I
Basic Principles of
CRM Middleware

In this chapter, we track the journey of data through CRM Middleware. During the course of the journey, we will briefly explain the main stops along the way and introduce you to the relevant terms of CRM Middleware.

1   A Journey Through CRM Middleware

This chapter is divided into different sections. First, we look at the flow of data from R/3 to CRM, and then at the data flow in the reverse direction. Next, we track the progress of a data change as it travels from CRM to a mobile client. Lastly, we look at the direction that the data takes from the mobile client back to CRM.

1.1   The Journey from R/3 to CRM

Marcus, who works in the Accounting department at Cheap Inc., creates a new customer in R/3. Once he has entered all the required data, he saves his changes. The new customer is now available in R/3 under the customer number 1234. What Marcus doesn't notice is that at the same time the new customer data has started on a journey into the connected CRM system.

At the first stop on its journey, the customer data is stored in a *BAPI structure* and – still in R/3 – written to an *outbound queue*. The BAPI structure is a unified data structure that is independent of object type and release. After the data is written to the outbound queue, R/3 doesn't have to wait for the new customer to be further processed. There are different outbound queues for different object types in R/3, so that customers and materials, for example, are written to different queues. There can also be different outbound queues for different objects with the same type.

Outbound queue in R/3

Inbound queue in
CRM

The outbound queue in R/3 is automatically activated, and the queue entries are processed sequentially. The new customer 1234 is then transferred to the *inbound queue* in CRM. The purpose of the inbound queue in CRM is to collect the data that comes from R/3. Because the same queue is used for changes to the same object, multiple changes to the same object are always processed in the correct order. The inbound queue in CRM has the same name as the outbound queue in R/3.

R/3 inbound
adapter

The inbound queue in CRM is also automatically activated, and the queue entries are processed sequentially. The *R/3 inbound adapter* now takes over the processing of the new customer 1234. The job of the inbound adapter is to convert the data received by CRM to a uniform internal format. To do this, a *mapping function module* reads the customer data from the BAPI structure and converts it to an *mBDoc (messaging BDoc)*. An mBDoc is a data container that transports data within CRM. Both the mapping function module and the structure of the mBDoc, the *BDoc type*, are defined for each object type, so there is a special mapping function module and mBDoc type for customer data. The mBDoc type for customers – and thus for the new customer 1234 – is called BUPA_MAIN.

Saving the mBDoc

The mBDoc with the new customer 1234 is saved in the BDoc store in CRM. This enables Rodney, who is responsible for regularly monitoring the CRM Middleware at Cheap Inc., to identify and solve any errors at an early stage.

Data validation by
the CRM
application

Before the new customer 1234 is saved by the CRM application, the system first has to check whether the data meets the requirements of the CRM application. This check is done using a *validation service*, which is specified for every mBDoc type. The validation service does not contain its own checks; instead, it calls up the checks of the CRM application, which are also used for dialog users. In the case of customer 1234, the checks detect whether mandatory fields, such as last name and address, have been filled, for example. The same checks are run if a user creates a new customer in the CRM application.

Online database

If the checks don't detect any errors, the customer data is saved to the *online database* of the CRM application and is thereby made available to the CRM application.

If the checks do detect errors, customer 1234 is not saved to the online database; instead, the status of the saved mBDoc is changed to *BDoc validation error* and the error information is saved along with the mBDoc. BDoc validation errors are Rodney's responsibility. He checks several times a day whether these kinds of errors or other errors have occurred in the CRM Middleware, and if they have, ensures that they are solved quickly. Only once Rodney has solved any errors can the mBDoc with customer 1234 continue on its journey through CRM Middleware.

In this case, customer 1234 successfully passes the validation, and is assigned the same number in CRM as in R/3.

That part of customer 1234's journey, where the validation service is called and the customer is saved to the CRM application, is known as *validation*. Figure 1.1 depicts this process.

Validation

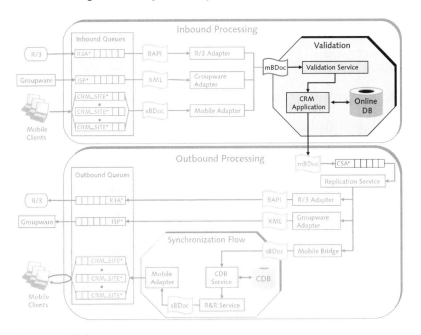

Figure 1.1 Validation

The part of customer 1234's journey from the inbound queue in CRM to validation is called *inbound processing* (see Figure 1.2).

Inbound processing

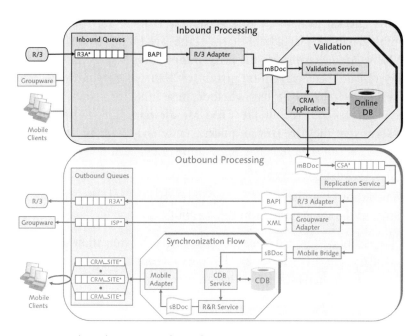

Figure 1.2 Inbound Processing of Data from R/3

1.2 The Journey from CRM to R/3

At Cheap Inc., customers are maintained in CRM as well as in R/3. This maintenance is one of the many tasks of Julie, who works in the company's call center. In a telephone conversation with the customer, Julie learns that customer 1234's address has changed. She makes the change in the CRM application and saves it. The changed address is then written to the CRM online database. At the same time, the changed data begins its journey to R/3.

Data validation by the CRM application

Data checks are also carried out for changes made directly in the CRM application. In this case, however, the data is checked not by a validation service, but directly in the dialog. Therefore, if Julie makes a mistake in entering the data, she immediately receives an error message and can correct the error there and then.

Saving the mBDoc

After the data validation, a new mBDoc is created that includes the change just made to customer 1234, and this mBDoc is saved in CRM.

Next, the change made to customer 1234 is written to a *CSA queue*, another inbound queue in CRM. The purpose of the CSA queue is to provide data in the CRM system to other systems. Using a second queue like this keeps the job of forwarding data to other systems separate from the processing of this data by the CRM system. This time, as before, there are different queues for different object types, and there can also be different queues for different objects with the same object type.

CSA queue

The CSA queue is processed sequentially. To process the change to customer 1234, a *replication service* is called that determines the systems to which the changed customer data is to be sent. Data changes can therefore be sent to, for example, an R/3 system, BW, and a non-SAP system. In our example, the data change is sent to the connected R/3 system.

Replication service

The *R/3 outbound adapter* is responsible for the further processing of the data change made to customer 1234. The task of this adapter is to convert the mBDoc data to a BAPI structure.

R/3 outbound adapter

In this next step, the change to customer 1234 is written to an *outbound queue* in CRM. As before, the task of the outbound queue is to collect data and to keep the processing in CRM separate from the further processing in R/3. The outbound queue is automatically activated, and the data is transferred sequentially to R/3.

Outbound queue in CRM

When the queue entry is processed, the address of customer 1234 in R/3 is changed to the new value. Julie's data change is now available to all R/3 users, such as Marcus in the Accounting department.

The part of customer 1234's journey from creating the new mBDoc to writing the data to the outbound queue is called *outbound processing*. Figure 1.3 depicts this process.

Outbound processing

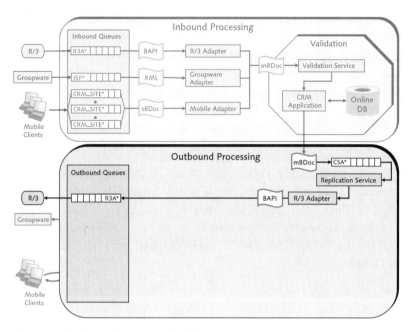

Figure 1.3 Outbound Processing for R/3

1.3 The Journey from CRM to a Mobile Client

Donna is a member of the external sales staff at Cheap Inc. and is responsible for customer 1234. As soon as this customer is changed on the CRM Server, the customer data automatically starts out on a journey from CRM to Donna's mobile client.

Mobile bridge Because Cheap Inc. uses the mobile client application, when the change to customer 1234 is processed in the CSA queue, a *mobile bridge* is automatically called after the R/3 outbound adapter (and any other outbound adapters).

The purpose of the mobile bridge is to convert the mBDoc containing the customer 1234 change to an *sBDoc (synchronization BDoc)*.

An sBDoc is a data container for the exchange of data between the CRM Server and mobile clients. An mBDoc can be converted to one or more sBDocs. Our customer is thus converted from an mBDoc with the BDoc type BUPA_MAIN to two different sBDocs: one with the BDoc type CAPGEN_OBJECT_WRITE, for the detailed customer data, and another with the BDoc type CUST_HIERARCHY, for an abbreviated form of the customer data that is used in the mobile client application for purposes such as search helps. The process of converting data from an mBDoc to one or more sBDocs is called *mapping*.

Like the mBDocs, sBDocs are saved in CRM, so that Rodney has access to information on the latest status, possible errors, and so on, for his monitoring tasks.

Saving sBDocs

First, the sBDocs with the new customer are further processed by the *CDB service (consolidated database service)*. This service saves the customer data to the CDB that contains all the data that can be sent to mobile clients. The data is not validated before it is saved to the CDB, as it is before it is saved to the online database, because the data has already been checked by the CRM application.

CDB service

After the CDB service, the *R&R service (replication and realignment service)* is the next stop on the journey for the customer 1234 change through CRM Middleware to the mobile client. The R&R service decides which mobile clients will receive the customer 1234 change.

R&R service

In many cases, the recipients have already been determined and now only have to be looked up in a *lookup table*. The process of determining recipients using existing entries in a lookup table is called *replication*.

However, in many cases, a field that is relevant to recipient determination will have changed, and consequently, the recipient determination has to be carried out again. This new recipient determination process is called *realignment*. The realignment process uses rules that are specified in the *administration console*. The set of rules in its entirety is called the *distribution model*.

The R&R service determines that Donna's mobile client is the sole recipient of the changes to customer 1234.

After the R&R service, the next stop for the changes to customer 1234 is the *mobile outbound adapter*. After the R&R service determines Donna's mobile client to be the sole recipient of this change, the mobile outbound adapter identifies the corresponding *outbound queue* and writes the changes to customer 1234 to that queue. Every mobile client has its own outbound queue on the CRM Server in

Mobile outbound adapter, outbound queue on the CRM Server

which all data for this mobile client is collected, regardless of object type.

Synchronization flow
The part of the journey from the saving of the sBDocs to the mobile outbound adapter is called *synchronization flow* (see Figure 1.4).

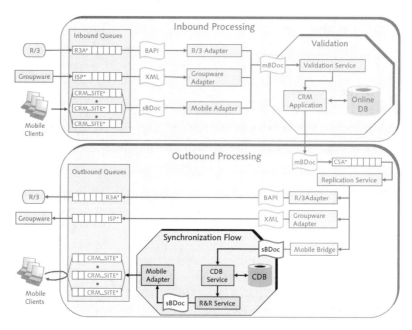

Figure 1.4 Synchronization Flow for Mobile Clients

ConnTrans, inbound queue of the mobile client
The changes to customer 1234 remain in Donna's outbound queue until she starts the *ConnTrans* application on her mobile client, and transfers the data to the *inbound queue* of the same name on her mobile client. After the transfer to the inbound queue of the mobile client has completed successfully, the change is deleted from the outbound queue of the CRM Server. When the inbound queue is processed, the customer 1234 change is written to the database of the mobile client and is then available to Donna in her mobile client application.

Outbound processing
The part of customer 1234's journey from creating the new mBDoc to writing the data to the outbound queue, is called *outbound processing*. Figure 1.5 depicts outbound processing.

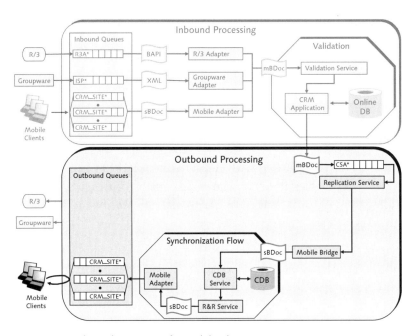

Figure 1.5 Outbound Processing for Mobile Clients

1.4 The Journey from a Mobile Client to CRM

At Cheap Inc., no new customers are created on the mobile clients, but it sometimes happens that a new contact is created in the mobile client application. During a visit to customer 1234, Donna creates a new contact with the name 1234-5 for this customer in her mobile client application. When this contact is saved, it is written to the database of the mobile client and is then made available to Donna in the mobile client application. At the same time, the new contact data starts its journey to CRM.

At the start of this journey, the new contact 1234-5 is written in an sBDoc to the *outbound queue* of Donna's mobile client. Each object type has its own sBDoc type; the sBDoc type for contacts is CONGEN_OBJECT_WRITE. The job of the outbound queue on the mobile client is to collect all data changes that are to be sent to the CRM Server.

Mobile client outbound queue

In the evening, Donna starts the ConnTrans application on her mobile client. The purpose of ConnTrans is to transfer the sBDocs from the outbound queue of the mobile client to the *inbound queue*

ConnTrans, inbound queue of the CRM Server

of the same name on the CRM Server. Only once the CRM Server has confirmed receipt of the sBDocs in its inbound queue are they deleted from the outbound queue on Donna's mobile client.

Mobile inbound adapter, saving the sBDoc

The inbound queue on the CRM Server is automatically activated and processed sequentially. The new contact 1234-5 is processed by the *mobile inbound adapter*. Like all inbound adapters, the purpose of this one is to convert data received from CRM to an mBDoc.

Prior to this, the sBDoc with the new contact 1234-5 is saved in CRM. This enables Rodney, who is responsible for regularly monitoring the CRM Middleware at Cheap Inc., to identify and solve any errors at an early stage.

The mobile inbound adapter, for its part, converts an sBDoc to an mBDoc using a *mapping method*. Every sBDoc type has its own mapping method. In the case of the new contact 1234-5, an sBDoc with the type CONGEN_OBJECT_WRITE is converted to an mBDoc with the type BUPA_MAIN. The mBDoc is *not* saved.

Data validation by the CRM application

Before the new contact 1234-5 is saved to the CRM online database, another check has to be carried out to verify whether the data meets the requirements of the CRM application. As before, the validation service for the BUPA_MAIN mBDoc type is used to check the new contact.

Online database

The new contact 1234-5 successfully passes the validation.

The data of the contact is saved to the CRM online database and is then made available in the CRM application (i.e., to Julie in the call center, for example).

If the validation had detected errors, contact 1234-5 would not be saved in the online database. In this case, because this contact was created on a mobile client and the mBDoc was therefore not saved, the status of the saved sBDoc and not the status of the mBDoc would be saved. The new status would then be *rejected (fully processed)*. BDocs with this status are not Rodney's responsibility (he is responsible for regularly monitoring the CRM Middleware), because no error has occurred on the CRM Server. While the data would not be correct, it was created on the mobile client and would therefore have to be corrected there too. This is why Donna would receive a rejection of the new contact on her mobile client and would have to solve the error in the mobile client application.

The part of contact 1234-5's journey, from the CRM application checking the mBDoc to the contact being saved to the CRM online database, is called *validation* (see Figure 1.1 earlier in this chapter).

Validation

The part of contact 1234-5's journey, from the inbound queue to saving the contact to the CRM online database, is called *inbound processing* (see Figure 1.6).

Inbound processing

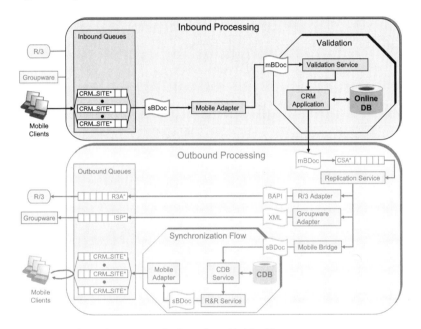

Figure 1.6 Inbound Processing for Data from Mobile Clients

This chapter provides a detailed description of the inbound processing of data that originates from other systems such as SAP R/3 or mobile clients. Here, the different processing stages are discussed and detailed information on the technical specifics of the involved components is provided.

2   Inbound Processing and Validation

Inbound processing represents the first major area of Middleware. At this stage, data that is received by the CRM system from other systems in various different formats is collected in *inbound queues* before it is converted by *inbound adapters* into a uniform data format. Then, the *validation* process checks data for correctness and saves it in the *online database* of the CRM application before it is forwarded to the next major area of SAP CRM Middleware: outbound processing. Figure 2.1 illustrates the process of inbound processing in SAP CRM Middleware.

Before we describe the individual stages of the inbound processing, we need to explain the terms *BDoc* and *flow* as these are basic concepts used throughout the entire SAP CRM Middleware.

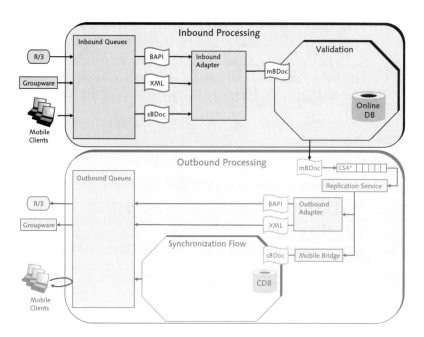

Figure 2.1 Inbound Processing in Middleware

2.1 BDoc

BDoc In Middleware, data is exchanged via *BDocs (Business Documents)*. A BDoc is a container that represents the smallest possible unit of business data that is needed to carry out a complete business process.

> **Examples**
>
> BUPA_MAIN is a BDoc for business partner data.
>
> BUPA_REL is a BDoc for business partner relationships.

BDoc class There are two different BDoc classes:

- ▶ **mBDoc**
  mBDocs (Messaging BDocs) are used for exchanging data within SAP CRM Middleware.

- ▶ **sBDoc**
  sBDocs (Synchronization BDocs) are used to exchange data between the CRM Server and mobile clients.

Examples

BUPA_MAIN is an mBDoc for the exchange of business partner data (e.g., between SAP R/3 and SAP CRM).

CAPGEN_OBJECT_WRITE is an sBDoc for exchanging business partner data between SAP CRM and mobile clients.

Figure 2.2 illustrates the use of mBDocs and sBDocs in SAP CRM Middleware.

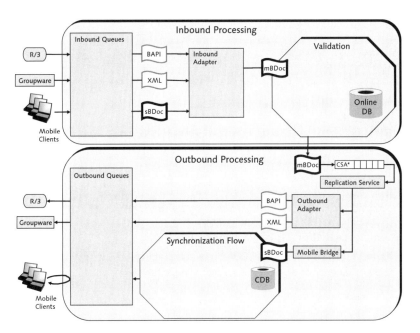

Figure 2.2 mBDocs and sBDocs in Middleware

The structure of a BDoc is referred to as the *BDoc type*. A *BDoc message* represents an instance of a BDoc type.

BDoc type and message

Examples

Strictly speaking, BUPA_MAIN is not a BDoc, but a BDoc type.

It is possible that several BDoc messages of the BDoc type BUPA_MAIN exist, for example, one BDoc message for creating business partner 12345, another BDoc message containing an update of business partner 12345, a third one for creating business partner 67890, and yet another BDoc message for deleting business partner 67890, and so on.

The term *BDoc instance* is used as a synonym for BDoc message. Chapter 4, *BDoc Modeling and Storage*, provides detailed information on the structure and modeling of BDocs.

2.2 Flow

Flow and service

The flow of data through SAP CRM Middleware is referred to as *flow*. The data itself is actually processed by services, each of which specializes in carrying out a certain task.

> **Examples**
>
> Data validation and the calling of outbound adapters are examples of services.

Flow context

A *flow context* represents the aggregation of different services at a certain stage within the Middleware. Services are defined per BDoc type and flow context.

> **Examples**
>
> The mBDoc validation is a flow context that involves calling a data validation service for the respective BDoc type.
>
> Another flow context is the sBDoc rejection, which includes calling a data rejection service and then a dispatcher service for calling outbound adapters.

A flow context is abbreviated via three characters:

1. The first character, **M** (messaging flow) or **S** (synchronization flow), indicates whether the flow context refers to mBDocs or sBDocs.

2. The second character, **I** (inbound) or **O** (outbound), indicates whether the flow context is processed in inbound or outbound processing.

3. The third character indicates the sequence in which the different flow contexts are executed. If this character is a number, it represents a standard SAP flow context, whereas a letter stands for a customer-specific flow context. By default, customer-specific flow contexts are always called after standard SAP flow contexts.

Examples

MIO signifies a flow context for mBDocs (M). This flow context is executed in inbound processing (I). It is the first flow context for mBDocs in inbound processing (0).

SO2 indicates a flow context for sBDocs (S). This flow context is executed in outbound processing (O). It is executed after flow context SO1 (2).

Figure 2.3 illustrates the use of flow contexts in SAP CRM Middleware.

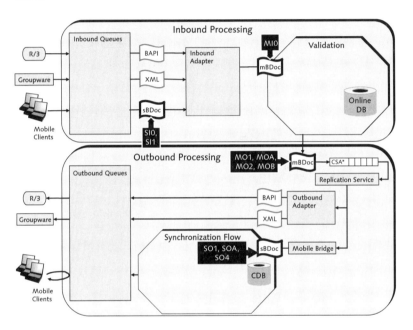

Figure 2.3 Flow Contexts in Middleware

2.2.1 Flow Contexts in Inbound Processing and Validation

Table 2.1 provides a list of flow contexts used in the inbound processing and validation processes for sBDoc messages.

Flow context	Description	Usage
SI0	sBDoc Validate	Is called by the mobile inbound adapter in order to transfer data to the CRM system. If the sBDoc type has been assigned an mBDoc type, the sBDoc message will be mapped to an mBDoc message; otherwise, outbound processing will be started immediately.
SI1	sBDoc Inbound (Before Validation)	Calls additional services prior to starting the mapping or outbound processing.

Table 2.1 Flow Contexts Used in the Inbound Processing and Validation for sBDoc Messages

Table 2.2 provides a list of flow contexts used in the inbound processing and validation for mBDoc messages.

Flow context	Description	Usage
MI0	mBDoc Validate	Is called by an inbound adapter in order to forward data to the CRM application. The BDoc is either accepted so that outbound processing can start, or the BDoc is rejected.

Table 2.2 Flow Contexts Used in the Inbound Processing and Validation for mBDoc Messages

2.2.2 Displaying Flow Definitions

Flow definition You can use Transaction SMO8FD or select **Architecture and Technology • Middleware • Message Flow • Display and Check Flow Definitions** from the SAP Easy Access menu in order to check which services have been defined for a specific BDoc type and for the different flow contexts (*flow definition*). Enter the desired BDoc type (or multiple BDoc types). Figure 2.4 shows the entry of BDoc type BUPA_MAIN as an example. After entering the BDoc type, click the **Execute** (F8) button, which is selected in Figure 2.4.

This will take you to the overview of services for the selected BDoc type. The services (names of function modules) for each flow context are displayed. Figure 2.5 shows the services for BDoc type BUPA_MAIN as an example.

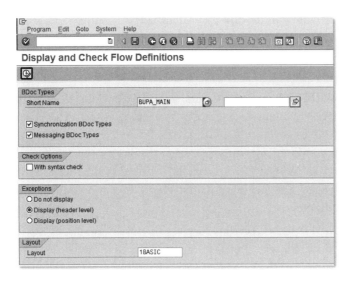

Figure 2.4 Selecting Flow Definitions for BDoc Type BUPA_MAIN

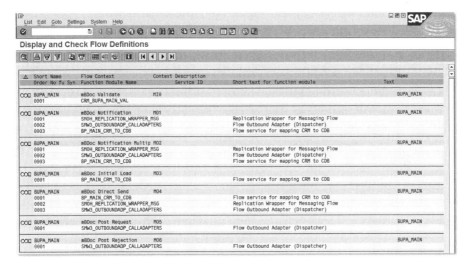

Figure 2.5 Services for BDoc Type BUPA_MAIN

2.2.3 Maintaining Flow Definitions

Flow definitions are stored in the following tables:

▸ Table SMW3BDOCIF contains interfaces between the CRM application and the Middleware. These interfaces represent a validation service, a service for mapping mBDoc messages to sBDoc messages, and a service for mapping sBDoc messages to mBDoc messages. If you want to display or maintain this table, call Transaction SMW3FDIF or select **Architecture and Technology · Middleware · Development · Message Flow · Define BDoc Type Specific Flow Attributes** from the SAP Easy Access menu.

▸ Table SMW3FDSTD contains standard flow definitions, which are specified per flow context and apply to all BDoc types. They can, however, be overridden by BDoc-specific entries. You should never make any changes to this table. To display the table, call Transaction SMW3FDSTD. Because the entries in this table must not be changed, the SAP Easy Access menu does not contain any corresponding entry.

▸ Table SMW3FDBDOC contains services that are defined per BDoc type and flow context. Entries contained in this table override possible entries for the same flow context in Table SMW3FDSTD. If you want to display or maintain this table, call Transaction SMW3FDBDOC or select **Architecture and Technology · Middleware · Development · Message Flow · Define BDoc TypeSpecific Flow** from the SAP Easy Access menu.

▸ Table SMW3FDCUST contains customer-specific services that are defined per BDoc type and flow context. Entries contained in this table override possible entries for the same flow context in Table SMW3FDSTD as well as possible entries for the same BDoc type and flow context in Table SMW3FDBDOC. To protect entries in the standard tables from being overridden, you can define services for specific flow contexts for additional calls. If you want to display or maintain Table SMW3FDCUST, call Transaction SMW3FDCUST or select **Architecture and Technology · Middleware · Development · Message Flow · Define Customer-Specific Flow** from the SAP Easy Access menu.

2.3   Inbound Queues

Inbound queues represent the first stop on the journey through inbound processing. Using inbound queues is helpful, because they enable you to separate the receipt of data from its further processing so that the sending system merely needs to write the data to the inbound queues and doesn't have to wait until the data is processed. Moreover, using inbound queues allows you to control the distribution of system resources, for instance, by defining the maximum number of queues that may be processed concurrently. Chapter 8, *Inbound Queues*, provides more details on this topic.

This section begins with the description of *qRFC*, which represents the basis for inbound queues. Then, it describes how the *QIN Scheduler* plans and starts the processing of data in the inbound queues. In addition, we'll introduce the *qRFC monitor for inbound queues* as well as name conventions that are used for inbound queues.

2.3.1 qRFC

In inbound processing, data is transferred from other systems (e.g., R/3 or mobile clients) to the CRM system via the qRFC (*queued Remote Function Call*) technology. The qRFC is an enhancement of a tRFC (*transactional Remote Function Call*). Both the qRFC and the tRFC, in turn, are based on the RFC (*Remote Function Call*). For this reason, we will describe the RFC before we explain the tRFC and the qRFC. Next, we'll illustrate how the qRFC is used in inbound processing.

A *remote function call* (RFC) is the call of a function module that runs   RFC
in a system that is external to the calling program. You can use RFCs to communicate between two SAP systems or between an SAP system and a non-SAP system. When two SAP systems communicate with each other, it is actually two ABAP programs that are doing the communicating; whereas the communication between an SAP and a non-SAP system is actually a dialogue between an ABAP program and a program that has been developed in a different programming language. Depending on the programming language used, different *RFC libraries* are available for that scenario:

1. *Java Connector* (JCo) for Java

2. *.NET Connector* for .NET

3. *RFC Software Development Kit* (SDK) for C and C++

> **Examples**
>
> For the purpose of exchanging data, the communication between SAP R/3 and SAP CRM is carried out via RFC. In this case, two ABAP programs communicate with each other (i.e., SAP CRM calls an RFC-enabled function module in SAP R/3 or vice versa).

To exchange data with mobile clients, the communication between SAP CRM and a connected communication station is also carried out via RFCs. Because this communication is really a dialogue between an ABAP program and a C program, the RFC Software Development Kit (SDK) is used in this case.

tRFC

tRFC (*transactional Remote Function Call*) enables you to execute RFC function modules, for example, to transfer data into another system, indirectly by first storing the function module call, including the associated parameters in database tables, and then running them asynchronously in a different work process.

This is quite useful, because it means that the receiver doesn't necessarily have to be available at the time the call is stored in the database tables. The function module can then be called once the receiver is available.

In addition, tRFCs ensure that each function module in the receiving system is executed exactly once, even if errors occur.

Process

The following steps are carried out during a tRFC:

1. The COMMIT statement, which is carried out in the calling application, writes the RFC function module that must be executed by the receiver, including status information and import parameters into the Tables ARFCSSTATE (tRFC status table of the sender) and ARFCSDATA (tRFC data table of the sender).

2. Along with the COMMIT statement in the calling application, the *scheduler* that plans the execution of the RFC function module is started asynchronously.

3. The scheduler calls function module ARFC_DEST_SHIP in the receiving system. In this context, the contents of Tables ARFCSSTATE and ARFCSDATA, which are included in this call, are used as parameters.

4. ARFC_DEST_SHIP first transfers the content of parameter ARFCSSTATE into Table ARFCRSTATE (tRFC status table of the receiver).

5. Then, ARFC_DEST_SHIP executes the function module.

6. Once the function module has been executed, the status of the execution is written to Table ARFCRSTATE of the receiver. In addition, ARFC_DEST_SHIP transfers the status of the execution (e.g.,

SUCCESS, SYSTEM FAILURE, or COMMUNICATION FAILURE) back to the sender.

7. If the sender receives the status *SUCCESS* or *SYSTEM FAILURE*, function module ARFC_DEST_CONFIRM is executed in an asynchronous RFC call. ARFC_DEST_CONFIRM deletes the corresponding entries from Table ARFCRSTATE of the receiver and then from Tables ARFCSSTATE and ARFCSDATA of the sender.

8. If the sender receives the status *COMMUNICATION FAILURE*, the function module has not been executed successfully on the side of the receiver. In this case, the tRFC call can be repeated at a later point in time.

In ABAP programs, the following call is used to execute a tRFC:

```
CALL FUNCTION ... IN BACKGROUND TASK
```

As mentioned in the above description of individual process steps, the following tables are used in tRFCs:

▶ Table ARFCSSTATE on the side of the sender contains the function modules to be called as well as the status of their execution. The keys used here are the so-called *TID* (*Transaction Identifier*), the receiver of the call, and a counter, which is used to summarize multiple tRFCs of the same LUW (*Logical Unit of Work*) under one TID.

▶ Table ARFCSDATA also on the side of the sender contains the import parameter data of these function modules. In addition to the key fields of Table ARFCSSTATE, this table uses a block number in the key. Thus, a 1-n relationship exists between Tables ARFCSSTATE and ARFCSDATA.

▶ Table ARFCSSTATE on the side of the receiver contains the function modules to be called as well as the status of their execution. The key is the same as the one used for Table ARFCSSTATE.

Although there's also an ARFCRDATA defined in the ABAP Dictionary, that table is not used by tRFCs. Figure 2.6 shows the different tRFC tables.

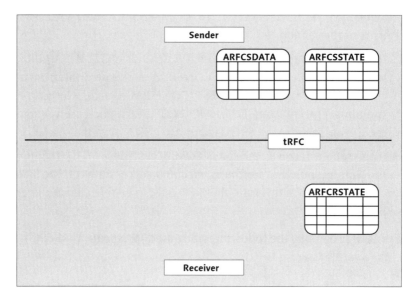

Figure 2.6 tRFC Tables

qRFC   qRFC (*queued Remote Function Call*) is an enhancement of tRFC, which enables you to execute LUWs in the receiving system sequentially. The order of processing is maintained even if errors occur.

A new LUW is always added to the end of the corresponding qRFC queue, and the first entry of a qRFC queue is always processed first. Some applications, such as those used on mobile clients, use a single queue for all data that is sent from a sender to a receiver. Other applications use multiple queues that can be processed concurrently.

> **Examples**
>
> Each mobile client has a separate inbound queue on the CRM Server. All data that is sent from the mobile client to the CRM system is written to that queue first. Consequently, the queue may contain changes to business partners as well as new sales orders, for example.
>
> Conversely, data that is transferred from the R/3 system to the CRM system is written to different queues, depending on the object. For example, changes to business partners are written to other queues than new sales orders.

qRFC uses *outbound queues* and *inbound queues*. When outbound queues are used, the LUWs in the sending system are first written to queues and then processed sequentially within each queue. Nevertheless, the receiver would immediately start processing the LUWs. However, if inbound queues are used as well, the LUWs (i.e., function module calls and associated data) are written to queues in the receiving system as well, where they are processed sequentially within each queue.

In ABAP programs, the syntax used to call tRFC and qRFC is the same. If you want to use qRFC inbound queues as well, you must additionally call one of the following function modules:

Additional function module call

```
TRFC_SET_QUEUE_NAME
TRFC_SET_QUEUE_NAME_LIST
```

Function module TRFC_SET_QUEUE_NAME defines a queue name only for the next qRFC call, while function module TRFC_SET_ QUEUE_NAME_LIST specifies a list of queue names for multiple subsequent qRFC calls.

Moreover, in order to use qRFC outbound queues, you must also call the following function module:

```
TRFC_SET_QUEUE_RECEIVER_LIST
```

In addition, you can use this function module to define multiple receivers that are supposed to execute the same function module.

Because qRFC is an enhancement of tRFC, the tables used in tRFCs are used in qRFCs as well. Apart from these tables, qRFC uses the following tables as well:

▶ Table TRFCQOUT on the side of the sender contains the outbound queues, that is, information about which entries are to be processed in which sequence in which outbound queue. The keys used here are the TID, the queue name, and a counter that specifies the sequence for processing the LUWs.

▶ Table QREFTID, which is also used on the side of the sender, represents the link between Tables TRFCQOUT and ARFCSDATA. Even if the same data is supposed to be sent to several receivers, it is stored only once in Table ARFCSDATA. Table QREFTID contains the mapping between the TID of Table TRFCQOUT and the TID used in Table ARFCSDATA.

▶ Table TRFCQIN on the side of the receiver contains the inbound queues, that is, information about which entries are to be processed in which sequence in which inbound queue. The key is the same as the one used for Table TRFCQOUT. The TID enables you to find the corresponding entries in Tables ARFCRSTATE and TRFCQDATA.

▶ Table TRFCQSTATE, which is also used on the side of the receiver, contains the status of inbound queue processing. The key is the same as the one used for Tables ARFCSSTATE and ARFCRSTATE.

▶ Table TRFCQDATA, also used on the side of the receiver, contains the data of the import parameters for the function modules called from within the inbound queues. The key is the same as the one used for Table ARFCSDATA. Table TRFCQDATA is required because tRFCs don't use Table ARFCRDATA due to the fact that they call function modules directly. Instead, Table TRFCQDATA is used for qRFC inbound queues.

Figure 2.7 shows the different qRFC tables.

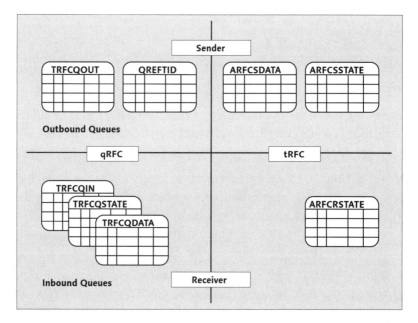

Figure 2.7 qRFC Tables

2.3.2 QIN Scheduler

The *QIN Scheduler* (*Inbound Scheduler*) plans and starts the processing of entries in the inbound queues. In addition to using the QIN Scheduler, each application can start the processing of entries in the inbound queues by using corresponding APIs (*Application Programming Interfaces*); however, QIN Scheduler was developed to avoid that.

QIN Scheduler

You can start the QIN Scheduler by calling Transaction SMQR or by selecting **Architecture and Technology • Middleware • Administration • Register / Deregister Queues** or alternatively **Architecture and Technology • Middleware • Monitoring • Queues • Register / Deregister Queues** from the SAP Easy Access menu.

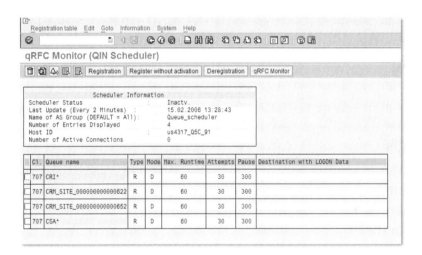

Figure 2.8 QIN Scheduler

Figure 2.8 shows the initial screen of QIN Scheduler. As you can see, all settings are based on queue names. Therefore, if you want to use new inbound queues, you must first register them and then set the respective parameters so that the entries in the new queues can be processed. When doing this, you can summarize multiple queue names by using the asterisk character (*), such as R3AD*.

Normally, the QIN Scheduler doesn't have to be working continuously because the inbound queues don't always contain entries that need processing. Therefore, the default status of the QIN Scheduler is *INACTIVE*, as shown in the example in Figure 2.9.

Status of the QIN Scheduler

Once an entry is written to an inbound queue, QIN Scheduler starts automatically, and its status changes to *STARTING*. When the QIN Scheduler is working, its status changes to *ACTIVE*. If QIN Scheduler waits for its next start, the status is *WAITING*.

Activating QIN Scheduler You can also activate QIN Scheduler manually. To do that, select **Edit • Activate Scheduler** from the QIN Scheduler menu.

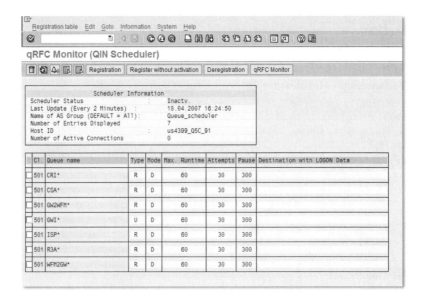

Figure 2.9 INACTIVE Status of QIN Scheduler

Registering an inbound queue To ensure that the entries of an inbound queue can be processed, the inbound queue must first be registered.

1. If the relevant queue name is already displayed in the QIN Scheduler, you must highlight it and click the **Registration** button. If the queue name is not yet displayed in the QIN Scheduler, then just click **Registration** without previously selecting a specific queue. Note that multiple queue names might have been summarized by using an asterisk (*) in the name. In that case, you may have to register a subset of the existing entry.

2. In both cases, the system displays the **Queue Registration** popup window. Enter the name of the queue to be registered — provided it doesn't display yet — as well as the corresponding parameters, as described below (see GWI* queues in Figure 2.10).

3. Then click the **Continue (Enter)** button in the popup window. This registers the inbound queue, which will then be displayed as a registered queue in QIN Scheduler (type **R**, see GWI* queues in Figure 2.11).

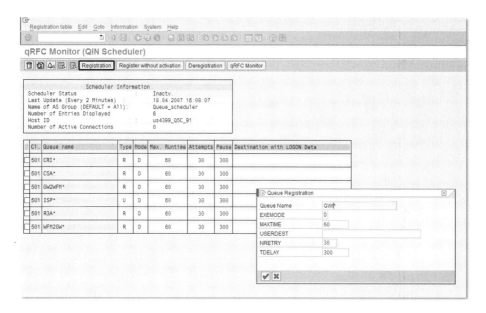

Figure 2.10 Queue Registration in QIN Scheduler

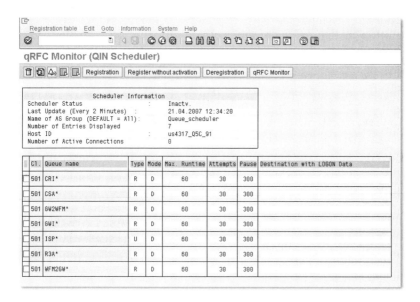

Figure 2.11 Registered Queues in QIN Scheduler

Whenever you use the **Registration** button, the registered queue is automatically activated at the same time. To avoid this, you can use the **Register without activation** button.

You can set the parameters listed below when registering a queue, as shown in Figure 2.10. Chapter 8, *Inbound Queues*, provides details on optimal parameter settings.

▶ EXEMODE determines whether the queue entries must be processed in a dialog or in the background.

▶ MAXTIME defines the maximum amount of time during which the scheduler processes entries of this queue before it starts processing entries of the next queue. You should not enter any value below the default value of 60 for this parameter. For larger queues that should have priority over others, you should enter a higher value.

▶ USERDEST specifies a logical destination that is used to process a queue (Transaction SM59 or **Architecture and Technology** • **System Administration** • **Administration** • **Network** • **RFC Destinations** in the SAP Easy Access menu). The logical destination must contain a relevant user, who will process the entries in this queue. If you don't enter a value for this parameter, you won't be able to determine exactly which user processes the queue entries; most often, this is the user who has written the entries to the queue.

▶ NRETRY defines the number of additional processing attempts if an error occurs, which allows for a renewed processing.

▶ TDELAY determines the delay time interval between individual processing attempts.

To prevent QIN Scheduler from processing the entries in an inbound queue automatically, you must deregister the queue. Even in deregistered queues, you can still start the processing the entries manually or by using the corresponding APIs. To deregister a queue, you must proceed as follows:

1. Highlight the name of the queue to be deregistered and click the **Deregistration** button. Note that multiple queue names may have been summarized by using an asterisk (*) in the name. In that case, you may have to deregister a subset of an existing entry.

2. The system then displays the **Queue Deregistration** popup window. Enter the name of the queue to be deregistered, provided it doesn't display yet (see GWI* queues in Figure 2.12).

3. Then click the **Continue (Enter)** button in the popup window. This deregisters the inbound queue, which will then be displayed as a deregistered queue in QIN Scheduler (type **U**, see GWI* queues in Figure 2.13).

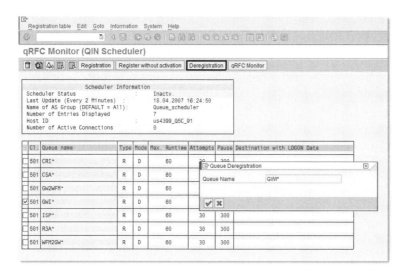

Figure 2.12 Queue Deregistration in QIN Scheduler

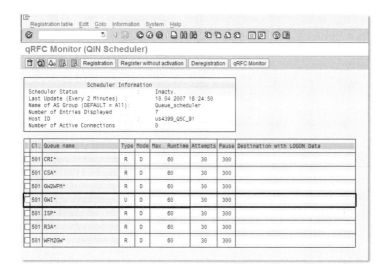

Figure 2.13 Deregistered GWI* Queues in QIN Scheduler

2.3.3 The qRFC Monitor for Inbound Queues

The *qRFC Monitor for Inbound Queues* enables you to view the status of inbound queues as well as the entries of individual inbound queues.

Displaying an overview of inbound queues

To access the qRFC monitor for inbound queues from within QIN Scheduler, you must click a queue name or select one or several queue names and click the **qRFC Monitor** button. Alternatively, you can start this monitor via Transaction SMQ2 or by selecting **Architecture and Technology · Middleware · Monitoring · Queues · Displays Inbound RFC Queues** from the SAP Easy Access menu. In the latter case, the system first displays a selection screen in which you must enter the queue name (or several queue names by using the asterisk character *****). Once you have entered the queue name, you can start the qRFC monitor for inbound queues by clicking the **Execute** button (F8, see Figure 2.14).

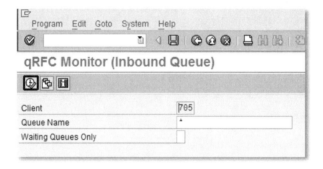

Figure 2.14 Selection Screen for Inbound Queues

The qRFC monitor for inbound queues initially displays an overview of all selected inbound queues, including the number of entries for each queue (see Figure 2.15).

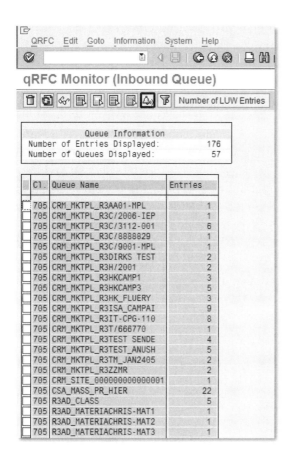

Figure 2.15 Overview of Inbound Queues

By clicking the **Change View** button, which is selected in Figure 2.15, you can open a detailed overview that contains the following additional information for each queue (see Figure 2.16):

▶ **Status**
Status of the queue

▶ **TID of First LUW**
TID of the first LUW in the queue

▶ **Date 1**
The date on which the oldest entry was written to the queue. This is the entry that is located at the beginning of the queue and will be processed first.

▶ **Time 1**
Time at which the oldest entry was written to the queue

▶ **Sender ID**
Logical destination of the system from which the data was sent

▶ **Wait for queue**
If the inbound queue is currently waiting for another queue to be processed, the name of that queue will be displayed here.

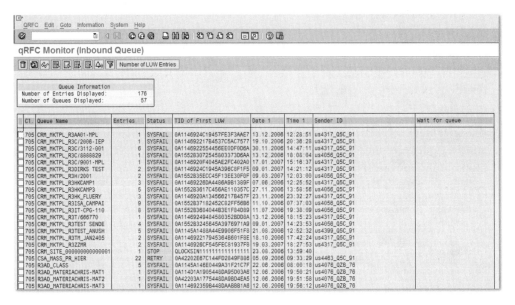

Figure 2.16 Detailed Overview of Inbound Queues

If you click the **Change View** button again, the system displays an overview of only those inbound queues from your selection, which are currently active (see Figure 2.17).

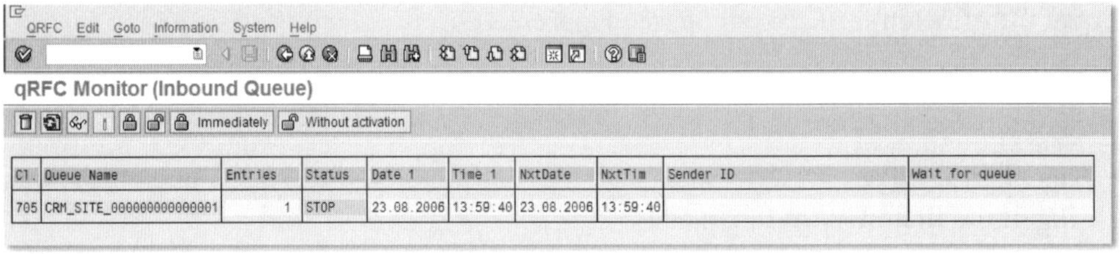

Figure 2.17 Overview of Active Inbound Queues

Status of an inbound queue   Inbound queues can have the following statuses:

▶ **READY**

The first queue entry is ready for processing.

▶ **RUNNING**

The first queue entry is currently being processed.

▶ **STOP**

The first queue entry is temporarily locked by the application.

▶ **WAITSTOP**

A dependency exists between the first queue entry and the first entry in another queue that is currently locked. The queue waits for the lock to be released.

▶ **WAITING**

A dependency exists between the first queue entry and an entry in another queue, which is not the first entry in that queue. The queue waits for the entry in the other queue to be processed.

▶ **SYSLOAD**

Currently, there is no free dialog work process to process the queue; the system will retry processing the queue.

▶ **CPICERR**

Network or communication error; the system will retry processing the queue.

▶ **ARETRY**

Temporary error; the system will retry processing the queue.

▶ **SYSFAIL**

Error; the system will not automatically retry to process the queue.

▶ **ANORETRY**

Severe error; the system will not automatically retry to process the queue.

▶ **NOEXEC**

The queue is waiting because the processing of the first queue entry is currently being debugged.

▶ **MODIFY**

The status of the first queue entry is currently being modified.

To display details for individual inbound queues, select the relevant queues in the overview and click **Display Selection**. Alternatively, you can double-click a queue name to navigate to the detail screen.

Displaying details for inbound queues

The detail screen displays the following information for the respective queues (see Figure 2.18):

▶ **Client, Queue Name, Entries**
Client, queue name and number of entries for each queue

▶ **Status**
Status of each queue

▶ **Date 1, Time 1**
The date and time when the first entry was written to the respective queue

▶ **NxtDate, NxtTim**
The date and time when the last entry was written to the respective queue

▶ **Sender ID**
ID of the sender that has written the entries to the respective queue

▶ **Wait for queue**
If the inbound queue is currently waiting for another queue to be processed, the name of that queue will be displayed here.

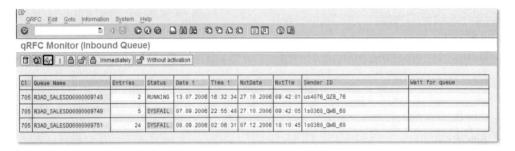

Figure 2.18 Detailed Display of Inbound Queues

Displaying entries of an inbound queue — If you want to view the individual entries of an inbound queue, select the relevant queue name in the detail screen and click the **Select** button, which is selected in Figure 2.18. Alternatively, you can also view the queue entries by double-clicking on the respective queue name. If an error occurred while the queue was being processed, a corresponding error message will display (see Figure 2.19). Double-click a field of an entry (e.g., **Function Module** or **Queue Name**) to obtain additional detailed information.

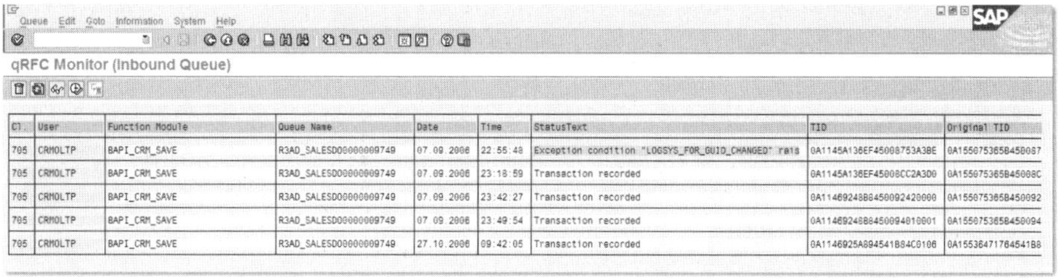

Figure 2.19 Displaying Entries of Inbound Queues

2.3.4 Naming Conventions for Inbound Queues

Usually, inbound queues for data from SAP R/3 have the same names in SAP CRM as the corresponding outbound queues in SAP R/3. Queue names for outbound queues in the R/3 system are defined in Table CRMQNAMES (in SAP R/3). Table 2.3 provides an overview of the naming conventions used for queue names for data from SAP R/3.

Queue Names for Data from SAP R/3

Type of Queue	Queue Name
Inbound queue for initial load from SAP R/3	R3AI_<OBJECT>*
Inbound queue for delta data transfer from SAP R/3	R3AD_<OBJECT>*
Inbound queue for requests from SAP R/3	R3AR_<OBJECT>*

Table 2.3 Queue Names for Data from SAP R/3

Chapter 8, *Inbound Queues*, contains detailed information about naming and parallelizing inbound queues for data from SAP R/3.

The naming convention for inbound queues for data from mobile clients is CRM_SITE*.

Queue names for data from mobile clients

You can find the exact queue name in the administration console (Transaction SMOEAC or by selecting **Architecture and Technology** • **Middleware** • **Administration** • **Administration Console** from the SAP Easy Access menu) by having the system display the site. The name of the inbound queue is listed under **Dependent Information** • **Queues** (see Figure 2.20).

The names of inbound queues for mobile clients are stored in Table SMOHQTAB.

Figure 2.21 shows a graphical overview of the names of inbound queues for data from different systems.

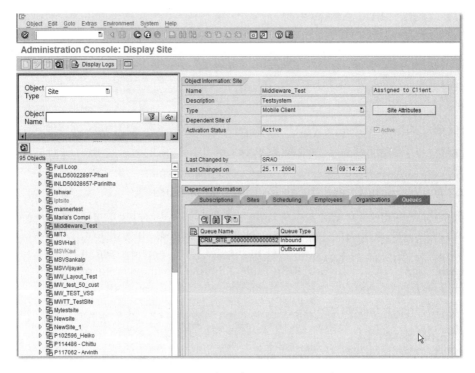

Figure 2.20 Queue Name in the Administration Console

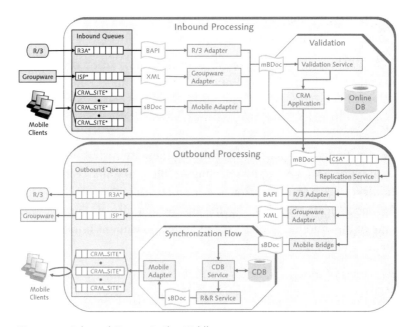

Figure 2.21 Inbound Queues in the Middleware

2.4 Inbound Adapters

Adapters are mappers between the different data formats used in the systems of a CRM system landscape. *Inbound adapters* are used in the inbound processing of SAP CRM.

Adapters and inbound adapters

2.4.1 Adapter Framework

The *adapter framework* is the foundation for data exchange in a CRM system landscape. It provides the basic functionality for the exchange of data between the following systems:

Adapter framework

- between SAP CRM and one or several SAP R/3 systems
- between SAP CRM and the CDB (consolidated database of mobile clients within SAP CRM)
- between SAP CRM and external systems

The adapter framework consists of the following components:

- **Initial Load**
  Transfers the entire dataset for specific objects (e.g., from SAP R/3 to SAP CRM). For this action, you can set filter criteria to transfer only those objects that meet these criteria.

- **Delta Data Transfer**
  Once the initial load has been completed, information regarding changes is permanently provided for specific objects (e.g., from SAP R/3 to SAP CRM). Here, you can set filter criteria as well.

- **Upload**
  Data from SAP CRM is made available to SAP R/3.

- **Synchronization**
  This component synchronizes the datasets of different systems. Again, you can set filter criteria to restrict the scope of data to be synchronized (e.g., by limiting it to a single sales order). You can use the synchronization component whenever a delta data transfer is not possible, or, for example, to cleanse inconsistent data.

2.4.2 Adapter Objects

Adapter objects are objects that are exchanged between source and target systems. The system distinguishes from among the following object types:

▶ Business objects for master and transaction data, such as business partners, materials, or sales orders

▶ Customizing objects for Customizing tables, such as transaction types, item categories, or activity types

▶ Condition objects for condition tables used for pricing

You can enter object-specific settings for each adapter object. To do that, you must use the following transactions:

▶ For business objects: Using Transaction R3AC1 or by selecting **Architecture and Technology · Middleware · Data Exchange · Object Management · Business Objects** from the SAP Easy Access menu.

▶ For customizing objects: Using Transaction R3AC3 or by selecting **Architecture and Technology · Middleware · Data Exchange · Object Management · Customizing Objects** from the SAP Easy Access menu.

▶ For condition objects: Using Transaction R3AC5 or by selecting **Architecture and Technology · Middleware · Data Exchange · Object Management · Condition Objects** from the SAP Easy Access menu.

Figure 2.22 shows the initial screen that displays when you call the above transactions. In this figure, we used business objects as an example. If you double-click an object or select the object and then click the **Details** button (see mouse pointer and object selection in Figure 2.22), the system displays the detail screen for the corresponding adapter object in which you can verify and change object-specific settings.

Each object is uniquely identified by the **Object Name** and **Subobject Name** fields. These fields are highlighted in the detail screen of adapter object BUPA_MAIN shown in Figure 2.23. Object names, subobject names, and the associated descriptions are stored in Table SMOFOBJECT.

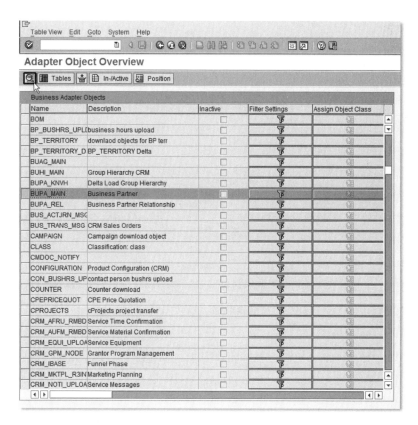

Figure 2.22 Overview of Business Objects

The **Linked BDoc** field displays the assignment of an object to a BDoc type. This assignment is a unique key that is generated and assigned in the BDoc Modeler. If you use the F4 help, the system displays the name of the BDoc type in addition to the GUID (see Figure 2.24). The purpose of linking an adapter object with the corresponding BDoc type is that the exchange of the adapter object occurs in data containers of that BDoc type. A BDoc that is linked with an adapter object is stored in Table SMOFOBJECT.

Assigning an adapter object to a BDoc type

> **Example**
>
> The exchange of data of adapter object BUPA_MAIN occurs in data containers of the BDoc type that has the same name.

The value displayed in the **Block Size** field indicates how many instances of an adapter object are selected and transferred commonly. This value is stored in Table SMOFOBJECT as well.

Block size

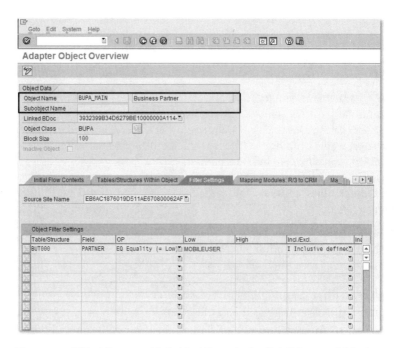

Figure 2.23 Object Name and Subobject Name in the Detail Screen of Adapter Object BUPA_MAIN

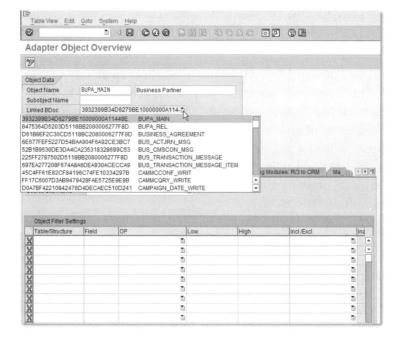

Figure 2.24 Names of BDoc Types for Adapter Objects

Example

If the block size set for adapter object BUPA_MAIN is 100, this means that 100 instances of this object are commonly selected and transferred.

In the case of a mass transfer of 1,340 business partners (adapter object BUPA_MAIN) from SAP R/3 to SAP CRM, this would mean that blocks of 100 business partners would be transferred 13 times, and a block of 40 business partners would be transferred once. In other words, the exchange would comprise 13 BDocs containing 100 business partners and one BDoc containing 40 business partners.

The **Object Class** controls the selection of the extractor module in SAP R/3. The extractor module for a specific object class is selected in Table CRMSUBTAB in the R/3 system. Alternatively, you can also store an extractor module directly with the adapter object in SAP CRM.

Object class

To change the assignment of the object class to an adapter object, you must click the **Assign Object Class** button (see Figure 2.25). This takes you to the **Assignment of object class for object** window in which you can directly assign an extractor module to the adapter object (see Figure 2.26). The object class for customizing objects is always CUSTOMIZING; the object class for condition objects is always CONDITIONS.

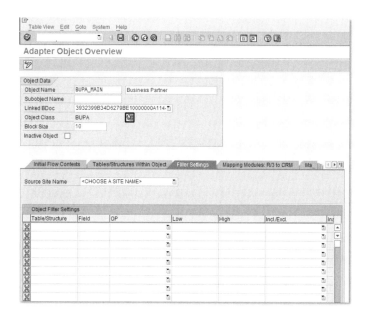

Figure 2.25 Assigning an Object Class to an Adapter Object

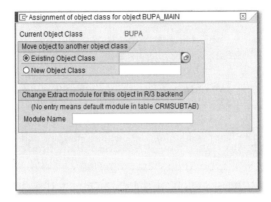

Figure 2.26 Assigning an Extractor Module to an Adapter Object

Object classes are stored in Table SMOFOBJCLA. The assignment of an adapter object to an object class is stored in Table SMOFOBJECT.

Activating and deactivating adapter objects

Only active objects can be exchanged via Middleware. You should therefore deactivate all objects that aren't needed. To do that, you must check the **Inactive Object** checkbox (see Figure 2.27). This value is stored in Table SMOFOBJECT.

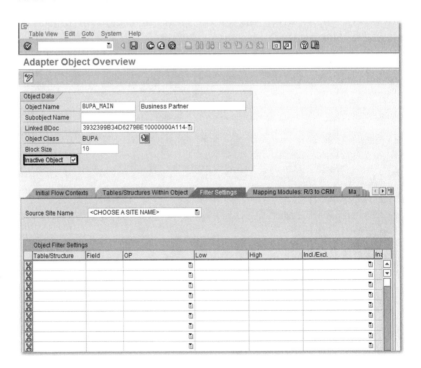

Figure 2.27 Deactivating an Adapter Object

Adapter objects are used to transfer data from other systems into the CRM system (*inbound adapter*) and to transfer data from the CRM system into other systems (*outbound adapter*). For this reason, you must specify for each adapter object the systems from and into which the data is to be transferred via this adapter object. To do this, you can make one or several entries.

Initial flow context

You can make these entries in the **Initial Flow Contexts** tab of the corresponding adapter objects. Once you have entered the **Source Site Type** and the **Target Site Type**, the system determines the consumer and flow context automatically. It selects the first flow context that is used for the transfer of data from the source site type to the target site type. The values are stored in Table SMOFINICON.

Examples

Adapter object CUSTOMER_MAIN is used for transferring customer data from SAP R/3 to SAP CRM. You can find the corresponding entry in the **Initial Flow Contexts** tab. The inbound processing in SAP CRM first processes flow context *MI0 – mBDoc Validate* (see Figure 2.28). This flow context is typically used for all adapter objects in order to transfer data from SAP R/3 to SAP CRM.

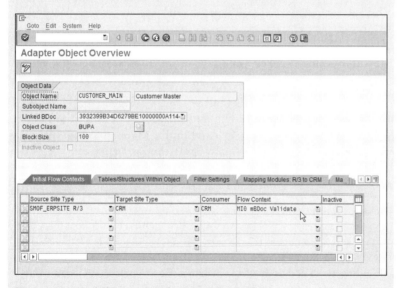

Figure 2.28 Initial Flow Context for CUSTOMER_MAIN

Adapter object BUPA_MAIN is used for transferring customer data from SAP CRM to various other systems such as SAP R/3, Groupware, or non-SAP systems. You can find a corresponding entry for each of these target systems in the **Initial Flow Contexts** tab. For the transfer of data to the R/3 system, for example, flow context *MO4 – mBDoc Direct Send* is executed (see Figure 2.29).

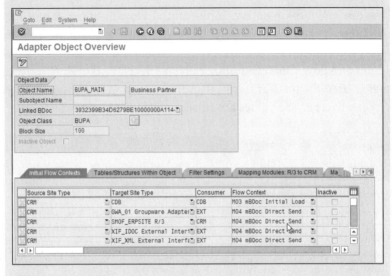

Figure 2.29 Initial Flow Context for BUPA_MAIN

Tables/structures for an adapter object

The **Table Name (Source Site)** field in the **Tables/Structures Within Object** tab contains a list of names of those tables, which are extracted by the adapter object in the source system. If a table in the source system can be uniquely mapped to a table in the target system, the name of that table is listed under **Mapped Table/Structure (Target Site)**. The data is stored in Table SMOFTABLES.

Examples

Adapter object CUSTOMER_MAIN is used to extract customer data from Tables KNA1, KNAS, KNBK, KNVA, KNVI, KNVK, KNVP, and KNVV in SAP R/3 and to transfer this data to SAP CRM. The **Table Name (Source Site)** field in the **Tables/Structures Within Object** tab contains a corresponding entry for each of these tables (see Figure 2.30). You cannot assign these tables uniquely to tables in the CRM system, which is why there are no entries under **Mapped Table/Structure (Target Site)**.

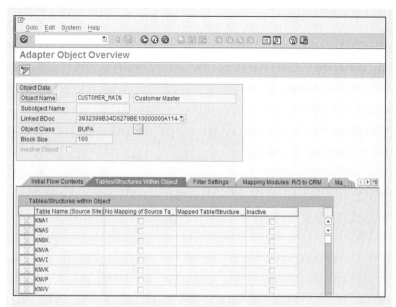

Figure 2.30 Tables/Structures for CUSTOMER_MAIN

Adapter object BUPA_MAIN is used for transferring customer data from Table BUT000 in SAP CRM to various other systems such as SAP R/3, Groupware, or non-SAP systems. The **Table Name (Source Site)** field in the **Tables/Structures Within Object** tab contains a corresponding entry (see Figure 2.31). As you cannot assign this table uniquely to a table in the target system, you won't find any entries under **Mapped Table/Structure (Target Site)**.

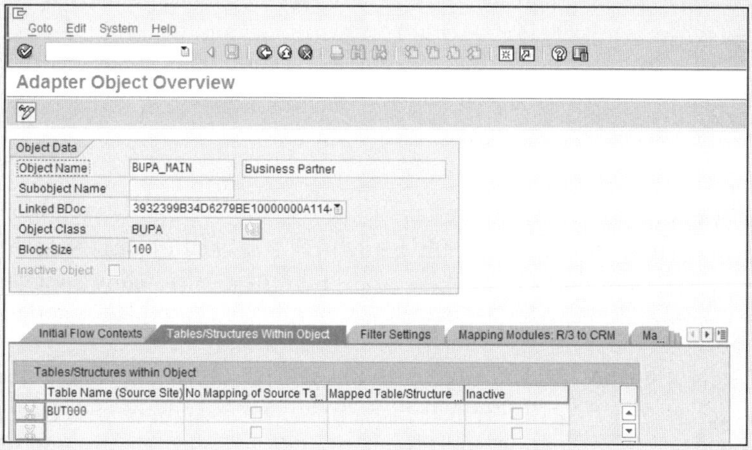

Figure 2.31 Tables/Structures for BUPA_MAIN

Filter settings for adapter objects are used to transfer only the data that fulfills defined filter criteria. You can define multiple filter criteria for the same field as well as filter criteria for different fields. In the first case, you must link the filter criteria using OR, whereas in the second case, you link them using AND. The data is stored in Table SMOFFILTAB.

Example

Adapter object MATERIAL is used to transfer materials from SAP R/3 to SAP CRM. Figure 2.32 shows a possible filter setting for this adapter object. This setting ensures that materials with material numbers (MARA-MATNR field) AM2-GT-V2, YCON, KMAT, or materials whose material numbers contain the BAR* pattern are excluded from the transfer.

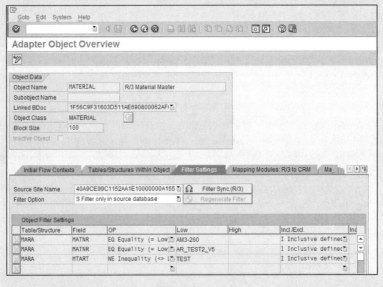

Figure 2.32 Filter Setting for MATERIAL

When new filter settings are saved, the corresponding filtering function modules are automatically generated. If these function modules are generated successfully, the system confirms this by outputting the message "Filter module for object <x> has been generated".

When you transfer data from SAP R/3 to SAP CRM, the source and target systems use different data models. The assignments between these data models are the responsibility of a mapping function module, which can be found under Module Name in the **Mapping Modules: R/3 to CRM** tab. If you want to use multiple mapping modules, you must store the sequence of the calls in the **Call Order** field. The data is stored in Table SMOFSUBTAB.

Example

Adapter object MATERIAL is used to transfer materials from SAP R/3 to SAP CRM. In the standard version, the assignment between the BAPI structure in which the data arrives in the CRM system and the corresponding data model in SAP CRM is established via the mapping function module COM_MAP_BAPIMTCS_TO_PROD_MAT.

When you transfer data from SAP CRM to SAP R/3, the source and target systems use different data models as well. The assignments between these data models are again carried out by a mapping function module, which can be found in the **Mapping Module for Load into R/3** field of the **Mapping Modules: CRM to R/3** tab. The data is stored in Table SMOFUPLMAP.

Mapping module CRM to R/3

Example

Adapter object PRODUCT_MAT is used to transfer materials from SAP CRM to various different target systems, such as SAP R/3. When you transfer data from SAP CRM to SAP R/3, the assignment between the data model in the CRM system and the BAPI structure in which the data is transferred to the R/3 system is carried out using the mapping function module, COM_MAP_PROD_MAT_TO_BAPIMTCS.

The **Parent Object** field in the **Parent Objects** tab lists the adapter objects that define the sequence during the initial load. The initial load for an adapter object is not started until the initial load for all parent objects has finished. The values are stored in Table SMOFOB-JPAR.

Parent objects

Example

The initial load for adapter object MATERIAL for the purpose of transferring materials from the R/3 system to SAP CRM doesn't start until the initial load of the corresponding customizing objects has finished.

2.4.3 Mobile Inbound Adapter

Changes to data in the mobile client application are written to the database of the mobile client. At the same time, an sBDoc message is written to the qRFC outbound queue of the mobile client in order to send the data change to the CRM Server.

Data changes in the mobile client application

The *ConnTrans* data transfer is started by the user of the mobile client, and transfers sBDoc messages from the qRFC outbound queue of the mobile client to the corresponding qRFC inbound queue of the CRM Server. Each queue entry represents a qRFC LUW that contains the call of a generated mobile inbound adapter.

Generated mobile inbound adapters

Each BDoc type has a separate *generated mobile inbound adapter*. Generated mobile inbound adapters are function modules with the following naming convention: <namespace><BDoc type>_I01.

You can determine the name of a mobile inbound adapter using the BDoc Modeler (via Transaction SBDM or by selecting **Architecture and Technology** • **Middleware** • **Development** • **Meta Object Modeling** • **BDoc Modeler** from the SAP Easy Access menu). You can then find the name of the mobile inbound adapter in the **Function module** field of the **BDoc Overview** tab.

Example

Figure 2.33 shows that function module /1CRMG0/CAPGEN_OBJ_WRITE_I01 is the generated mobile inbound adapter for BDoc type CAPGEN_OBJECT_WRITE.

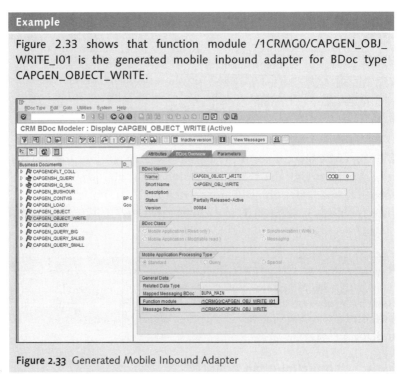

Figure 2.33 Generated Mobile Inbound Adapter

Generic mobile inbound adapter

All generated mobile inbound adapters use the same function module (SMO8_MOBILEINBOUND_PROCESSMSG) in order to start a synchronization flow using flow context *SIO – sBDoc Validate*. This function module is referred to as *generic mobile inbound adapter*.

The sBDoc message is locked and the header data, that is, the following information, is updated:

▸ Flow context: *SI0 — sBDoc Validate*

▸ Date and time when the BDoc message was received

▸ Initial status: *I01 — Received (intermediate state)*

Then, the name of the qRFC inbound queue is determined and the qRFC LUW is deleted from the inbound queue.

Lastly, the sBDoc message is written to the *BDoc store* and a COMMIT WORK is executed to store the changes in the database. If an error occurs in the subsequent steps, which leads to a ROLLBACK WORK, the sBDoc message is preserved in this status.

Then, the services for flow context *SI1 – sBDoc Inbound (Before Validation)* are called. However, at present, no known usage for this flow context does exist.

After that, the sBDoc message is validated. Here, you have several options:

▸ Typically, the sBDoc message is mapped to an mBDoc message and the data is validated in such a way that the mBDoc message is actually validated. For this purpose, the sBDoc type must be assigned a corresponding mBDoc type.

▸ If, in exceptional cases, the sBDoc type is not assigned an mBDoc type, the synchronization flow is started directly via flow context *SO1 — sBDoc Notification* without any further validation. In this case, the updated data won't be written to the online database of the CRM application and no data can be sent to receivers other than mobile clients. For this reason, this kind of validation is referred to as *Mobile Client Only*. Chapter 3, *Outbound Processing*, provides more information on the synchronization flow.

There are also various ways of *mapping* an sBDoc message to an mBDoc message:

▸ In static mapping, the sBDoc type is assigned a fixed mBDoc type. The sBDoc message is actually mapped to the mBDoc message via the implementation of the MAP_SYN2MSG method of ABAP interface IF_SMW_MAP.

▶ In dynamic mapping, the sBDoc message is mapped to an mBDoc message as well. However, in this case, the mBDoc type is determined dynamically. The determination of the mBDoc type and the mapping of the sBDoc message to the mBDoc message occur via the implementation of the MAP_SYN2MSG method of ABAP interface IF_SMW_DYNMAP.

How can we find out whether an sBDoc type is mapped to an mBDoc type? Start Transaction SMW3FDIF, which you can also find in the SAP Easy Access menu by selecting the following path: **Architecture and Technology · Middleware · Development · Message Flow · Define BDoc Type Specific Flow Attributes**. If an implementing class (of the MAP_SYN2MSG method) is specified for the sBDoc type in the **Mapper Class** column, the sBDoc type will be mapped to an mBDoc type (see Figure 2.34).

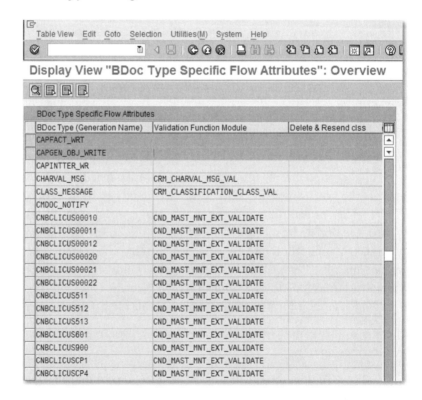

Figure 2.34 Mapping an sBDoc Type to an mBDoc Type

Example

In Figure 2.34, you can see that both the sBDoc type CAPFACT_WRT (business partner information sheet) and the sBDoc type CAPGEN_OBJ_ WRITE (customer) are assigned mapper classes. Therefore, the two sBDoc types are mapped to mBDoc types.

To determine whether static or dynamic mapping is being used, double-click a row within Transaction SMW3FDIF to navigate to the detail screen for the BDoc type. The **sBDoc In IF Type** field (see Figure 2.35) enables you to distinguish between static and dynamic mappings.

Example

Figure 2.35 shows that the sBDoc type CAPFACT_WRT (business partner information sheet) is dynamically mapped to an mBDoc type.

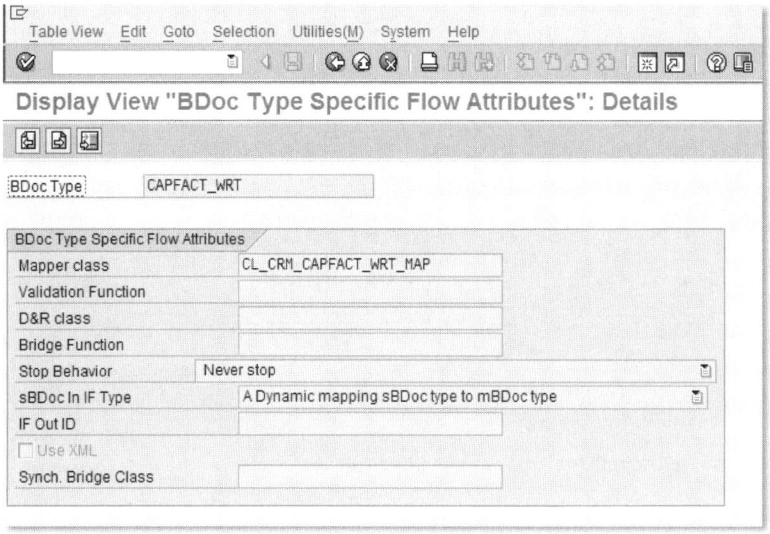

Table View   Edit   Goto   Selection   Utilities(M)   System   Help

Display View "BDoc Type Specific Flow Attributes": Details

| BDoc Type | CAPFACT_WRT |

BDoc Type Specific Flow Attributes	
Mapper class	CL_CRM_CAPFACT_WRT_MAP
Validation Function	
D&R class	
Bridge Function	
Stop Behavior	Never stop
sBDoc In IF Type	A Dynamic mapping sBDoc type to mBDoc type
IF Out ID	
☐ Use XML	
Synch. Bridge Class	

Figure 2.35 Static or Dynamic Mapping

In BDoc Modeler (Transaction SBDM), you will find an assigned **[!]** mBDoc type for some sBDoc types in the **Mapped Messaging BDoc** field of the **BDoc Overview** tab (see Figure 2.36). This means that the sBDoc type is mapped statically to this mBDoc type. If this entry is missing, it doesn't necessarily mean that the sBDoc type won't be mapped to an mBDoc type. Instead, it can mean that dynamic mapping to an mBDoc type is taking place here.

Note that once the sBDoc message has been mapped to an mBDoc message via flow context *MI0 — mBDoc Validate*, the mBDoc message is not written to the BDoc store. In this case, a successful validation is recorded in the status information in the header data of the sBDoc message. Even the error-handling process is not carried out by the message flow, but by the synchronization flow.

Temporary errors When processing the sBDoc message, the system checks whether a temporary error exists, which would cause an automatic retry of the process. If the maximum number of processing attempts has been reached, the error is treated as a non-temporary error.

Figure 2.36 An mBDoc Type Assigned to an sBDoc Type

Error handling In case of an error, the mobile client that has sent the data receives a rejection message. For more details on this topic, please refer to Chapter 3, *Outbound Processing*. In addition, the automatic error handling process is started by the Error Handler. Section 2.6 contains further details about the Error Handler. The error status is recorded in the header data of the sBDoc message, while the errors are written to the error segment of the sBDoc message.

The change to the sBDoc message is written to the BDoc store and a COMMIT WORK is executed to store the changes in the database. Chapter 4, *BDoc Modeling and Storage*, provides further details on the status of BDoc messages.

2.5 Validation

The *validation* process is called by the inbound adapters (see Section 2.4). The inbound adapters generate an mBDoc message and the flow is started using flow context *MI0 — mBDoc Validate*.

If the mBDoc message did not originate from an sBDoc message (from the mobile client) by means of a mapping, the mBDoc message is locked first, while header data such as flow context *MI0 — mBDoc Validate*, the date and time at which the mBDoc message was received, and the initial *Status I01 — Received (intermediate state)* are maintained. After that, the name of the qRFC inbound queue is determined and the qRFC LUW is deleted from the inbound queue. Then, the mBDoc message is written to the *BDoc store*. Finally, a COMMIT WORK is executed.

Validation Service and CRM Application

Then, a *validation service* is called to check the data contained in the mBDoc message for correctness. Figure 2.37 shows that the validation service is the only service that is called in the flow via flow context text *MI0 — mBDoc Validate*.

A validation service is a function module that is defined for each mBDoc type. You can find the validation service for the respective mBDoc type in Table SMW3BDOCIF. If you want to display or maintain this table, call Transaction SMW3FDIF or select **Architecture and Technology · Middleware · Development · Message Flow · Define BDoc Type Specific Flow Attributes** from the SAP Easy Access menu. Alternatively, you can determine the validation service for a specific BDoc type by using Transaction SMO8FD. As shown in the example of mBDoc type BUPA_MAIN in Figure 2.38, the validation service is located under flow context *MI0*.

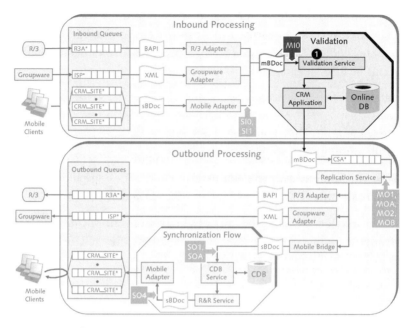

Figure 2.37 Calling the Validation Service

Figure 2.38 Validation Service for mBDoc Type BUPA_MAIN (Business Partner)

Table 2.4 contains a list of validation services for several important BDoc types in standard SAP versions.

BDoc type	Description	Validation service
BUPA_MAIN	Business partners	CRM_BUPA_MAIN_VAL
BUPA_REL	Business partner relationships	CRM_BUPA_REL_VAL
BUS_TRANS_MSG	Sales orders	CRM_DOWNLOAD_BTMBDOC_VAL
PRODUCT_MAT	Materials	COM_PRODUCT_MAT_VALIDATE

Table 2.4 Validation Services for Important BDoc Types

Validation services don't carry out any validations by themselves. Instead, they call the validations of the CRM application, which are used when you enter data directly through the CRM application.

If the validation process is successful, the data is stored in the online database of the CRM application and then forwarded to other systems such as SAP R/3 or mobile clients through outbound processing. Chapter 3, *Outbound Processing*, contains a detailed description of the outbound processing process.

When the data is validated via the validation service, various errors may occur.

Examples

A change of addresses is supposed to be transferred from the R/3 system to SAP CRM. However, at this time, the business partner is locked in the CRM system because a different user is currently editing the data. Consequently, the BDoc message about the business partner triggers an error.

A relationship between two business partners is supposed to be transferred from the R/3 system to SAP CRM. But, one of the two business partners does not exist in the CRM system because of a validation error that occurred when the data was created. Consequently, the BDoc message about the business partner relationship triggers an error.

The tax ID of a business partner that is supposed to be transferred from the R/3 system to the CRM system contains characters that are not permitted for tax IDs in SAP CRM. Consequently, the BDoc message about the business partner triggers an error.

A sales order, which has been created on a mobile client, contains a product that doesn't exist in the CRM system. Consequently, the BDoc message about the sales order triggers an error.

If the mBDoc message didn't originate from an sBDoc message (from a mobile client), the Error Handler starts the automatic error handling process in case of an error. Section 2.6 has more details about the Error Handler. The error status is recorded in the header data of the mBDoc message, while the errors are written to the error segment of the mBDoc message.

2.6 Handling Errors When Processing BDoc Messages

Errors that occur during the processing of BDoc messages, such as validation errors, represent one of the core areas of Middleware monitoring. Therefore, you should monitor this area on a daily basis and eliminate errors immediately.

2.6.1 Error Handler

If errors occur during the processing of BDoc messages, the *Error Handler* automatically takes the necessary action to troubleshoot these errors. The following types of error actions are possible:

▶ Triggering a workflow event. This enables a responsible person to view a BDoc message and to decide on how to process this message further (e.g., to determine that the BDoc message should be processed again or deleted).

▶ Sending an email to specific recipients.

Error actions can be defined on the basis of the following parameters:

▶ Suggested error action for all errors that occur during the processing of BDoc messages

▶ Error action for a specific BDoc type only and for all error statuses or for only a specific one

▶ Error action for a specific site type (of the sender) only and for all sites of this site type, or for only a specific site of this site type

▶ Error action for canceled BDoc messages only

Most of the error actions are predefined by SAP; however, you can also define your own ones. To do this, you must enter the corresponding settings in Customizing.

To define your own troubleshooting actions, you must start Customizing via Transaction SPRO or by selecting **Architecture and Technology** • **Configuration** • **Customizing** from the SAP Easy Access menu. Then click on the **SAP Reference IMG** button. You can find the corresponding IMG activity under **Customer Relationship Management** • **CRM Middleware and Related Components** • **Message Flow Setup** • **Assign Error Actions to Messages**.

2.6.2 Displaying and Processing Erroneous BDoc Messages

You can display BDoc messages in the BDoc store using Transaction SMW01 or by selecting **Architecture and Technology • Middleware • Monitoring • Message Flow • Display BDoc Messages** from the SAP Easy Access menu:

Displaying BDoc messages

▸ Enter the relevant selection criteria. Figure 2.39 shows that erroneous BDoc messages have been selected (**Errors**) which haven't been completely processed yet (**Non Final**), as well as BDoc messages that are currently in an intermediate state (**Intermediate State**). Rejected BDoc messages (**Rejected**) and those that have already been processed (**Processed**) were not selected in this example because such BDoc messages wouldn't require any further action to be taken. Chapter 4, *BDoc Modeling and Storage*, provides further details on the status of BDoc messages. In order to avoid extensive selection results, you should limit the date and time as much as possible, for example, by setting the **Send Date and Time** to today, as shown in Figure 2.39. In addition, the selection screen enables you to select BDoc messages of specific BDoc types (**BDoc Type (Generation Name)**) as well as individual BDoc messages (**BDoc Message ID**), BDoc messages of specific users (**User (Creator)**), and BDoc messages containing specific flow contexts (all fields in the **Flow Context** section; to display more fields, you would have to scroll down in the selection screen shown in Figure 2.39).

▸ By clicking on the **Expand Additional Selection Options** button, which is marked in Figure 2.39, you can display other interesting selection criteria, as shown in Figure 2.40. The selection options provided in the **Site Information** section allow you to select BDoc messages that originate from individual sender sites or will be sent to individual receiver sites. The **Message validation type** field enables you to select by different message types. For more details on the topic of message types, please refer to Chapter 3, *Outbound Processing*. Moreover, you can use the **Root ID** field to select all BDoc messages relating to a specific object instance. The root ID represents the GUID of the object instance. For example, in BDoc messages of BDoc type BUPA_MAIN, it is the GUID of the business partner. You can find this GUID in the **PARTNER_GUID** field of Table BUT000.

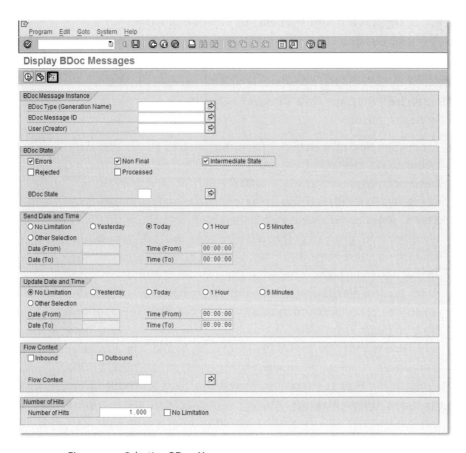

Figure 2.39 Selecting BDoc Messages

The **Queue name** field enables you to search for BDoc messages originating from specific queues. By checking the **Only Queue Stopper (MI0, SI1)** option, you can restrict the selection to erroneous BDoc messages that may block a queue and must therefore be handled with top priority.

▶ Start your selection by clicking the **Execute** button.

▶ The system displays a list of BDoc messages that meet the selected criteria. BDoc messages containing errors are indicated by a red traffic light; messages that are still being processed are indicated by a yellow traffic light; and BDoc messages that have been processed successfully are indicated by a green traffic light.

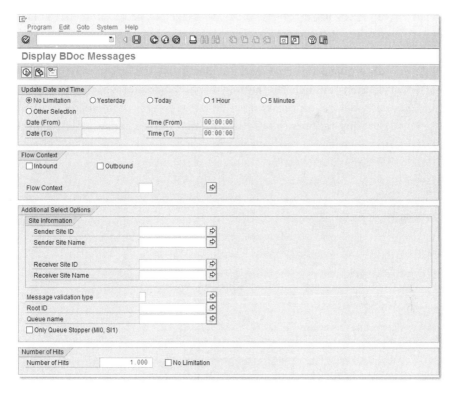

Figure 2.40 Additional Selection Options for BDoc Messages

▶ To see the error message regarding an erroneous BDoc message, select the BDoc message and click the **BDoc Message Error/Receiver** button, which is selected in Figure 2.41. This figure shows how the error message is displayed in the system.

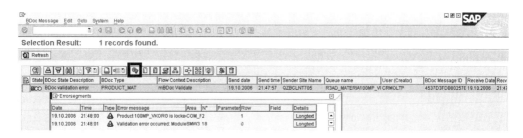

Figure 2.41 Error Messages for BDoc Messages

▶ BDoc messages that contain errors can be procesed again. To do that, click the **Reprocess BDoc Message** button (see Figure 2.42).

[!] Reprocessing erroneous BDoc messages can entail inconsistencies if other BDoc messages for the same object instance have been successfully processed in the meantime. (BDoc messages for the same object instance have identical root IDs and can be selected via their root ID). Therefore, you should ensure whether this is the case before reprocessing a BDoc message. Immediate troubleshooting reduces the probability that other changes to the object instance have already been processed.

Figure 2.42 Reprocessing BDoc Messages

> **Example**
>
> A validation error occurred in the Middleware when the name of product HT-1060 was changed from "Old Name" to "New Name", which was transferred from SAP R/3 to the CRM system. However, in the meantime, the name of the product was changed to "Brand New Name" in the R/3 system, and this change was processed successfully by the Middleware. If the erroneous BDoc message containing the change to "New Name" is reprocessed now, the product is assigned the name "New Name" in the CRM system, whereas in R/3, its name is "Brand New Name."

▶ Furthermore, you can mark erroneous BDoc messages for deletion. To do that, you must click the **Mark to be deleted** button (see Figure 2.43).

[!] Note that this can also result in inconsistencies. For this reason, you should delete erroneous BDoc messages only if their contents are transferred to the system in different ways (e.g., via a request).

Figure 2.43 Marking BDoc Messages for Deletion

You can display a summary of BDoc messages via Transaction SMW02 or by selecting **Architecture and Technology · Middleware · Monitoring · Message Flow · Display BDoc Message Summary** from the SAP Easy Access menu.

Displaying a BDoc message summary

To view a total of the different errors that occurred during the processing of BDoc messages, you can either call Transaction SMW02A or select **Architecture and Technology · Middleware · Monitoring · Message Flow · BDoc Message Error Analysis** from the SAP Easy Access menu.

Displaying the error total

You can display a summary of BDoc messages that haven't been processed yet via Transaction SMW03 or by selecting **Architecture and Technology · Middleware · Monitoring · Message Flow · Display Unprocessed BDoc Message Summary** from the SAP Easy Access menu.

Summary of BDoc messages to be processed

This chapter provides a comprehensive description of outbound processing in SAP CRM Middleware, which involves the transfer of data from the CRM system to other systems, such as SAP R/3 or mobile clients.

3   Outbound Processing

Besides inbound processing and validation, *outbound processing* represents the third major area within Middleware. The outbound processing determines which data is supposed to be sent to which systems, then converts the data into the required formats and forwards it to the *outbound queues* for the respective systems.

Figure 3.1 illustrates the process of outbound processing in SAP CRM Middleware.

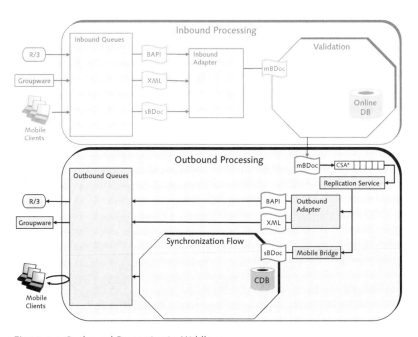

Figure 3.1 Outbound Processing in Middleware

Outbound processing consists of four major stages: Outbound data is converted by *outbound adapters* into the required formats and then forwarded to outbound queues for the receiver systems. If mobile clients are used, a *mobile bridge* converts the data into the data format that is required for the *synchronization flow*. The synchronization flow determines which data is supposed to be sent to which mobile clients and places this data into outbound queues as well. Before describing these four stages in greater detail, we will first introduce the *replication model* in which the rules for data distribution in outbound processing are defined.

3.1 Replication Model

In outbound processing, data is replicated from the CRM system to other systems, such as SAP R/3 or mobile clients according to different rules. These rules are defined in the *replication model*.

Administration console

The replication model must be maintained in the *administration console*. You can start the administration console by calling Transaction SMOEAC or by selecting **Architecture and Technology · Middleware · Administration · Administration Console** from the SAP Easy Access menu.

The following sections describe the components of the replication model:

▸ Lookup tables

▸ Replication objects

▸ Replication object types

▸ Publications

▸ Sites

▸ Site types

▸ Subscriptions

Lookup tables

Lookup tables are a central component of the replication model. They contain information about which data are supposed to be sent to which sites.

Replication objects

A *replication object* is a logical unit that is exchanged between different datasets. Each replication object is based on a BDoc type. In other

90

words, there is a direct relationship between a replication object and a BDoc type.

To display or modify replication objects in the administration console, you must select the **Replication Object** entry in the **Object Type** field. The **Object Name** field enables you to select replication objects with specific names, while the **Filter** button allows you to enter additional selection criteria. By clicking the **Display Objects** button, you can view all replication objects that meet the selection criteria you entered. Figure 3.2 shows the selection of object type **Replication Object**, the **Display Objects** button, as well as the selected replication objects. In this display, the replication objects are divided into *replication object types*.

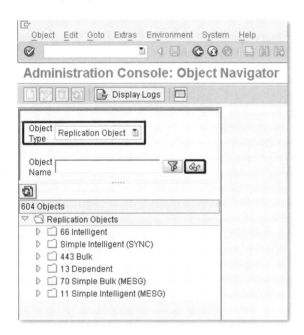

Figure 3.2 Replication Objects in the Administration Console

To display the replication objects of a replication object type, you must open the corresponding folder by clicking the arrow next to the folder. Figure 3.3 shows an open folder containing the replication objects of replication type **Intelligent**.

To view the details of an individual replication object, you must double-click the relevant object. Figure 3.4 shows the detail screen of replication object CAPGEN_OBJ_WRITE. The **BDoc Name** field displays BDoc type CAPGEN_OBJ_WRITE, which is used as a basis for this replication object.

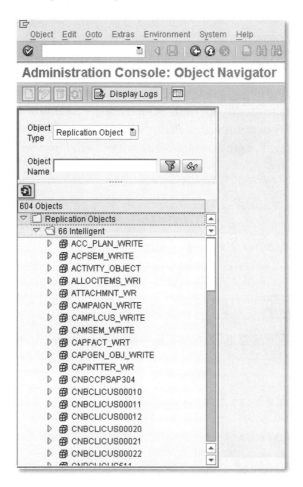

Figure 3.3 Replication Object Types in the Administration Console

Replication objects are stored in Table SMOHREPOBJ.

Replication object types
Replication object types determine according to which type of rules data is exchanged via a replication object. There are different replication object types for mBDocs and sBDocs. Because sBDocs are used to exchange data with mobile clients, the system uses the corresponding replication object types for sBDocs that enable the dispatch of data to mobile clients. Correspondingly, replication object types for mBDocs are used for sending data to other systems.

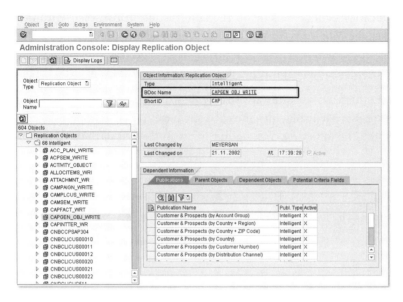

Figure 3.4 BDoc Type of a Replication Object in the Administration Console

Publications can be referred to as data containers that summarize data logically. They are based on replication objects, that is, each publication is assigned a replication object. One replication object can be used for several publications. In a publication, individual criteria fields are selected out of a set of possible criteria fields of the replication object.

To display or modify publications in the administration console, you must select the **Publication** entry in the **Object Type** field. Here again, you can enter different selection criteria. The **Display Objects** button enables you to view all publications that meet the selection criteria you entered.

The display of publications is also subdivided by replication object types. To display the publications that belong to a specific replication object type, you must once again open the corresponding folder. By double-clicking a publication, you can display the detail screen.

Publications are stored in Table SMOHPUBL.

BDoc messages are not replicated to individual users, but to *sites* (local databases). Sites are created for other systems such as SAP R/3 or Groupware, as well as for each mobile client to which data should be sent.

Publications

Sites

To display or modify sites in the administration console, you must select the **Site** entry in the **Object Type** field. Again, you can enter different selection criteria and display the respective sites by clicking the **Display Objects** button. Sites are stored in Table SMOHSITEID.

Site types   In the display, the sites are subdivided into *site types*, as shown in Figure 3.5. To display the sites of a site type, you must open the corresponding folder by clicking the arrow to the left of the folder.

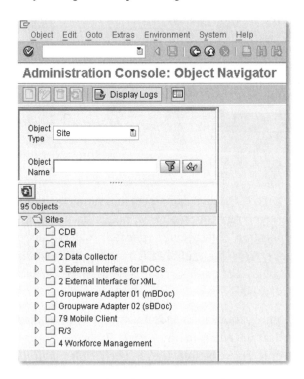

Figure 3.5 Sites in the Administration Console

All sites of the same site type use the same outbound adapter to send data to other systems. Different standard site types such as R/3, Groupware adapters, or mobile clients with corresponding outbound adapters are available.

Subscriptions   Subscriptions are assignments of sites to publications.

To display or modify subscriptions in the administration console, you must select the **Subscription** entry in the **Object Type** field. The **Object Name** field allows you to select the subscriptions by entering specific names. By clicking the **Display Objects** button, you can view all subscriptions that meet the selection criteria you entered.

Subscriptions are based on publications, that is, each subscription is assigned a publication. One publication can be used for several subscriptions. Moreover, in a subscription, values are defined for the criteria fields of the assigned publication. Furthermore, a subscription is assigned sites that are supposed to receive the respective data.

Subscriptions are stored in Table SMOHSUBSCR, while the assignments of sites to subscriptions are stored in Table SMOHSUBSIT.

Figure 3.6 illustrates the relationship between replication objects, publications, subscriptions, and sites.

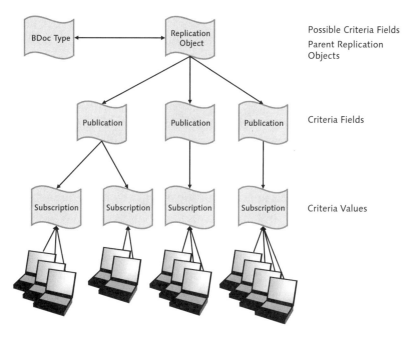

Figure 3.6 Relationships Between Replication Objects, Publications, Subscriptions, and Sites

The following replication object types exist for mBDocs (i.e., for sending data to other systems, such as SAP R/3):

Replication object types for mBDocs

▶ *Simple Bulk (MESG).* This replication object type means that all object instances for the replication object are completely replicated to a site that has the corresponding subscription.

▶ *Simple Intelligent (MESG)*. Using this replication object type means that possible distribution criteria are defined for the replication object, based on which a decision is made concerning which object instances will be replicated to a site that has the respective subscription.

Examples

The BUPA_MAIN replication object of type *Simple Bulk (MESG)* enables you to replicate all business partner data from the CRM system to an R/3 system, for example.

The PRODUCT_INDOBJ replication object of type *Simple Intelligent (MESG)* enables you to replicate individual objects from the CRM system to an R/3 system, for example.

Replication object types for sBDocs

The following replication object types are available for sBDocs (i.e., for exchanging data with mobile clients):

▶ *Bulk* means that all object instances for the replication object are replicated to a site that has the relevant subscription, which is why no possible distribution criteria need to be defined. A single lookup table called SMOHLUBULK is created for all replication objects of this type. This table stores information about which publication (replication object plus selected criteria fields) is to be replicated to which site. A bulk type replication object can neither have a parent object nor can it be the parent object of another replication object.

▶ *Simple Intelligent (SYNC)* means that possible distribution criteria are defined for the replication object, based on which a decision is made concerning which object instances will be replicated to a site that has the relevant subscription. However, in this case no lookup table is created that stores information regarding which object is supposed to be replicated to which site. For this reason, the receivers must be determined anew for each object. In addition, no automatic realignment is carried out that would ensure that the datasets of the sites are identical to the entries contained in the lookup table. A replication object of the *Simple Intelligent (SYNC)* type can neither have a parent object, nor can it be the parent object of another replication object.

▶ *Intelligent* means that possible distribution criteria are defined for the replication object in question, based on which a decision is made concerning which object instances will be replicated to a site that has the relevant subscription. A lookup table is created for the replication object that stores information regarding which object is supposed to be replicated to which site. This means that the receivers of a specific object don't need to be determined repeatedly. Lookup tables for intelligently replicated replication objects as well as the associated indexes and lock objects are generated. The naming convention for lookup tables is as follows: <namespace><industry><short ID of replication object>RRL. An automatic realignment service is carried out for intelligently replicated replication objects, which ensures that the datasets of individual sites are identical to the entries contained in the lookup table. A replication object of the *Intelligent* type can have a parent object and it can also be the parent object of another replication object.

▶ *Dependent* means that no individual distribution criteria are defined for a replication object and also that no separate lookup table is created. Instead, a parent object must be specified for a replication object of this type, whose distribution is followed by the dependent replication object.

Examples

Usually, Customizing data is replicated bulk to the individual sites. For example, Customizing data for organizational management is replicated using replication object CRM_DNL_ORGMAN.

Language-dependent components of mobile applications are replicated *Simple Intelligent (SYNC)* using replication object WD_BLOB_LD_WRITE.

Replication object CAPGEN_OBJ_WRITE, which is used to replicate customer data, represents one out of many examples of intelligent distribution. Possible criteria fields are, for example, Country, ZIP, Region, the Customer No., and many others.

Replication object CUST_MAT_INFO serves as an example of dependent distribution. This object is used to replicate customer material information based on the respective customer, that is, an object is replicated to exactly the same sites as the associated customer.

The detail screen of a replication object displays the replication object type in the **Type** field.

Table 3.1 provides a list of the different replication object types including their characteristics.

Replication Object Type	Assigned BDoc Type	Possible Distribution Criteria	Lookup Table	Parent Object
Simple Bulk (MESG)	mBDoc	No	No	No
Simple Intelligent (MESG)	mBDoc	Yes	No	No
Bulk	sBDoc	No	SMOHLUBULK	No
Simple Intelligent (SYNC)	sBDoc	Yes	No	No
Intelligent	sBDoc	Yes	Yes	Yes
Dependent	sBDoc	No	No	Yes

Table 3.1 Replication Object Types and Their Characteristics

Wizards

To create new replication objects, publications, and subscriptions, the administration console provides specific *wizards*. To start a wizard, select **Replication Object**, **Publication**, or **Subscription** from the **Object Type** field and click **Create Object**. Alternatively, you can select **Object • Create** from the menu.

Interlinkages

Interlinkages are links between two intelligent replication objects that are related to each other via a link table. If an instance of the leading object is replicated to a specific site, an instance of the following object, which is linked through the interlinkage, will be replicated to the same site.

To display or modify interlinkages in the administration console, you must select the **Interlinkage** entry in the **Object Type** field. Then click the **Display Objects** button to display all existing interlinkages.

By double-clicking an interlinkage you can display the detail screen. As shown in Figure 3.7, a **Leading Object**, a **Following Object**, and a **Link Table** are defined for each interlinkage. Furthermore, it must be defined which two fields in the link table should be linked with each other so that an object instance of the dependent replication object can be replicated with the corresponding object instance of the leading replication object (**Source Field** and **Dest Field**). In addition, you can filter the link table by specific entries: Only if the entry in the **Relation Field** field corresponds to the value in the **RelValue** field will an entry in the link table be considered for the interlinkage.

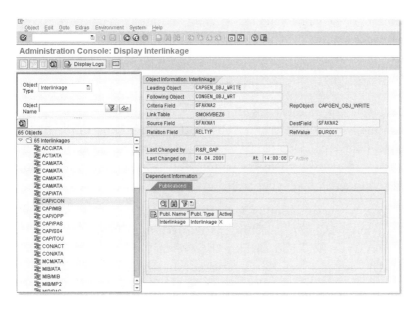

Figure 3.7 Interlinkages in the Administration Console

Example

There are plans to replicate the customer master data along with the contact persons to the mobile clients. For this purpose, an interlinkage called CAP/CON was defined, which contains the leading replication object CAPGEN_WRITE (customers) and the following replication object CONGEN_WRT (contact persons). The relevant link table is called SMOKVBEZ6. This table contains relationships between individual customers, as well as relationships between customers and individual contact persons. Because in this example, we only want to evaluate relationships between a customer and a contact person, the table is filtered by the respective relationship type (RELTYP = BUR001). The source field is SFAKNA1, while the destination field is SFAKNA2. This means that if a customer is replicated whose unique key is contained in the SFAKNA1 field of link table SMOKVBEZ6, all contact persons whose keys are assigned to the respective entries in the SFAKNA2 field will follow.

Interlinkages are stored in Table SMOHILTP.

The *subscription agent* is a tool that enables you to generate subscriptions, assign sites to subscriptions, and assign employees to sites.

Subscription agent

For this purpose, *subscription generators* are used. Subscription generators are based on publications. For each subscription generator, rules are defined to determine the criteria values for the subscrip-

Subscription generators

tions to be generated and for assigning the sites and employees. SAP provides a number of predefined subscription generators.

Active subscription generators are included in a background job and executed at regular, customer-specific intervals.

To display or modify subscription generators in the administration console, you must select the **Subscription Agent** entry in the **Object Type** field. Again, there are various selection criteria available. By clicking the **Display Objects** button, you can view the subscription generators that meet your selection criteria.

To create new subscription generators, you can use a specific wizard. Start this wizard by selecting the **Subscription Agent** entry in the **Object Type** field and clicking the **Create Object** button. Alternatively, you can select **Object • Create** from the menu.

Header information for subscription generators is stored in Table SMOEGENHEA, whereas detail information is stored in Table SMOEGENDET.

Table 3.2 provides a list of the tables that are available for the different elements in the administration console.

Elements in the Administration Console	Table
Replication objects	SMOHREPOBJ
Publications	SMOHPUBL
Sites	SMOHSITEID
Subscriptions	SMOHSUBSCR
Assignment of sites to subscriptions	SMOHSUBSIT
Interlinkages	SMOHILTP
Subscription generators (header information)	SMOEGENHEA
Subscription generators (details)	SMOEGENDET

Table 3.2 Tables for the Different Elements in the Administration Console

3.2   Messaging Flow

Once the data has been checked for correctness and written to the CRM database by the CRM application, the data is written to an mBDoc message and a *messaging flow* starts in order to notify interested parties about the data changes.

3.2.1 CSA Queues

In the messaging flow, the mBDoc messages are first stored in the BDoc store in an initial status and then written to *CSA queues*. Although it is actually an outbound flow, inbound qRFC queues are used for CSA queues for performance reasons. Chapter 2, *Inbound Processing and Validation*, contains detailed information about inbound queues, for example, with regard to monitoring or registration and deregistration.

Inbound queue names for CSA queues are defined in Table SMOFQFIND. The naming convention for these names is CSA_<OBJECT>*.

Queue names for CSA queues

Please refer to Chapter 8, *Inbound Queues*, for more detailed information on naming and parallelizing CSA queues.

You can switch the messaging flow in outbound processing on and off. You can only switch off the messaging flow for this BDoc type if it is ensured that there are no interested parties for modified object instances of a BDoc type. To do that, you must use Transaction SMW3_00 and create an entry for the respective BDoc type. When doing this, you must check the **Do Not Send** field (see Figure 3.8).

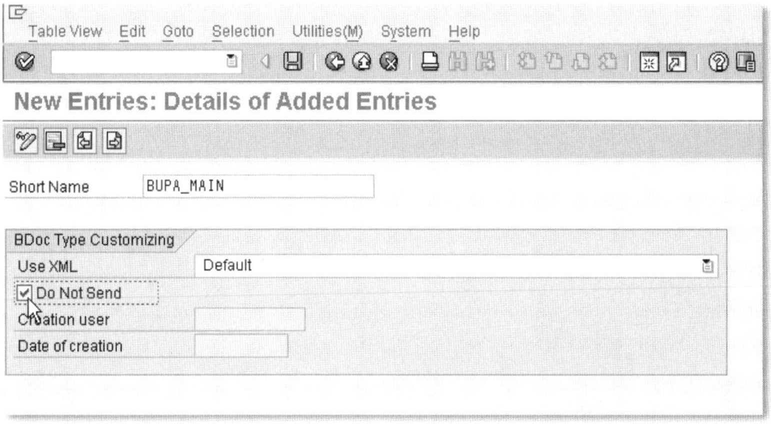

Switching the messaging flow on or off

Figure 3.8 Switching Off the Messaging Flow for a BDoc Type

Example

You operate a CRM system as a standalone system in which you manage your business partners. There are no other systems that are interested in business partner changes in your CRM system. Therefore, you can switch off the messaging flow for BDoc type BUPA_MAIN.

3.2.2 Replication Service and Outbound Adapters

When an mBDoc from the CSA queues is processed, a *replication service* is called, which is supposed to replicate the data that is contained in the mBDoc into other systems, such as SAP R/3. After that, the relevant *outbound adapters* are called, which convert the data into the required formats and forward it to the respective outbound queues.

Both the replication service and the outbound adapters are called in the messaging flow (flow context *MO**). This procedure consists of two steps. The first step calls the replication service, while the outbound adapters are called in the second step. In a third step, a *mobile bridge* is called, which is described in greater detail in Section 3.2.3. Figure 3.9 illustrates the call of the replication service, outbound adapters, and mobile bridge in the messaging flow.

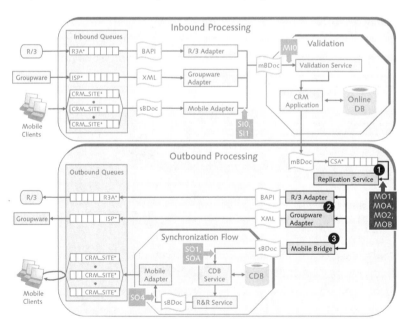

Figure 3.9 Messaging Flow in Outbound Processing

To replicate data from the CRM system into other systems, a *replication wrapper* is called first — for mBDocs that's function module SMOH_REPLICATION_WRAPPER_MSG. This function module is usually the first service that is called for flow contexts *MO1* (mBDoc Notification), *MO2* (mBDoc Notification Multiple), and *MO4* (mBDoc Direct Send). Figure 3.10 illustrates the call of the replication wrapper within the flow definition for mBDoc type PRODUCT_MAT (material).

Replication service

Then, the replication wrapper calls a *replication service* for the respective mBDoc type. This replication service is a generated function module with the following naming convention: <namespace><industry><BDocType>_RRR. The replication service determines the receivers of the data, which is contained in the mBDoc.

In the case of a bulk replication (*Simple Bulk (MESG)*), the contents of the BDoc don't affect who receives the data. The receivers are determined directly on the basis of the corresponding subscriptions.

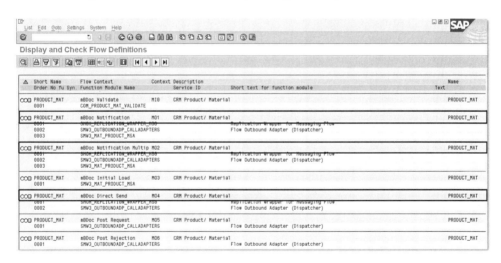

Figure 3.10 Calling the Replication Wrapper in the Flow Definition for BDoc Type PRODUCT_MAT

In the case of intelligent replication (*Simple Intelligent (MESG)*), the receivers are dependent on the contents of the root segment of the BDoc. Chapter 4, *BDoc Modeling and Storage*, provides further details on the structure of BDoc messages. Because a BDoc message can contain several object instances for different receivers, a separate receiver determination process is carried out for each of these instances based on the subscriptions. All receivers determined in this manner are then included in the list of receivers for this BDoc. In addition, this list is complemented with references to object instances that are supposed to be sent to the individual receivers. These references are evaluated by the outbound adapters at a later stage.

Outbound adapters

Outbound adapters are called in the messaging flow, as shown in Figure 3.11, for BDoc type PRODUCT_MAT (material).

When an outbound adapter is called, the system first calls function module SMW3_OUTBOUNDADP_CALLADAPTERS as a dispatcher. This function module groups the receiver sites of a BDoc according to the site type and then calls the relevant outbound adapters, such as R/3, BW, or XIF adapters.

The outbound adapters are responsible for converting data into the formats required by the receivers and for forwarding the data to the outbound queues of the receivers.

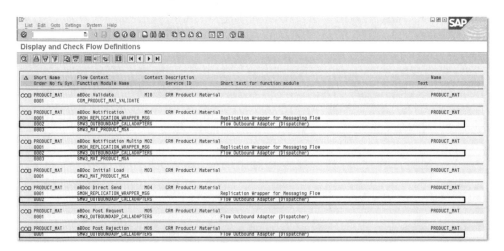

Figure 3.11 Calling the Outbound Adapters in the Flow Definition for BDoc Type PRODUCT_MAT

Chapter 2, *Inbound Processing and Validation*, provides more detailed information on adapter objects.

3.2.3 Mobile Bridge

Once the replication service and outbound adapters have been called for an mBDoc, the next step consists of calling the *mobile bridge*. For each mBDoc, a separate mobile bridge exists, which is responsible for converting mBDocs generated by the CRM application into sBDocs, which are used for updating the CDB (*Consolidated Database*) and mobile clients. Like the replication service and the outbound adapters, the mobile bridge is called in the messaging flow.

Because not every CRM system uses the mobile scenario, all mobile bridges are deactivated by default. Not until a mobile bridge has been activated will the CDB and mobile clients be provided with data of the corresponding BDoc type.

From a technical point of view, a mobile bridge is a function module that converts a specific mBDoc type into the corresponding sBDocs. The names of mobile bridges must be maintained in Table SMW3FDBDOC. If you want to display or maintain this table, call Transaction SMW3FDBDOC or select **Architecture and Technology • Middleware • Development • Message Flow • Define BDoc Type Specific Flow** from the SAP Easy Access menu. Figure 3.12 shows a list of entries in Table SMW3FDBDOC. Apart from other flow services, mobile bridges are listed in the **Funct.Name** column. The checked field in the **Active** column indicates that the associated mobile bridge is active.

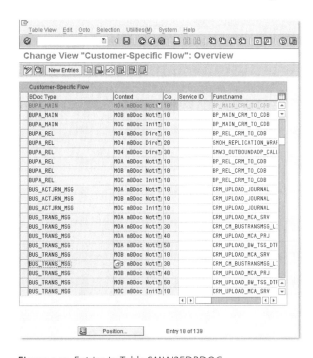

Figure 3.12 Entries in Table SMW3FDBDOC

> **Example**
>
> Function module BP_MAIN_CRM_TO_CDB represents a mobile bridge
> for BDoc type BUPA_MAIN for business partners. On the basis of an
> mBDoc of type BUPA_MAIN, this mobile bridge generates sBDocs of type
> CAPGEN_OBJ_WRITE for customers, CONGEN_OBJ_WRITE (short name
> CONGEN_OBJ_WRT) for contacts, EMPLOYEE_WRITE for employees,
> and CUST_HIERARCHY for an abbreviated form of the business partner.

3.2.4 Flow Contexts in the Messaging Flow

Table 3.3 provides an overview of the flow contexts in the messaging
flow, that is, during the outbound processing of mBDoc messages.

Flow Context	Description	Usage
MO1	mBDoc Notification	Notifies other systems about a change in an object instance.
MOA	mBDoc Notification (additional calls)	Calls additional services when an object instance has changed.
MO2	mBDoc Notification Multiple	Notifies other systems about changes in multiple object instances.
MOB	mBDoc Notification Multiple (additional calls)	Calls additional services when multiple object instances have changed.
MO3	mBDoc Initial Load	Initial load from the CRM online database to the CDB.
MOC	mBDoc Initial Load (additional calls)	Calls additional services for the initial load from the CRM online database to the CDB.
MO4	mBDoc Direct Send	Direct send of data from the CRM system to systems that have been previously determined.
MO5	mBDoc Post Request	Used for requests to send data to other systems.
MO6	mBDoc Post Rejection	Returns the receiver database into a consistent state when data has been rejected. Usually, rejections are not used in the messaging flow.
MOF	mBDoc Post Rejection (additional calls)	Calls additional services when data has been rejected.

Table 3.3 Flow Contexts Used for Outbound Processing of mBDoc Messages

3.3 Synchronization Flow

Once the mobile bridge has generated sBDocs from an mBDoc, the *synchronization flow* makes sure that the mobile clients are provided with the required data.

Synchronization flow

The synchronization flow consists of three steps:

1. In the first step, the *CDB service* updates the CDB.

2. In the second step, the *R&R service* identifies the mobile clients that are supposed to receive the data.

3. In the third, step, the *mobile adapter* forwards the data into the outbound queues of the corresponding mobile clients.

As shown in Figure 3.13, these three steps are called in the synchronization flow using flow context *SO1 — sBDoc Notification*.

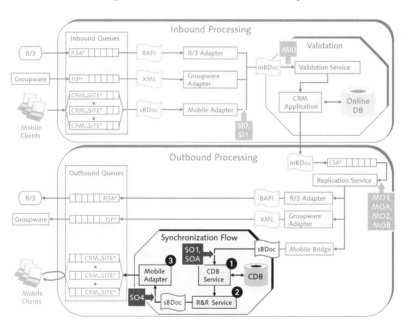

Figure 3.13 Synchronization Flow in Outbound Processing

3.3.1 CDB Service

The CDB is the logical database of the CRM Mobile. It contains all the data that can be sent to mobile clients in consolidated form. The tables of the CDB are located in the same database as the tables of

CDB

CRM Online. The CDB is actually just a set of separate tables that can usually be recognized by the prefix SMO. CRM Online tables don't have this prefix.

> **Examples**
>
> SMOKNA1 is a CDB table for customer data; SMOMARA is a CDB table for product data.

CDB service   As shown in Figure 3.13, a *CDB service* is called in the synchronization flow using flow context *SO1 — sBDoc Notification*. A CDB service is responsible for updating the CDB.

For each sBDoc type, there is a separate CDB service. The CDB service is a generated function module whose name is structured according to the following naming convention: <namespace><BDoc Type>_CDB.

> **Example**
>
> Figure 3.14 shows the call of the CDB service for customer data for which BDoc type CAPGEN_OBJ_WRITE is used. The name of the associated CDB service is /1CRMGC/CAPGEN_OBJ_WRITE_CDB.

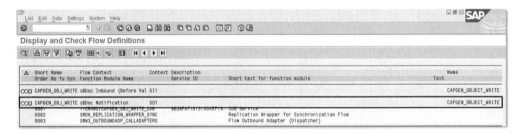

Figure 3.14   Calling the CDB Service for BDoc Type CAPGEN_OBJ_WRITE

3.3.2   R&R Service

The *R&R service* replicates object instances to receivers that are already known (replication), and determines the receivers if they are not yet known (realignment).

Replication   If it is already apparent which sites are supposed to receive a specific object instance, the *replication* process handles distributing the corresponding BDoc message to the relevant sites. Determining which object instances should be replicated to which sites is done on the basis of lookup tables. After that, the mobile adapter forwards the BDoc message into the outbound queues of the sites that have been determined in this manner.

If it is not yet apparent which sites are supposed to receive a specific object instance, or if due to a change of distribution-relevant fields, an object needs to be sent to different sites than before, the replication starts the *realignment* process, which determines the receiver sites. The realignment service determines the information regarding which objects are supposed to be replicated to which sites on the basis of the replication model and writes that information into the lookup tables. In order to replicate the BDoc message to the newly determined sites, the realignment service starts data extracts, which ensure that the mobile adapter forwards the BDoc message into the outbound queues of the sites that were newly determined.

Realignment

Figure 3.15 illustrates the interaction between replication and realignment.

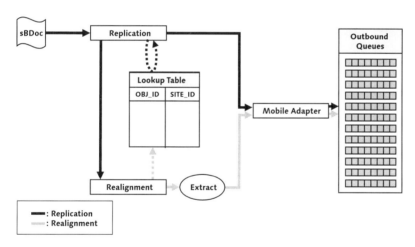

Figure 3.15 Interaction Between Replication and Realignment

As described above, the lookup tables represent the link between replication and realignment. Based on the lookup tables, replication determines which data must be replicated to which sites, while realignment maintains this information in the lookup tables. Lookup tables contain the following fields:

Lookup tables

▶ **OBJ_ID**
GUID of an object instance (intelligent distribution) or publication (lookup table SMOHLUBULK in the case of bulk distribution).

▶ **SITE_ID**
GUID of the site to which the object instance (or all object instances) that belongs to the publication is supposed to be replicated.

▶ **EXTRACTED**
This flag indicates whether or not the object instance (or all object instances) that belong to the publication have already been sent to the site ("T" = TRUE or "F" = FALSE). If an object instance (or all object instances) that belongs to the publication has not been sent to a site yet, changes to this object instance (or these object instances) won't be replicated to the respective site either.

▶ **ASSIGNMENT**
This flag indicates whether the object instance was directly assigned to the site via a subscription or indirectly through an interlinkage.

▶ **ACCDATE, ACCTIME**
Date and time of the last change.

Examples

Short information about business partners (replication object CUSTOMER_ HIERARCHY) is replicated to the mobile clients via bulk distribution. Lookup table SMOHLUBULK, which is relevant for objects replicated in this manner, contains an entry for each site to which this data is supposed to be replicated. The OBJ_ID field contains the GUID of the publication from Table SMOHPUBL, while the SITE_ID field contains the GUID of the corresponding site from Table SMOHSITEID.

Customers (replication object CAPGEN_OBJ_WRITE) are replicated intelligently to the mobile clients. Entries contained in the lookup table indicate that the object instances are replicated to the corresponding sites. Here, the OBJ_ID field contains the GUID of the object instance (i.e., in this case that's the GUID of the customer from CDB table SMOKNA1), while the SITE_ID field contains the GUID of the corresponding site from Table SMOHSITEID.

R&R queues | Because various tasks of the R&R, such as the realignment and extraction of data, can be very time-consuming, an *R&R queue framework* is used to separate those tasks from the synchronization flow and dialog steps in the administration console. Unlike inbound and outbound queues, the R&R queue framework is not based on the technology of qRFC, but on that of tRFC.

The following R&R queues exist:

▶ **AC_EXTRACT queue**
If a user starts an AC extract in the administration console, corresponding entries are placed in the AC_EXTRACT queue in order to provide the requested data for the sites.

▶ **EXTRACTBLK queue**
The R&R processes place entries for extracts of replication objects that have been replicated in a bulk process into the EXTRACTBLK queue in order to provide the data to the relevant sites.

▶ **EXTRACT queue**
The R&R processes place entries for extracts of individual intelligently and dependently replicated object instances (of individual customers, for example) into the EXTRACT queue in order to provide the data to the relevant sites.

▶ **REALIGN queue**
The R&R processes place entries of individual intelligently and dependently replicated object instances (of individual customers, for example) into the REALIGN queue in order to determine the relevant sites and to maintain the lookup tables accordingly.

▶ **SUBCHECK queue**
Once the assignment of sites to subscriptions has been changed in the administration console, entries are placed into the SUBCHECK queue in order to extract the relevant data for the sites.

For each entry in the R&R queues, a corresponding entry is created in Table SMOHMSGQ. If the queue entry is linked to a list of sites (this refers to entries in the AC_EXTRACT, EXTRACT, EXTRACTBLK, and SUBCHECK queues), you can find this list in Table SMOHSITEQ. The status of the individual R&R queues is indicated in Table SMOHSGQST.

To display R&R queues, you must either call Transaction SMOH-QUEUE or select **Architecture and Technology • Middleware • Monitoring • Queues • Monitor R&R Queues** from the SAP Easy Access menu. The system then displays the status of the queue demon as well as the status and number of entries in the individual R&R queues as shown in Figure 3.16

Displaying R&R queues

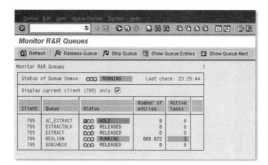

Figure 3.16 Display of an Overview of R&R Queues

If you click on a queue (in the **Queue** column) or after clicking the **Show Queue Entries** button, the system displays the entries of an individual R&R queue, as shown in Figure 3.17 for the AC_EXTRACT queue.

R&R queue demon   The *R&R queue demon* is responsible for triggering the processing of the R&R queues once the queues contain entries and the queue status permits the processing of the entries. The queue demon always runs in client 000, but you can start it from any other client.

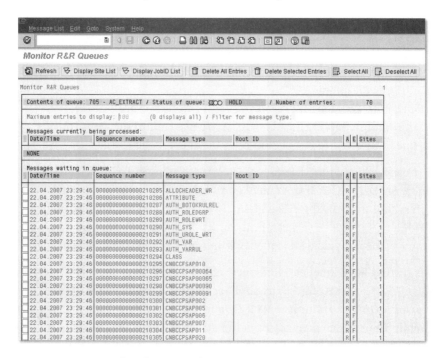

Figure 3.17 Display of Entries in the R&R Queue

The R&R queue demon can assume one of the following statuses:

▶ **RUNNING**

The queue demon is active, that is, it starts the processing of R&R queues as soon as they contain entries and the queue status permits the processing of these entries.

▶ **STOPPING**

The queue demon has been stopped. In this case, the status is first set to STOPPING before the queue demon discontinues its work and the status is set to HOLD.

▶ **HOLD**

The queue demon has been stopped and therefore cannot trigger the processing of entries in the R&R queues.

▶ **STARTING**

The queue demon has been started. In this case, the status is first set to STARTING before the queue demon actually starts working and the status is set to RUNNING.

To start or stop the queue demon, click the **Start Queue Demon** or **Stop Queue Demon** buttons in Transaction SMOHQUEUE (see Figure 3.18).

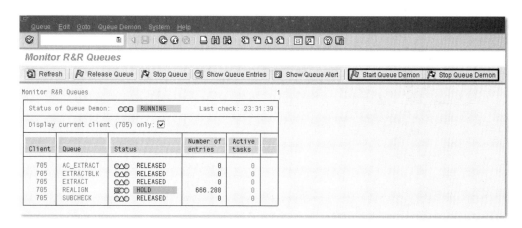

Figure 3.18 Starting and Stopping the Queue Demon

R&R queues can assume one of the following statuses:

▶ **HOLD**

The processing of entries in the queue has been stopped. Entries in the queue are not processed in this status.

113

► **RELEASED**

The processing of entries in the queue is permitted, but the process is currently inactive.

► **STARTING**

The queue demon has detected that there is at least one entry to be processed in a queue that has the RELEASED status. The status of the queue is first set to STARTING. Then the processing of the queue is triggered and the status changes to RUNNING.

► **RUNNING**

The entries in the queue are currently being processed.

► **STOPPING**

The processing of entries in the queue has been stopped. No new queue entries will be processed, whereas the processing of entries that are already being processed will be completed before the status is set to HOLD.

Starting and stopping R&R queues | To start or stop R&R queues, click the **Release Queue** or **Stop Queue** buttons in Transaction SMOHQUEUE. Alternatively, you can click the traffic light icon that indicates the status of the respective queue (see Figure 3.19).

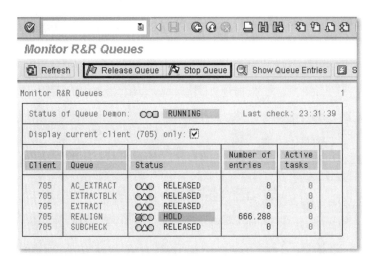

Figure 3.19 Starting and Stopping R&R Queues

Replication | Like the CDB service, the *replication* is also called in the synchronization flow using flow context *SO1 — sBDoc Notification*. First, a replication wrapper is called, which then calls the *replication service* for the respective BDoc type. The replication wrapper for sBDocs is actually the function module, SMOH_REPLICATION_WRAPPER_SYNC; the replication services for the individual BDocs are generated function modules with the following naming convention: <namespace><industry><BDoc Type>_RRR.

Based on the lookup tables, the replication service determines the sites to which the data is supposed to be sent. If necessary, the realignment service and the extraction of data are triggered at this stage as well.

The following section describes the steps involved in bulk replication. Figure 3.20 illustrates which queues are processed in which sequence. The numbers used in the description below refer to the corresponding steps in the figure.

Bulk replication

▶ The replication service is started in the synchronization flow. ❶

▶ The receiver sites for the sBDoc message are determined in lookup table SMOHLUBULK. The receiver determination process only takes active sites into account that have already received an extract of the publication (EXTRACTED = "T"). The list of receivers is then transferred to the mobile outbound adapter, which, in turn, writes the sBDoc message into the outbound queues of the receiver sites. ❷

A bulk replication doesn't involve any realignment.

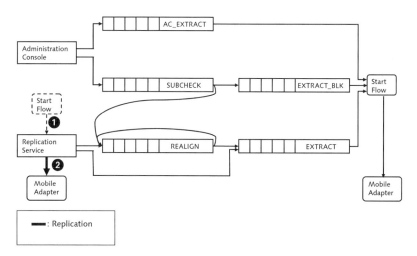

Figure 3.20 Bulk Replication

The following section describes the individual steps carried out in the case of intelligent replication and realignment. Figure 3.21 illustrates which queues are processed in which sequence. The numbers used in the description below refer to the corresponding steps in the figure.

▸ The replication service is started in the synchronization flow. **❶**

▸ The receiver sites for the sBDoc message are determined based on the generated lookup tables for the respective BDoc types. The receiver determination process only takes active sites into account that have already received an extract of the object instance (EXTRACTED = "T"). The list of receivers is then transferred to the mobile outbound adapter, which, in turn, writes the sBDoc message into the outbound queues of the receiver sites. **❷**

▸ For active sites that are determined on the basis of the lookup table but haven't received an extract of the object instance yet (EXTRACTED = "F"), an entry is written to the EXTRACT queue. **❸**

▸ During the processing of entries in the EXTRACT queue, new sBDoc messages are generated using flow context *SO4 − sBDoc Direct Send* and the list of receivers is populated. **❹**

▸ The new sBDoc messages are stored in the BDoc store, while the list of receivers is forwarded to the mobile outbound adapter, which writes it into the outbound queues of the receiver sites. **❺**

▸ Then, a check is made to determine whether the contents of the generated lookup table relevant to the BDoc type must be changed. This is the case whenever an object instance is created or deleted or if at least one criteria field of the publication has changed. If the contents of the lookup table must be changed, the object instance is written to the REALIGN queue. **❻**

▸ During the processing of an entry in the REALIGN queue, the entries for the object instance that are contained in the lookup table are compared with the relevant sites that have been calculated on the basis of subscriptions and interlinkages. Sites that have been determined in the lookup table, but that haven't been calculated based on the subscriptions ("old" sites) are deleted from the lookup table, and deletions for the object instance are written to the EXTRACT queue. For sites that have not been determined in the lookup table, but that have been calculated based on the subscriptions ("new" sites), new entries are written into the lookup table, and entries for extracts of the object instance are written to the EXTRACT queue. Moreover, for sites that have initiated the creation of a new object instance but aren't responsible for this object instance themselves, deletions are written into the EXTRACT queue. **7**

▶ If dependent object instances exist for an object instance in the REALIGN queue and that object instance is processed, then new entries are generated for the dependent object instances in the REALIGN queue. **8**

▶ During the processing of entries in the EXTRACT queue, new sBDoc messages are generated using flow context *SO4 — sBDoc Direct Send* and the list of receivers is populated. **9**

▶ The new sBDoc messages are stored in the BDoc store, while the list of receivers is forwarded to the mobile outbound adapter, which writes the sBDoc message into the outbound queues of the receiver sites. **10**

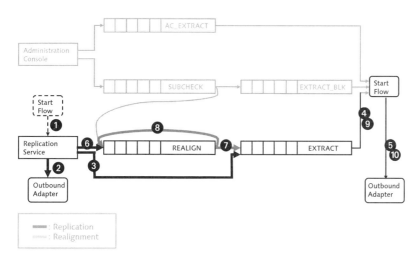

Figure 3.21 Intelligent Replication and Realignment

Example

The replication model defines that customers are replicated to mobile clients of sales representatives based on the customers' ZIP codes. Because mobile client A is used by a regional sales manager who is responsible for the entire area of Germany, he receives all customers with ZIP codes from 00000 through 99999.

Mobile client B is used by a sales representative who is responsible for the area with ZIP codes from 60000 through 69999. Therefore, this sales representative receives the data corresponding to that area.

Then, a new customer is created with customer number 1 and ZIP code 31311. During replication and realignment, the following steps are carried out:

▶ The replication service is started in the synchronization flow. ❶

▶ Because customer 1 is new, the lookup table doesn't contain any entries for this customer yet. Therefore, Steps ❷ through ❺ (see Figure 3.21) can be omitted.

▶ It turns out that the lookup table for customers must be changed now because a new customer is being created. For this reason, an entry is written to the REALIGN queue. ❻

▶ During the processing of an entry in the REALIGN queue, the entries for the object instance that are contained in the lookup table are compared with the relevant sites that have been calculated on the basis of subscriptions and interlinkages. The lookup table doesn't contain any entries for the new customer 1. However, based on the subscriptions, it can be calculated that mobile client A is responsible for this customer. For this reason, a new entry for customer 1 and mobile client A is written into the lookup table and an entry for an extract of customer 1 for mobile client A is written to the EXTRACT queue. ❼

▶ No dependent data currently exists for customer 1 in the REALIGN queue. So, Step ❽ can be omitted.

▶ During the processing of entries in the EXTRACT queue, a new sBDoc message is generated using flow context *SO4 — sBDoc Direct Send* for customer 1. The list of receivers is populated with mobile client A. ❾

▶ The new sBDoc message is stored in the BDoc store, while the list of receivers is forwarded to the mobile outbound adapter, which writes the sBDoc message into the outbound queues of mobile client A. ❿

Now, the data of the customer with customer number 1 is changed, and because the customer relocates to a different place, the ZIP code changes from 31311 to 68723. During replication and realignment, the following steps are carried out:

▶ The replication service is started in the synchronization flow. ❶

▶ Based on the generated lookup table for customers, mobile client A is determined as the receiver of the sBDoc message containing the change to customer 1. This receiver is transferred to the mobile outbound adapter which, in turn, writes the sBDoc message into the outbound queues of mobile client A. ❷

▶ Because mobile client A has already received an extract of customer 1, the entry in the lookup table reads EXTRACTED = "T". Therefore, Steps ❸ through ❺ (see Figure 3.21) can be omitted.

▶ It now turns out that the lookup table for customers must again be changed because the ZIP code is a criteria field of the publication for distributing customers. For this reason, an entry is written to the REALIGN queue. ❻

▶ During the processing of an entry in the REALIGN queue, the entries for the object instance that are contained in the lookup table are compared with the relevant sites that have been calculated on the basis of subscriptions and interlinkages. Based on the lookup table, mobile client A is determined as the receiver for the new customer 1. However, based on subscriptions, both mobile clients A and B are calculated as receivers. For this reason, a new entry for customer 1 and mobile client B is written into the lookup table, and an entry for an extract of customer 1 for mobile client B is written to the EXTRACT queue. ❼

▶ No dependent data does exist yet for customer 1 in the REALIGN queue. Therefore, Step ❽ can be omitted.

▶ During the processing of entries in the EXTRACT queue, a new sBDoc message is generated using flow context *SO4 — sBDoc Direct Send* for customer 1. The list of receivers is populated with mobile client B. ❾

▶ The new sBDoc message is stored in the BDoc store, while the list of receivers is forwarded to the mobile outbound adapter, which writes the sBDoc message into the outbound queues of mobile client B. ❿

With the exception of replication and realignment, the R&R queues are also required for *AC extracts*. An AC extract is started in the administration console in order to send selected data manually to mobile clients. Chapter 10, *Outbound Queues*, contains instructions on how to perform an AC extract. Figure 3.22 illustrates which queues are processed in which sequence. The numbers used in the description below refer to the corresponding steps in the figure.

AC extract

▶ A user starts an AC extract in the administration console. This can either be a complete extract comprising all data for selected sites, extracts for selected subscriptions of one site only, or extracts for selected replication objects of a subscription. Along with the sites to which they are supposed to be sent, the selected replication objects are written to the AC_EXTRACT queue. This process also includes dependent replication objects and replication objects that are linked to a replication object to be extracted via an interlinkage. If, at the same time, an AC extract of the same objects for multiple sites is carried out, only one entry containing all receivers will be written to the AC_EXTRACT queue. ❶

► During the processing of entries in the AC_EXTRACT queue, new sBDoc messages are generated using flow context *SO4 — sBDoc Direct Send*, and the list of receivers is populated. ❷

► The new sBDoc messages are stored in the BDoc store, while the list of receivers is forwarded to the mobile outbound adapter, which writes the sBDoc message into the outbound queues of the receiver sites. ❸

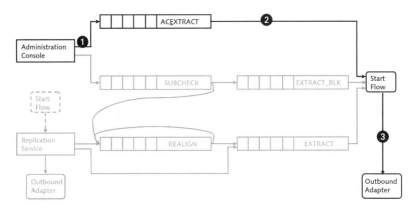

Figure 3.22 AC Extract

Changing the assignment of sites to subscriptions

R&R queues are also used for changing the assignment of sites to subscriptions in the administration console. Figure 3.23 illustrates which queues are processed in which sequence. The numbers used in the description below refer to the corresponding steps in the figure.

► A user creates or removes the assignment of a site to a subscription in the administration console. This causes an entry containing the subscription and receiver site to be written to the SUBCHECK queue. ❶

► During the processing of entries in the SUBCHECK queue, a separate entry is written to the EXTRACTBLK queue for each replication object, which is replicated in a bulk process. If the SUBCHECK queue contains multiple entries for the same subscription, an optimization process ensures that the required entries are written to the EXTRACTBLK queue only once (containing multiple receivers). ❷

▶ During the processing of entries in the EXTRACTBLK queue, new sBDoc messages are generated using flow context *SO4 — sBDoc Direct Send*, and the list of receivers is populated. ❸

▶ The new sBDoc messages are stored in the BDoc store, while the list of receivers is forwarded to the mobile outbound adapter, which writes it into the outbound queues of the receiver sites. ❹

▶ In the case of intelligently replicated replication objects, a separate entry is written into the REALIGN queue for each object instance in order to determine to which sites the object instances are supposed to be replicated. If the SUBCHECK queue contains multiple entries for the same subscription, an optimization process makes sure that the required entries are written to the REALIGN queue only once (containing multiple receivers). ❺

▶ During the processing of an entry in the REALIGN queue, the entries for the object instance that are contained in the lookup table are compared with the relevant sites that have been calculated on the basis of subscriptions and interlinkages. Sites that have been determined in the lookup table, but that haven't been calculated based on the subscriptions ("old" sites) are deleted from the lookup table, and deletions for the object instance are written to the EXTRACT queue. For sites that have not been determined in the lookup table, but that have been calculated based on the subscriptions ("new" sites), new entries are written into the lookup table, and entries for extracts of the object instance are written to the EXTRACT queue. ❻

▶ If dependent object instances exist for an object instance in the REALIGN queue and that object instance is processed, then new entries are generated for the dependent object instances in the REALIGN queue. ❼

▶ During the processing of entries in the EXTRACT queue, new sBDoc messages are generated using flow context *SO4 — sBDoc Direct Send*, and the list of receivers is populated. ❽

▶ The new sBDoc messages are stored in the BDoc store, while the list of receivers is forwarded to the mobile outbound adapter, which writes the sBDoc message into the outbound queues of the receiver sites. ❾

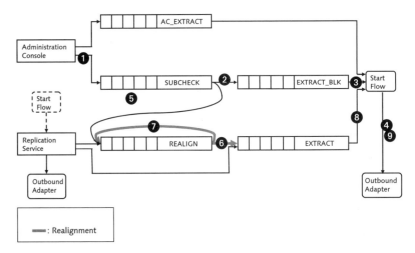

Figure 3.23 Changing the Assignment of Sites to Subscriptions

3.3.3 Mobile Outbound Adapter

After the CDB service and the replication service, the *mobile outbound adapter* is called in the synchronization flow using flow context *SO1 — sBDoc Notification*. The mobile outbound adapter is also called for extracts in the synchronization flow (flow context *SO4 — sBDoc Direct Send*).

The mobile outbound adapter is not supposed to carry out mappings to other data formats or to generate new sBDoc messages. It is merely responsible for forwarding an existing sBDoc message to the outbound queues of previously determined receivers.

In order to call the mobile outbound adapter in the synchronization flow, function module SMW3_OUTBOUNDADP_CALLADAPTERS is first called as a dispatcher. This function module then calls the mobile client outbound adapter, which is the generic function module, SMW1_SAPMOBILE_OUTADAPTER. This function module determines the names of the qRFC outbound queues for the individual receivers, which are maintained in the administration console. In addition, it determines which message types are supposed to be sent to the individual mobile clients. A client that has initiated a data change receives a *confirmation message*, whereas all other receivers receive a BDoc message that contains only the modified data. In the case of extracts, the following other message types are sent to the clients: *current state messages* containing the complete current dataset of an object from the CDB, *ZAP messages* for deleting all instances of an object type, *deletion messages* for individual object instances, and *bulk messages* for the simultaneous creation of multiple object instances. After that, a generated function module is called, which writes the data into the outbound queues of the receivers.

3.3.4 Rejection Messages

In Chapter 2, *Inbound Processing and Validation*, we already mentioned that if an error occurs in the case of data changes that are initiated by a mobile client, a *rejection message* is sent to that mobile client. The purpose of the rejection message is to re-establish a state of consistency in the database of the mobile client, that is, the status of the database must be identical with that of the CDB. Moreover, the rejection message enables the user of the mobile client to realize that an error occurred with regard to the data change and to rectify that error in the mobile client application.

In inbound processing, the CRM Server receives an sBDoc message from the mobile client, which contains information about the data changes. The rejection message is a copy of that sBDoc message. All changes contained in the sBDoc message are read from the CDB ("before image") and written into the rejection message. The only receiver of a rejection message is the mobile client that initiated the rejected data change. The rejection message is transferred to the mobile outbound adapter, which, in turn, writes it into the outbound queues of the mobile client.

3.3.5 Flow Contexts in the Synchronization Flow

Table 3.4 provides an overview of the flow contexts in the outbound synchronization flow, that is, during the outbound processing of sBDoc messages.

Flow Context	Description	Usage
SO1	sBDoc Notification	In the case of delta processing, this flow context is responsible for updating the CDB and the subscribed mobile clients.

Table 3.4 Flow Contexts Used for Outbound Processing of sBDoc Messages

Flow Context	Description	Usage
SOA	sBDoc Notification (additional calls)	Calls additional services for delta processing.
SO2	sBDoc Rejection	In the case of an error, the mobile client that initiated a change receives a rejection message, including a "before image," in order to re-establish a consistent state in its database.
SOB	sBDoc Rejection (additional calls)	Calls additional services if an error occurs in a change that was initiated by a mobile client.
SO3	sBDoc Initial Load	In the case of an initial load, this flow context is responsible for updating the CDB and mobile clients.
SOC	sBDoc Initial Load (additional calls)	Calls additional services for initial load.
SO4	sBDoc Direct Send	Is called by the extract function of the R&R service in order to send current state, ZAP, deletion, or bulk messages to the receivers (mobile clients) determined by the R&R.

Table 3.4 Flow Contexts Used for Outbound Processing of sBDoc Messages (cont.)

3.4 Outbound Queues

Outbound queues

Outbound queues represent the final stage in CRM outbound processing. The use of queues ensures that the processing of data in the CRM system is separated from further processing in the external system. The CRM system merely needs to write the data into the relevant outbound queue without the need for the external system to be available at that point in time. The CRM system, in turn, doesn't need to wait for the data to be further processed. Moreover, using outbound queues enables you to control the distribution of system resources for processing the data.

The following section provides a brief description of qRFC, which represent the basis of outbound queues. Next, we'll describe how the QOUT Scheduler plans and starts the processing of data in the outbound queues. We'll also introduce the qRFC monitor for outbound queues, as well as naming conventions that are used for outbound queues.

3.4.1 qRFC

As is the case with inbound queues, the qRFC (*queued Remote Function Call*) technology is also used for outbound queues. Chapter 2, *Inbound Processing and Validation*, has a detailed description of the basic principles of qRFC. Figure 3.24 once again shows the tables used by qRFC. This figure contains both the tables for inbound queues and those for outbound queues.

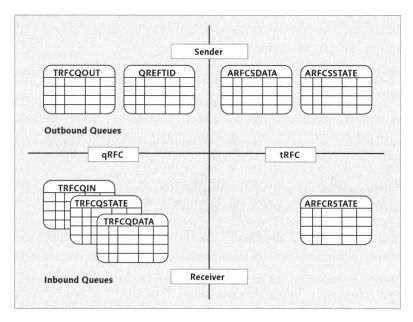

Figure 3.24 Tables of qRFC

3.4.2 QOUT Scheduler

The *QOUT Scheduler* (*Outbound Scheduler*) plans and starts the processing of entries in the outbound queues. You can use Transaction SMQS to control and modify the settings of the QOUT Scheduler.

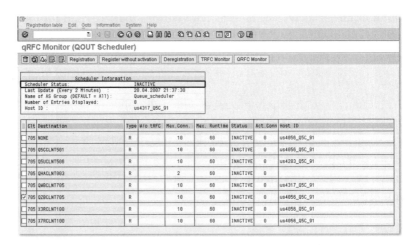

Figure 3.25 QOUT Scheduler

Figure 3.25 shows the initial screen of the QOUT Scheduler. In contrast to the QIN Scheduler in which all settings are based on queue names, the settings of the QOUT Scheduler are based on destinations, that is, the settings refer to multiple outbound queues that have the same destination.

Usually, you don't have to register destinations in the QOUT Scheduler. If the destinations are TCP/IP connections (type T) or ABAP connections (type 3) to other SAP systems in which the logon information is maintained completely, these destinations are registered automatically. You can determine the type of a destination using Transaction SM59 or by selecting **Architecture and Technology • System Administration • Administration • Network • RFC Destinations** from the SAP Easy Access menu.

Status of the QOUT Scheduler Usually, the QOUT Scheduler is not constantly active because the outbound queues do not always contain entries to be processed. For this reason, the default status of the QOUT Scheduler is *INACTIVE*, as shown in Figure 3.25.

Once an entry is written to an outbound queue, the QOUT Scheduler starts automatically, and its status changes to *STARTING*. When the QOUT Scheduler is working, its status changes to *ACTIVE*. If the QOUT Scheduler waits for a free work process, its status is *WAITING*.

Activating the QOUT Scheduler You can also activate the QOUT Scheduler manually. To do that, select **Edit • Activate Scheduler** from the QOUT Scheduler menu.

To register or deregister a destination (for debugging purposes), select the relevant destination and click the **Registration** or **Deregistration** button, highlighted in Figure 3.26. The **Type** column indicates the status of the destinations, "R" representing registered and "U" deregistered destinations.

Registering and deregistering a destination

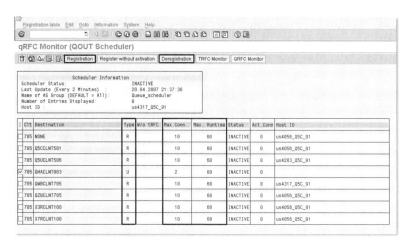

Figure 3.26 Parameters of the QOUT Scheduler

You can set the following parameters during the registration of a destination:

Parameters for destinations

▶ The **Max. Conn.** parameter defines the maximum number of concurrent connections to a destination (i.e., work processes in the CRM system).

▶ The **Max. Runtime** parameter specifies the maximum amount of time during which the scheduler processes data of an outbound queue for the destination before it begins processing data of the subsequent outbound queue.

As shown in Figure 3.26, the QOUT Scheduler also displays the current settings of these two parameters.

You can exclude destinations from being processed by the QOUT Scheduler. The difference between deregistered and excluded destinations is that no data is sent to deregistered destinations, whereas data that is sent to excluded destinations is processed immediately, but not by the QOUT Scheduler.

Excluding a destination

To exclude a destination, select the destination in the QOUT Scheduler and choose **Edit • Exclude** from the menu.

3.4.3 The qRFC Monitor for Outbound Queues

The *qRFC Monitor for Outbound Queues* enables you to view the status of outbound queues as well as the entries of individual outbound queues.

Displaying an overview of outbound queues

By selecting a destination in the QOUT Scheduler and clicking the **QRFC Monitor** button, you can open the qRFC monitor for the outbound queues assigned to the selected destination. Alternatively, you can start the qRFC monitor via Transaction SMQ1 or by selecting **Architecture and Technology • Middleware • Monitoring • Queues • Displays Outbound RFC Queues** from the SAP Easy Access menu. In the latter case, the system first displays a selection screen in which you must enter the queue name (or several queue names by using the asterisk character *****). Once you have entered the queue name, you can start the qRFC monitor for outbound queues by clicking the **Execute** button (F8, selected in Figure 3.27).

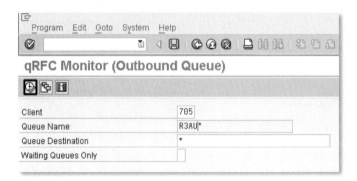

Figure 3.27 Selection Screen for Outbound Queues

The qRFC monitor for outbound queues initially displays an overview of all selected outbound queues, including the number of entries for each queue (see Figure 3.28).

By clicking on the **Change View** button, which is selected in Figure 3.28, you can access various other views, which are similar to the views available in the QIN Scheduler, as described in detail in Chapter 2, *Inbound Processing and Validation*. These other views also include detail views that display the status of each individual outbound queue.

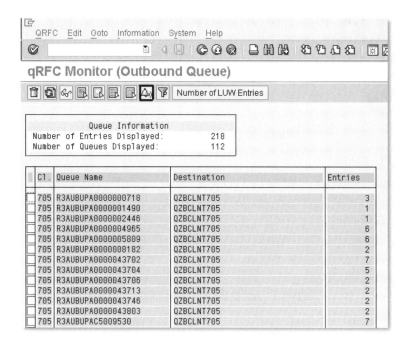

Figure 3.28 Overview of Outbound Queues

Outbound queues can have the following statuses:

▸ **READY**
The first queue entry is ready for processing.

▸ **RUNNING**
The first queue entry is currently being processed.

▸ **EXECUTED**
The first queue entry has been processed and is now waiting for a confirmation by the receiver.

▸ **NOSEND**
The entries in this queue are not actively sent; instead, the receiver (e.g., a mobile client) must retrieve the data.

▸ **STOP**
The first queue entry is temporarily locked by the application.

▸ **WAITSTOP**
A dependency exists between the first queue entry and the first entry in another queue that is currently locked. The queue waits for the lock to be released.

▶ **WAITING**

A dependency exists between the first queue entry and an entry in another queue that is not the first entry in that queue. The queue waits for the entry in the other queue to be processed.

▶ **WAITUPDA**

The first queue entry contains an update task, and the queue is waiting for this task to be executed.

▶ **SYSLOAD**

Currently, there is no free dialog work process to process the queue; the system will retry processing the queue at a later stage.

▶ **CPICERR**

Network or communication error; the system will retry processing the queue.

▶ **ARETRY**

Temporary error; the system will retry processing the queue.

▶ **SYSFAIL**

An error occurred on the side of the receiver. You must search for a short dump in the receiver system and eliminate the cause of the error. The system will not automatically retry to process the queue.

Displaying details for outbound queues

To display details for individual outbound queues, select the relevant queues in the overview and click **Display Selection**. Alternatively, you can double-click a queue name to navigate to the detail screen.

The detail screen displays the following information for the respective queues (see Figure 3.29):

▶ **Cl.** (Client): The system displays only outbound queues of the client to which you have logged in.

▶ **Queue Name**

▶ **Destination** of the queue

▶ **Entries**: Number of entries that are currently contained in the queue

▶ **Status** of the queue

▶ **Date 1, Time 1**: Date and time when the first entry was written into the respective queue.

▶ **NxtDate, NxtTim**: Date and time when the last entry was written into the respective queue.

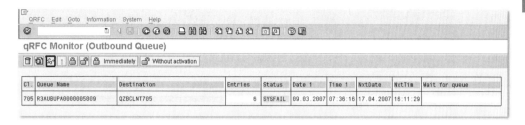

Figure 3.29 Detailed Display of Outbound Queues

If you want to view the individual entries of an outbound queue, select the relevant queue name in the detail screen and click the **Select** button, which is highlighted in Figure 3.29. Alternatively, you can also view the queue entries by double-clicking the respective queue name. As shown in Figure 3.30, the system then displays the following information:

Displaying entries of an outbound queue

▶ **Cl.** (Client)

▶ **User** that has written the entry to the queue

▶ **Function Module**: RFC function module that is executed during the processing of the queue entry in the receiver system

▶ **Queue Name**

▶ **Destination** of the queue

▶ **Date, Time**: Date and time at which the entry was written to the queue

▶ **Status**: Processing status of the queue entry:

▷ The status of non-processed queue entries is: Transaction recorded

▷ The status of a queue entry that is currently being processed is: Transaction executing.

▷ If errors occur, the status text contains an error description, such as the following: "The current application triggered a termination with a short dump."

Double-click a field of a queue entry (e.g., **Queue Name** or **Destination**) to obtain additional detailed information.

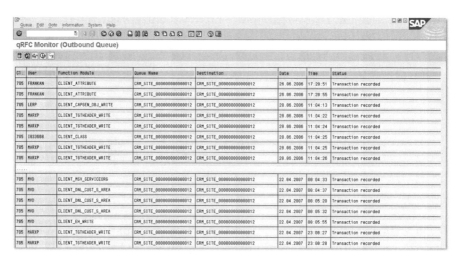

Figure 3.30 Displaying Entries of Outbound Queues

3.4.4 Naming Conventions for Outbound Queues

Outbound queues
for R/3

For outbound queues that are used for uploading data to the R/3 system, the following naming convention is used: R3AU<object part><objectID>. Both the <object part> and <objectID> for the respective BDoc type are defined in Table SMOFQFIND: <object part> is contained in the **Queue Object Part** field, while <objectID> can be found in the field specified in **Segment Field Name**.

> **Example**
>
> R3AUBUPA0000004711 is an outbound queue for business partner data (BUPA object) from the CRM system to R/3.

Outbound queues
for mobile clients

The naming convention for outbound queues for data that is to be sent to mobile clients is CRM_SITE*. You can determine the exact queue name in the administration console (Transaction SMOEAC). To do that, you must display the details of the corresponding site. The name of the outbound queue is listed under **Dependent Information · Queues** (see Figure 3.31). The names of outbound queues for mobile clients are stored in Table SMOHQTAB.

Figure 3.32 provides a graphical overview, which includes the names of outbound queues for data to be sent to different systems.

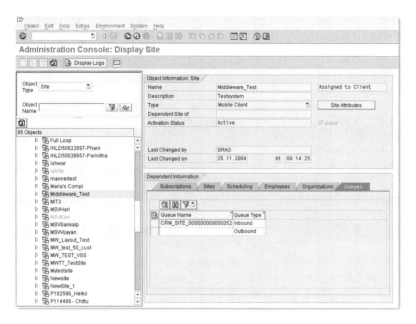

Figure 3.31 Outbound Queue Name for Mobile Clients in the Administration Console

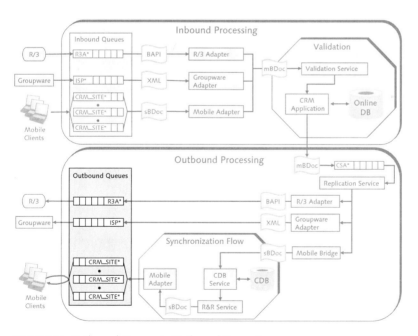

Figure 3.32 Outbound Queues in Outbound Processing

Additional
outbound queues When you start an initial load, a request, or a comparison using DIMa (Data Integrity Manager), an outbound queue is generated in the CRM system before the data is sent from the R/3 system. Table 3.5 lists the naming conventions used for these types of outbound queues.

Type of Queue	Queue Name
Outbound queue at the start of an initial load from R/3 to CRM	R3AI_<OBJECT>
Outbound queue at the start of an initial load from CRM to the CDB	CDBI_<OBJECT>
Outbound queue at the start of a request from R/3 to CRM	R3AR_<OBJECT>
Outbound queue at the start of a request from CRM to the CDB	CDBR_<OBJECT>
Outbound queue at the start of DIMa for comparing data between R/3 and CRM at header level	R3AH_<DIMAINSTANCE>
Outbound queue at the start of DIMa for comparing data between R/3 and CRM at details level	R3AD_<DIMAINSTANCE>
Outbound queue at the start of DIMa for comparing data between CRM and CDB at header level	CDBH_<DIMAINSTANCE>
Outbound queue at the start of DIMa for comparing data between CRM and CDB at details level	CDBD_<DIMAINSTANCE>

Table 3.5 Names of Additional Outbound Queues

In the names listed in Table 3.5, <OBJECT> represents the name of the respective adapter object, while <DIMAINSTANCE> stands for the respective name of the DIMa instance, which you can determine using Transaction SDIMA (Data Integrity Manager).

In this chapter, we go into more detail as we describe what BDocs are, how you can model them, and what steps you need to take to keep system performance high.

4   BDoc Modeling and Storage

CRM Business Documents (BDocs) are data containers for transporting and processing business objects. The benefit of a BDoc is that it enables business objects to be transported as a self-contained unit without the user having to know anything about the technical structure of the object in the database ("What belongs in which table?"). Besides the object data, BDocs also contain all the information on the processing status of a Middleware object.

BDocs are similar in structure to the IDoc; however, they go beyond IDocs in that they can also be easily extended via a framework that is available in the Middleware. You have to manually create very few function modules in Middleware to use an extended BDoc in CRM Middleware; you can automatically generate most of the required Middleware routines without knowing ABAP or SQL. Therefore, while an IDoc is only an intermediary document, a finished BDoc provides an application that you can use immediately to process your data. In other words, if you didn't use BDocs, you would have to write an application that deletes associated item data when the object header is deleted. With a BDoc, on the other hand, a cascading delete process is triggered automatically. The only information that has to be explicitly provided is the instruction to delete the object.

4.1   Definition and Structure of BDocs

As we have seen in the previous chapters on inbound processing, validation, and outbound processing, there are two basic classes of BDocs: *synchronization BDocs* (sBDocs) and *messaging BDocs* (mBDocs). Besides these two main classes, there is also a third: *mobile*

BDoc classes

application BDocs (query BDocs). A mobile application BDoc type is used by CRM mobile applications to query data from the mobile client's local database. This chapter explains in detail the technical structure of the three types, the basic differences between them, and how to model BDocs.

[»]   SAP Customer Relationship Management (SAP CRM) contains two integration models that are different in terms of message exchange and synchronization. The message layer uses mBDoc types to exchange data between applications on the CRM Server and the relevant backend (R/3 or a third-party system). The synchronization layer, on the other hand, uses sBDocs and allows access to a fully functional replication and realignment mechanism (see Chapter 9, *Replication Model and R&R*). The CRM Server and external clients (mobile client or a GWA_02 instance of the groupware adapter; see Chapter 5, *Groupware Integration*) are synchronized in this case.

Structure of an sBDoc   Synchronization BDocs are used to exchange data with external clients using the synchronization layer of CRM Middleware (described above). An sBDoc contains data on the header and detail level, and this data is divided into segments. The header level has only one segment, which contains the control data. Besides the data segments themselves, which contain the application data, the detailed level — also known as the body level — also contains an error segment that is used to store any error and status information. Database table fields are assigned to the fields in every data segment of an sBDoc. These assignments are made on the basis of a 1-n relationship; in other words, every segment can be assigned to one or more database tables (see Figure 4.1). Mobile application BDocs have a similar structure to sBDocs. In this BDoc class, too, the segments of the mobile application BDoc type are mapped to tables, like those of the sBDoc type.

If a segment is assigned to multiple tables, write access can be gained to only one of these tables, and read access applies to all other tables. Besides pure database tables, the data segments of the sBDoc types can also be assigned to database views or joins. However, in this case too, only one read access is allowed, which is why this method is used in mobile application BDocs only. This class of BDocs queries data from the mobile client's local database, which is why read access is used exclusively.

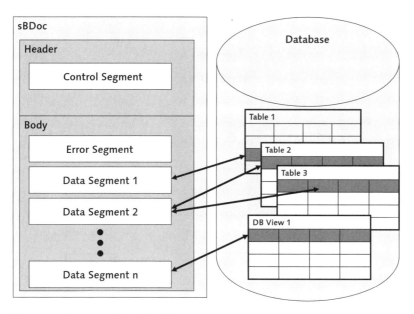

Figure 4.1 Structure of an sBDoc Type

Like sBDocs, an mBDoc consists of two basic parts; however, the definition of these parts and how they function between the BDoc classes are very different. While an sBDoc is divided into a header and a detail part, an mBDoc is usually divided into a *classic part* and an *extension part*, a structure that was introduced with SAP CRM Release 3.0 (see Figure 4.2). The classic part is used for recipient determination and is therefore mandatory. It consists of a header segment and other, sometimes hierarchically structured segments. Contrary to the sBDoc segment, however, the latter type of segments do not contain any application data and are not assigned to any database table. For this reason, all segment fields of an mBDoc are completely filled at runtime by the application. The extension part is optional and contains the actual transactions data. Every extension part of an mBDoc represents its own structure in the database (contrary to the sBDoc, whose data part is defined by means of its assignment to the database structures).

Structure of an
mBDoc

137

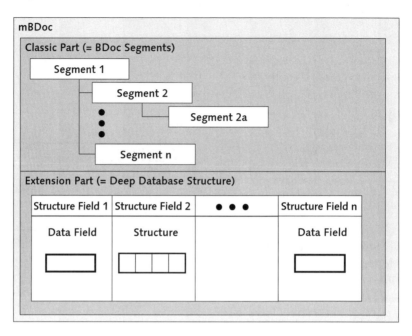

Figure 4.2 Structure of an mBDoc

mBDoc types support the simple type of replication, the intelligent and unfiltered type (bulk replication), only. They cannot handle realignments and dependencies between mBDoc types (see Chapter 3, *Outbound Processing*).

Table 4.1 contains a final overview of the structure of sBDocs and mBDocs.

BDoc Component	Usage	Comment
Header	sBDoc and mBDoc	
Body segments	sBDoc and mBDoc	Created in the BDoc Modeler and, together with the header segment, also known in mBDocs as the classic part. In an mBDoc, these segments contain information for recipient determination. In an sBDoc, this part contains the BDoc information.

Table 4.1 Overview of BDoc Structure Elements

BDoc Component	Usage	Comment
Extension	mBDocs	Modeled in the Data Dictionary, it contains the application data.
Error segment	sBDocs and mBDocs	

Table 4.1 Overview of BDoc Structure Elements (cont.)

Because the data in the synchronization layer also has to be exchanged with the backend via the normal communication channels (and vice versa), an mBDoc is usually assigned to one or more sBDocs. Conversely, however, in static mapping with the BDoc Modeler, every sBDoc can be assigned to only one mBDoc. Figure 4.3 illustrates the assignment between the sBDoc CAPGEN_OBJ_WRITE, which is used to exchange business partner data via the synchronization flow (to mobile clients, for example), and the mBDoc BUPA_MAIN.

Relationship between sBDocs and mBDocs

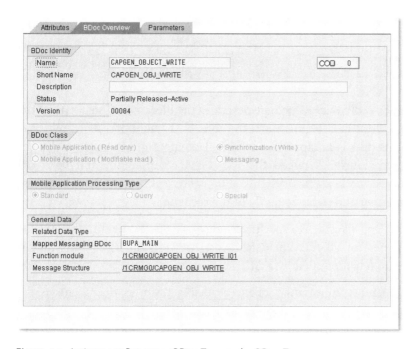

Figure 4.3 Assignment Between sBDoc Type and mBDoc Type

The conversion between the types is based on these assignments. In the outbound interface, conversion takes place in the mobile bridge while the messaging flow is being processed, and in the inbound interface via the mapping service of the mobile adapter (see Figure 4.4).

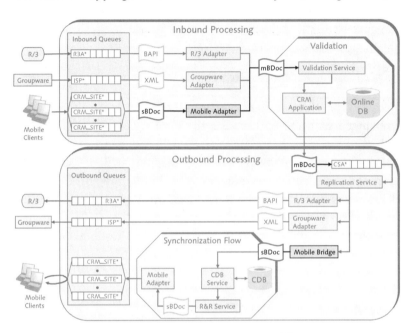

Figure 4.4 Conversion Between mBDoc and sBDoc in Middleware

BDoc types

Each individual BDoc type describes the hierarchical structure of the business data segment and the control segment of a BDoc message. This data is encapsulated in the BDoc messages, which enables the data transfer between the SAP CRM components, and the CRM Server and external systems to be processed in a unified, consistent manner and independently of the content.

BDoc instances

A BDoc instance is a specific instance of a BDoc type that contains the values for all relevant data fields. An individual BDoc instance is uniquely identified by a GUID.

BDoc Modeler and rules

The most important tool for modeling business documents is the CRM Business Document Modeler, which is started by Transaction SBDM. The BDoc Modeler can process BDoc types of all BDoc classes in the CRM system: messaging BDocs, synchronization BDocs and mobile application BDocs. The BDoc Modeler lets you create your own BDocs, and display and extend existing ones. When you start the transaction, you can first filter the BDoc types that are available for display and processing (see Figure 4.5). You can choose to display only BDoc types of a certain BDoc class, select individual BDoc types, or select BDoc types in accordance with organizational criteria, such as activation status. Enter the filter you require and either click the **Execute** button or press the F8 button to open the detailed view of the BDoc types you selected.

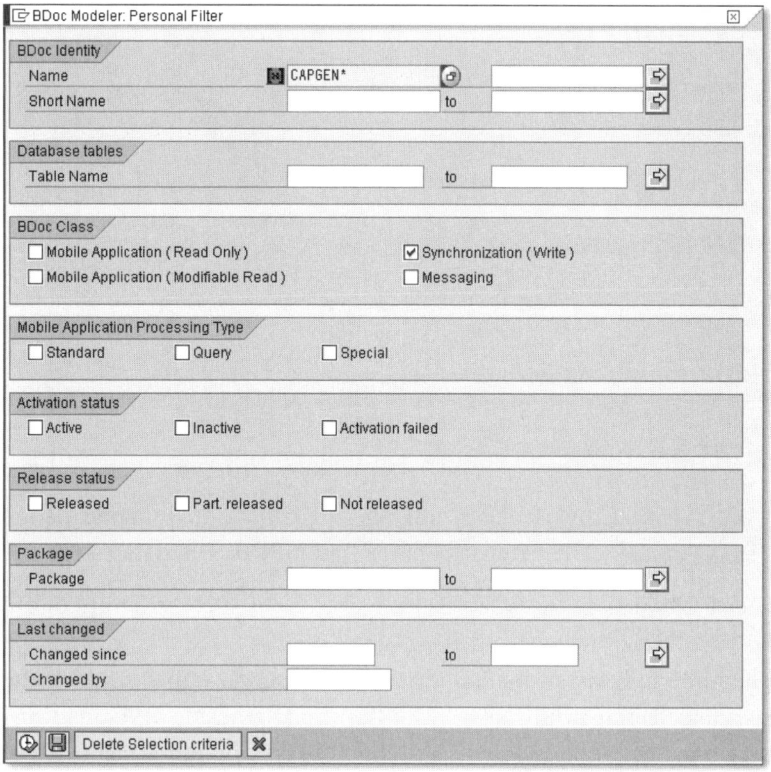

Figure 4.5 Filter Options in the BDoc Modeler

Now, the overview of the selected BDocs opens (see Figure 4.6). Here, you can either create new BDoc types or edit existing ones, in accordance with certain rules.

When creating your own BDocs or segments in the BDoc Modeler, always place a "Z" at the start of the name. Similarly, always place "ZZ" at the start of the names of segment fields that you want to add to a standard segment. However, if the segment to which you want

Namespace

141

to add the new field already exists in the customer namespace, the segment field does not have to start with "ZZ".

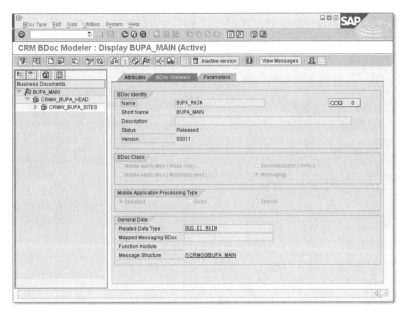

Figure 4.6 BDoc Overview of Transaction SBDM

Only the classic part of an mBDoc type can be maintained in the BDoc Modeler. The extension part of an mBDoc is a database structure that has to be created using Transaction SE11 before the classic part is created.

The left-hand area of the BDoc Modeler contains an overview of the selected BDocs. In this area, click the triangle beside a BDoc to display a list of the individual segments. In Figure 4.6, we see that the BDoc type BUPA_MAIN consists of the segments CRMW_BUPA_HEAD and CRMW_BUPA_SITES. This area also has a toolbar containing the most important actions. This toolbar enables you to release and transport a BDoc and to generate where-used lists, for example. The right-hand area of the BDoc Modeler is the actual work area. Its content and functions are specific to whether you have selected an individual segment of a BDoc or a full BDoc, and to the BDoc class. The **BDoc Overview** tab shows the BDoc class to which the selected BDoc type belongs. You can see that BUPA_MAIN is an mBDoc and is used for message exchange. The **General Data** section of this tab shows the data type of this BDoc and, in the case of sBDocs, any assigned mBDoc types (see Figure 4.3). If you have created any BDocs of your own, you can maintain their assignments here. You can also assign a site type to the individual BDoc types. This assignment is then ultimately analyzed in the administration console if you want to assign a subscription to a site.

Which of the tabs you can activate will depend on the BDoc class in question. For example, while query BDocs can use parameters to execute queries in the local database of the mobile client, this is not possible for mBDocs. Consequently, if you try to go to the **Parameters** tab to edit parameters for mBDoc types, an error message is displayed. If you click a segment in the left-hand area of the screen, the work area changes as shown in Figure 4.7.

Context-sensitive options

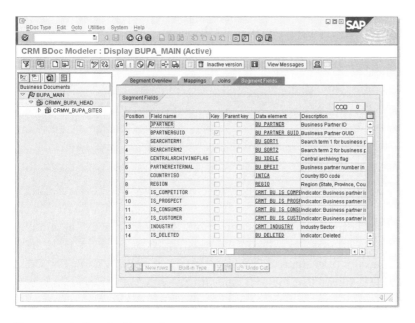

Figure 4.7 Options for Segments

Because mBDoc segments are not assigned to any database tables, an mBDoc type cannot contain any joins or WHERE clauses. The **Mappings** and **Joins** tabs are therefore inactive for mBDocs in the segment view. Figure 4.8 shows the assignment between a segment of an sBDoc and a CDB database table. You can see that segment CAPGEN_OBJECT is assigned to the database table SMOKNA1. If you want to assign a CDB table to one of your own sBDoc segments, this table has to have the client field and only one GUID field in the

WHERE clauses

format CHAR32 or RAW16 as a primary key. Other fields may not be available in the primary key, but may of course be defined as secondary keys. All GUID fields that are used in an sBDoc type as key fields or superordinate key fields have to have the same type (i.e., they must all be either CHAR32 or RAW16).

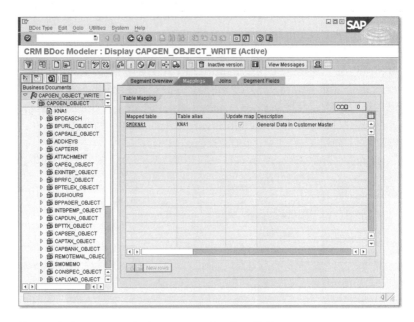

Figure 4.8 Assignment of a Segment to a Database Table

To further specify the assignment of a segment to a database table, you can also specify a WHERE clause, which restricts the table area. The example in Figure 4.9, which contains the sBDoc CAPGEN_OBJ_WRITE, shows that the only relevant SMOKNA1 entries are those in which the **Source** field has the value "CAP". Thus, the selection is restricted to business partners and interested parties. A similar WHERE clause could be defined for the BDoc CONGEN_OBJ_WRITE, with the difference that the restriction would be to source CON (i.e., contact persons).

If you want to assign a table to the topmost segment of two sBDocs in the BDoc Modeler, you have to define your own WHERE clause that enables a fixed, unique assignment of table rows to BDocs (similarly to the example of CAPGEN_OBJECT_WRITE and CONGEN_OBJECT_WRITE). This kind of WHERE clause is then called a *static WHERE clause*.

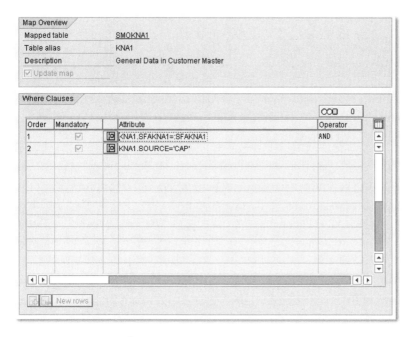

Figure 4.9 WHERE Condition in an sBDoc

The reason for the unique assignment is that without it, a data record would be assigned to two BDoc instances. Because only one BDoc instance is created when a data record is updated, this change then may not reach all the intended recipients, depending on the subscription model.

If you modify WHERE clauses provided by SAP, these are not automatically merged when you implement an upgrade version of SAP BDocs. **[«]**

Also, when creating your own BDoc types, ensure that these have only one topmost segment; that is, a segment without any other superordinate segments. This kind of topmost segment is called the *root segment*. If you want to create a hierarchical structure, note that the keys of the topmost segments also have to exist in the subordinate segment. Thus, there can only be a 1:n relationship between superordinate and subordinate segments of a BDoc type, as a segment can contain only one primary key. CDB tables and their associated BDoc type segments always have to have the key of the table that is directly superordinate to them or the key of their superordinate segment. Every primary key of an sBDoc segment should be a key field in the assigned table that is marked "updatable".

You can also use the BDoc Modeler to release BDocs. However, because released BDocs can no longer be extensively edited, you should do this only if you are certain that no further changes will be made to the BDoc definition. The main restrictions that apply once a BDoc is released are as follows:

▶ Only the description can be edited in the BDoc overview screen.

▶ In the parameter screen, new parameters can be added only at the end, and released parameters cannot be modified or deleted. Thus, if you realize that the existing parameters don't fulfill all the requirements, you may not be able to include any overlooked requirements at this stage.

▶ Restrictions also apply after release to the assignment of a site type to a BDoc definition. Released site types cannot be changed or deleted, and new site types can be added only at the end.

▶ While you can add new segments or segment fields of any hierarchy to a released BDoc type, released segments or segment fields cannot be changed or deleted.

▶ Released static WHERE clauses cannot be changed, but all dynamic WHERE clauses — that is, both released and non-released ones —can be changed. New WHERE clauses can be added only at the end.

[»] Partially released BDocs can be changed only if the BDoc types are custom-defined (i.e., if they are BDocs in the customer namespace).

As is the case for other objects in an SAP system, a locking logic applies on the object level in the BDoc Modeler. Therefore, when you're editing a BDoc type, a lock is placed on this BDoc type so that no other users can edit this type at the same time. However, during the lock period, the locked BDoc type can still be used for data exchange. The table in which the BDoc types are saved is called SMOGTRANS.

4.2   Data Storage for BDoc Messages

So far in this chapter, we have focused on the BDoc classes and the basic structures of the BDoc types of the individual classes. Now, we will turn our attention to actual instances of the data, how the data is stored, and the meanings of individual values in the main generic fields of a BDoc instance.

Many BDocs contain only delta data. Therefore, besides the actual application values, a BDoc message also has to contain information on what is to happen with this data (i.e., whether it will be created, deleted, or modified) so that it can be correctly processed in the target system. This is done using the *task type* that specifies which action is to be executed, and also using what are known as *sendbits*, which specify the fields that are affected by this action.

Data model of a BDoc

The header data of a BDoc message is stored in the SMW3_BDOC database table and is filled via the CL_SMW_MFLOW=>SET_ HEADER_FIELDS method. Besides the standard fields, which are filled in every BDoc, other fields can also be set by the application. Apart from the client, one of the most important standard fields is the BDOC_TYPE field, which usually contains the generation ID of a BDoc, such as BUPA_MAIN. Another standard field is SITE_ID, which defines the logical destination of the sender. Normally, this field is initial if the sender site is online or if it is an external system, such as an XIF adapter, that is not recognized via the administration console. Another very important standard field is ROOT_ID, which is the instance ID of the content of an sBDoc. This field contains the value of the primary key field of the root segment (i.e., the GUID of the affected object). It is filled by the sender, but doesn't contain any value if the sBDoc message contains unfiltered data (BULK data). The BDOC_ID field contains the GUID that defines the actual BDoc instance.

The status of a BDoc instance indicates the extent to which this instance has already been processed and whether any errors have occurred so far. Usually, the status of an instance is set by the messaging flow and not by the application. However, the application is responsible for validating the message and possibly also for the error updating process, which is then used in the flow to determine the BDoc status. Table TSMW3_STAT determines which actions can still

BDoc status

be executed for a BDoc instance with a certain status; in other words, whether processing can continue with this status. The various possible statuses are roughly divided into three classes:

▶ **Intermediate State**
An instance in intermediate state is one that has not yet been fully processed; in other words, processing can and should continue. A BDoc message should not be allowed to remain in interim status for long. The various statuses of this class are as follows:

  ▶ **I01 — Received (Intermediate State)**
  This status means that the data has been received and has been set up for further inbound processing in the inbound queue.

  ▶ **I02 — Written to qRFC Queue (Intermediate State)**
  This BDoc instance status means that the data for outbound processing has been posted to the queue and is now ready for further processing.

  ▶ **I03 — After qRFC Step (Intermediate State)**
  This status follows on from status I02 and means that the data for outbound processing has been extracted from the queue. Therefore, this data is no longer in the queue.

  ▶ **I04 — BDoc Saved Before Update Task**
  When a BDoc instance has this status, all update functions are executed only once a COMMIT WORK has been issued. This status is set before the status of the BDoc message changes to I02.

[»]   If a BDoc instance has an interim status for longer than usual, this often means that an error has occurred that cannot be propagated to the supporting programs (this kind of error is usually connected to a short dump). If this is the case, open Transaction ST22, check whether there is a corresponding dump, and analyze the root cause.

▶ **Error State**
Errors occurred when an instance was being processed. Processing of the message will continue, or the error can be analyzed in more detail. The error statuses are as follows:

  ▶ **E01 — Technical Error (incomplete)**
  This status applies not so much to application errors as errors

that occur due to a missing function, for example, and are purely technical in nature.

▷ **E02 – Partially Send, Receivers Have Errors**
These are errors that occur when data is sent to target systems such as R/3 or groupware.

▷ **E03 – BDoc Cannot Be Read From Database**
In this case, the BDoc cannot be found in the database. This error occurs very rarely.

▷ **E04 – BDoc Validation Error**
The validation process has failed.

▷ **E05 – Inbound Processing Failed**
This is a relatively new status that was introduced with CRM 4.0. If the BDoc message in inbound processing retains status I01 for longer than usual, the status is changed by SMW3WD to E05 after a specified interval.

▷ **E06 – Outbound Processing Failed**
This is also a new error that was introduced with CRM 4.0. If the BDoc instance retains the interim status I02, I03 or I04 for a very long time during outbound processing, the status is automatically changed from SMW3WD to E06.

▷ **E07 – XML Conversion Error During Outbound Processing**
This status is set if an error occurs during the XML conversion process.

Statuses E05 and E06 were introduced to reduce the workload required to monitor and reorganize Middleware processing. Whereas previously, for error monitoring, the interim statuses also had to be checked, now, only the error statuses of the system have to be monitored. **[«]**

▷ **Final status**
An instance with this status has been fully processed and no further action is required.

The fact that an instance has "final status" does not automatically mean that it was processed correctly, only that that it does not need further processing. Final status can also be set for a BDoc instance that has errors but that is deliberately not being further processed, or cannot be further processed. Thus, error status E03, for example, is also a final status. **[!]**

> ▶ **F01 — Rejected (Fully Processed)**
> This status is set in the synchronization flow if the document is technically correct but is rejected by the application validation process for business reasons (e.g., the object cannot be currently processed without causing inconsistencies). The message sender is informed about this status.

> ▶ **F02 — Confirmed (Fully Processed)**
> This status is set if the BDoc has been fully processed.

> ▶ **F03 — Set to "Processed" (Fully Processed)**
> This status is set manually as part of system monitoring and error correction. It should be set only if the BDoc has been checked and no further processing is required. In particular, if you are setting this status, you should ensure that it would not cause inconsistencies between the sender and recipient systems.

> ▶ **F04 — Confirmed (Fully Processed by All Recipients)**
> This status is set if the BDoc has been successfully processed in all recipient systems and is therefore used in the outbound flow only.

> ▶ **F05 — Information (No Processing)**
> This status is set if the data cannot be processed (e.g., if no recipients could be determined).

Important fields in SMW3_BDOC

These statuses are also determined by the relevant application during the flow processing and validation processes. Depending on whether an error has occurred or processing was successful, the data either has to be posted to the database or a rollback has to be carried out. The field VAL_STATE is used to specify which of these actions should take place. Thus, this field defines what the flow should do with the data. It is filled by the application. The possible values of this field are as follows:

▶ **S — Success (COMMIT WORK)**
This status means that the BDoc was processed successfully and the data should be posted (COMMIT WORK).

▶ **P — Partial Success (COMMIT WORK)**
This status is set in the process of validating orders, for example, if only individual messages are to be rejected and if the application allows partial validation.

- ▶ **E — Validation Error (COMMIT WORK)**

  An error occurred in the validation process, but the process of posting the BDocs should still be started. When this status is set, the application checks that no database operations were carried out.

- ▶ **A — Validation Error (ROLLBACK WORK)**

  A serious validation error occurred and the data is to be rolled back.

- ▶ **T — Temporary Validation Error (COMMIT WORK)**

  When this status is set, the application checks that no database operations were carried out.

- ▶ **Q — Partial Error (ROLLBACK WORK + Recall Again)**

  This status is set if a BDoc has multiple business object instances and only some of these were successfully validated. If partial validation is not allowed, status A is also set in this case.

Another central consideration in determining statuses is the point in the messaging flow at which the message is currently located in the system. This information is stored in the field FCTXT and is set by the flow during the actual inbound and outbound processing processes. The allowed values correspond to the usual flow contexts, as discussed in Chapter 2, *Inbound Processing and Validation*, and Chapter 3, *Outbound Processing*.

The date and time at which the BDoc was created are stored in the SND_DATE and SND_TIME fields. Besides the creation time, the time at which the BDoc was last modified is also stored in two other fields: UPD_DATE and UPD_TIME. These fields are changed to the time of the last processing if a message is re-processed. The timestamps stored here are analyzed in the reorganization process. For more information on the reorganization options in CRM Middleware, see Chapter 12, *Reorganization*.

The information about the DDIC structures that are linked to a BDoc is stored in two fields in Table SMW3_BDOC: DDIC1, which contains the DDIC type of the classic part of the BDoc, and DDIC2, which contains the DDIC type of the extension part of the BDoc. In a BDoc, the latter contains the actual data in mBDoc format. This segment is empty in an sBDoc.

The field DBGMODE is an important one, particularly for examining message errors in Transaction SMW01. It enables the user to debug the Middleware flow during BDoc post-processing. This field can be set for mBDoc messages only. If its value is "X", debugging mode is active.

Robust data storage If you change DDIC structures that are used in BDoc types, it may no longer be possible to read BDoc messages after these structure changes are activated. Therefore, if possible, you should fully process all BDoc messages before activating the structure changes. Only if this is not possible (e.g., because the maintenance window is too small) can you use what is known as *robust data storage*. Robust data storage means that BDoc data is stored in an XML format, and it can usually still be read after the change.

However, note that robust BDoc message storage requires considerably more system resources, such as CPU and disk space. Therefore, you should deactivate this storage option after you have successfully activated the structure change and fully processed all old data. Before you use robust data storage in a live system, you should always implement the structure changes and process the old messages in your test landscape first.

To activate robust data storage for a specific BDoc type, open Transaction SM30 and, in Table SMOFPARSFA, enter the value "FLOW" in the **Key** field, enter the value "USE_XML_BDOCTYPE" in the **Paramname** field, and enter the value "X" as a parameter value. Assign the generation ID of the BDoc as a value to the field **Paramname2** (see Figure 4.10). If you want to activate robust data storage for multiple BDoc types, you have to create an individual entry for every type.

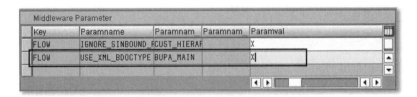

Figure 4.10 Activating Robust Data Storage

In summary, the overall procedure for making DDIC structure changes using robust storage is as follows:

1. Activate robust storage using Table SMOFPARSFA for the BDoc type in question.

2. Check that old BDoc messages that were created before robust data storage was activated are fully processed, as there is no automatic conversion of existing BDoc messages to robust message storage.

3. Activate the DDIC changes.

4. Deactivate robust storage in order to bring resource consumption back to a normal level for new messages.

SAP's CRM solution also supports data exchange with groupware solutions, such as Microsoft Outlook. This chapter will give you an understanding of the Middleware mechanisms and components that are the heart of groupware integration (GWI).

5 Groupware Integration

The SAP Customer Relationship Management (SAP CRM) environment provides a number of different ways of integrating business processes with an existing groupware solution in your company. In addition to exchanging data — such as a business appointment — via ConnTrans between different clients in a mobile sales scenario, and then synchronizing this data on the mobile client using the groupware client software, you can also exchange business data directly and bi-directionally between the CRM server and a groupware server. The former example is referred to in groupware integration as a *client-client scenario*, and the latter as a *server-server scenario*. Because, in terms of Middleware, the data exchange process in the client-client scenario is not significantly different from a normal data exchange in the CRM mobile sales scenario, we'll restrict ourselves here to the server-server scenario.

Integration scenarios

5.1 Server-Server Scenario in Groupware Integration

The Middleware has two tasks in a server-server scenario in *groupware integration* (GWI). One is to take data that is sent from groupware servers to CRM in different formats, convert it to a unified data format, and forward it for validation. The other is to transfer data generated in the CRM Server to these external groupware servers in a suitable format. Figure 5.1 illustrates how GWI is incorporated into CRM Middleware.

GWI overview

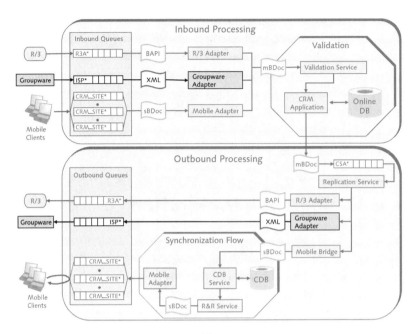

Figure 5.1 Groupware Integration in Middleware

As you can see from the figure, the *groupware adapter* (GWA) is the core of Middleware on the CRM Server. It is responsible in the flow for administrating the various queues for converting groupware messages to an internal format, and vice versa. The GWA is based on the standard inbound/outbound adapter of the mobile sales scenario, the sync adapter. Therefore, no new technology was developed for data exchange control in GWI; instead, the tried-and-tested framework for controlling the data flow between CRM Middleware and external sites is used, with the addition of some GWI-specific modifications.

[»] When discussing the server-server GWI in this chapter, we use the single general term *groupware adapter* (GWA), even though strictly speaking, there are two different groupware adapters, the groupware adapter 01 (GWA_01) and the groupware adapter 02 (GWA_02). GWA_02 enables data to be exchanged with individual users' *private* contacts folder, while GWA_01 only enables data to be exchanged with the *public* folder of the groupware solution. Similarly, GWA_01 is based on mBDoc messages, while GWA_02 is based on sBDocs. The data mapping to the individual user folders in the case of GWA_02 is the reason for this difference, as the CRM Middleware replication and realignment mechanism is used to implement this functionality. In cases where the differences are important, we will mention this explicitly.

Besides the internal components illustrated in Figure 5.1, various external components are also involved in the process of data exchange with the groupware solution. Figure 5.2 illustrates the process of communication with these external components.

External components

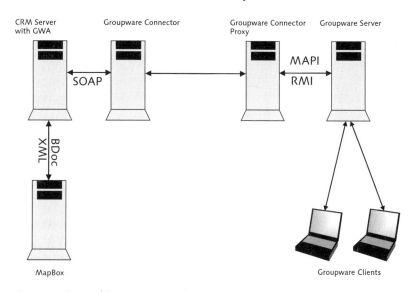

Figure 5.2 External Components in Groupware Integration

The format in which data is exchanged between CRM and the external world of the groupware solution uses the *vCard* and *iCalendar* standards. Therefore, the internal CRM BDoc format has to be converted to a format that is based on these standards. The external component that performs this task is called the *MapBox*. The MapBox uses the J2EE stack of the SAP NetWeaver Application Server as a Java application. Thus, to summarize, the GWA is responsible for the technical processing of incoming and outgoing messages, and the MapBox is responsible for communication with the external world.

MapBox

The MapBox can be installed on the CRM Server, but if a J2EE release of 6.40 or lower is used, the MapBox should be installed on its own system for performance and stability reasons.

[«]

The combination of MapBox, GWA, and the generic Middleware message interface (the payload interface, PLIF) is known as the *internal SyncPoint* (ISP). The PLIF provides the technical framework for data exchange, but it does not interpret the data; the sender and the recipient of the message define and execute the data interpretation process.

Therefore, the GWA, which is written in ABAP, must communicate with the MapBox, an external application. Because of the different technologies that are used, the GWA converts the messages to its own format, *BDoc XML*, which, as is always the case in CRM, is exchanged with the MapBox via queues. Therefore, the MapBox must be maintained as an RFC destination. This is done in Transaction SM59. It is important here that you assign the **Registered Server Program** activation type to the unique program ID MAPBOX (see Figure 5.3). You must also specify this program ID in the MapBox basic settings.

Another GWI component is the *groupware connector* (GWC). The GWC is responsible for the final conversion of the iCalendar/vCard format to the specific format of the groupware solution in question. Because this is a specific format, there are various connectors for the individual groupware solutions such as MS Exchange and Lotus Domino. In a CRM landscape with GWI, there is a single GWC component, which can communicate with multiple GWC proxies. For performance reasons, we recommend that you also install another, separate proxy, besides the default proxy, for every local LAN in a distributed organization.

GWI Middleware details

So far, we have described the data flow between CRM and the GW solution on the level of the systems involved. Now, building on this basic knowledge, we will turn our attention to the technical details of individual steps and internal system processing. We will restrict ourselves here to internal processing procedures on the CRM Server, and will not go into detail on the specific functioning of external components, such as the GWC.

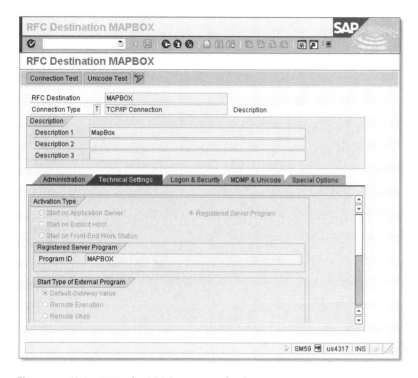

Figure 5.3 Maintaining the RFC Destination for the MapBox

As you can see from the figures, the data exchange process between the GWC and the GWA uses the SOAP protocol. This data exchange is organized via queues, as is always the case in CRM. Outgoing messages are placed in the relevant outbound queue by the GWA and are then collected there by the GWC.

We will now use the example of an appointment to explain the exact interaction between GWA, the MapBox, and the GWC.

When an appointment is created in CRM Online for an employee who is involved in the data exchange with the GW solution, the appointment is first validated, and then the replication service triggers the GWA (see Figure 5.4).

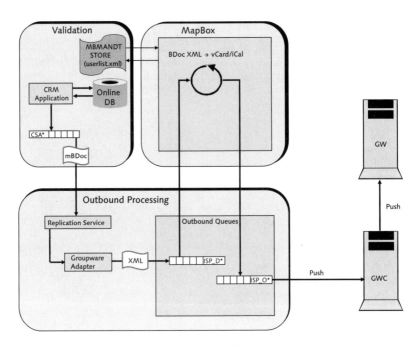

Figure 5.4 Outbound Processing in the Server-Server Scenario

The outbound data exchange between the GWA and the GWC begins when the GWA creates a corresponding entry in the *secondary* data queue, ISP_D*, of the user in question. The MapBox collects the data here and converts it to the external iCalendar-based format. The modified data is then written to the *primary* data outbound queue, ISP_O*, of the user. The queues retain the status *NOSEND*, like in mobile sales.

[»] User-specific queues are created in the internal SyncPoint for inbound data (ISP_I*) and outbound data (ISP_O*). The exact, unique name of this queue is created automatically and is linked to the user's email address in Table ISPQTAB. Also, secondary queues are generated for communicating with the MapBox (ISP_S*, ISP_D*). While all queues are user-specific, there is a maximum of two ISP_D* queues: one for data exchange with public folders, and one for data exchange with private folders on the groupware server.

System queues Besides these data queues, other queues are also required to monitor the data exchange process. These are known as *system queues* and are also created in the system with the prefix ISP_I* or ISP_O*, but are assigned specific names because of their meaning (see Figure 5.5).

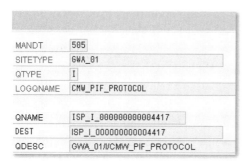

Figure 5.5 System Queue CMW_PIF_PROTOCOL in ISPQTAB

Thus, for example, the data queue itself is filled, and the name of this data queue is also set in the system queue _ISP_QFILLED. This system queue is checked regularly by a queue dispatcher that is located on the GWC. If the queue dispatcher finds an entry in _ISP_QFILLED, the processor module of the GWC that is responsible for inbound messages is started. This module then processes all outbound data queues on the CRM Server sequentially, reads the individual messages from the queues (e.g., an appointment), and saves these messages in the relevant format on the groupware server.

Because the GWC has to create messages for multiple users centrally **[«]** on the groupware server, it needs the corresponding administration rights on this server.

If the creation of the appointment fails, an error entry is created and written to another system queue called CMW_PIF_PROTOCOL. If the appointment is created successfully, a link has to be created between the appointment on the groupware server and the CRM Server, so that changes to the appointment can be exchanged accordingly. Therefore, the internal ID of the appointment on the groupware server is also specified in the XML response message. The CMW_PIF_ID_QUEUE system queue contains this data in the CRM Server once the message has been processed in the ISP_I* queue.

Conversely, that is, from the viewpoint of CRM inbound data processing (see Figure 5.6), the GWC reads all data sequentially in the groupware server for the users who are involved in the data exchange, and writes any changes (in our example, the change to the appointment) to the corresponding inbound queue on the CRM Server. Besides the data record mapping that is required, the groupware server users also have to be assigned to the correct users on the CRM Server; otherwise, the correct assignment of data records and users required cannot be set up. The user mapping is done by assigning each user's email address to the business partner GUID in CRM. The information about which users are relevant at this point is provided by CRM in a list, in the file *userlist.xml*. However, this data is saved in the CRM groupware solution in multiple places, and in multiple forms. For example, the MapBox uses a form of the *userlist* that is stored on the CRM Server in the database table MBMANDT-STORE. On the GWC, on the other hand, it is available in the form of the *userlist.xml file*. Figure 5.7 shows an example of a data record for a user both as an XML file and as an entry in the database table.

The technical details of how the data is read on the groupware server depend on the groupware solution that is used in each case, and are not dealt with further here.

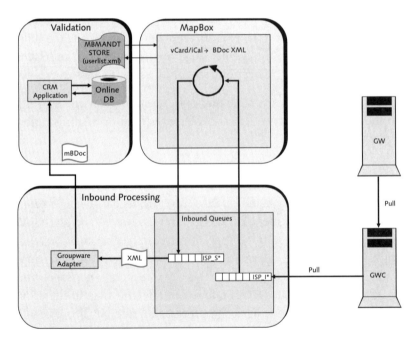

Figure 5.6 Inbound Processing in the Server-Server Scenario

Figure 5.7 Various Instances of "userlist.xml"

As we saw earlier, the data has to be mapped in both environments so that it can be exchanged correctly between the groupware solution and the CRM solution. In terms of mapping the actual data in the MapBox, as mentioned above, we use the term *mapping*, as in "the BDoc ID is mapped with the UID of the GW solution." This BDoc ID can be the GUID of the appointment, for example.

Thus, when an appointment is processed in the GW solution, the solution first checks whether there is already a BDoc ID for this incoming UID. If there is, the solution creates a change message to this effect. If not, the process of creating a new appointment begins.

As we have seen in our example, there are several system queues within the GWA besides the *primary* and *secondary* data queues. The number of these other queues depends on the number of users involved in the data exchange process.

Queues in the GWI

Departing from this rule, there is only one ISP_D* queue for synchronization using GWA_01 or GWA_02.

[«]

The following is a summary of information provided by the main system queues on the CRM Server about the data exchange between CRM and groupware:

▶ **_ISP_QFILLED**
In this queue, the GWA provides a list of the data queues currently filled on the CRM side. This information is then used by the GWC to collect the data from the data queues.

▶ **CMW_PIF_ID_QUEUE**
In this inbound queue, the GWC writes the IDs of the newly-created messages on the GW server. These IDs enable CRM data to be mapped to the relevant data on the GW server so that changes can be made synchronously.

▶ **USER_LIST**
This queue contains a list of all employees whose data is to be exchanged between groupware and the CRM Server. It is also used for mapping between users on the CRM Server and the email addresses of users on the GW server.

▶ **CMW_PIF_PROTOCOL**
If errors occurred in the data exchange process, the GWC places them in this system queue. The error information is therefore centrally available on the CRM Server. Also, status information on the replication process is updated in both directions in the relevant log files on the connector, the MapBox and the connector proxy.

5.2 Analyzing Groupware Integration

As in every IT solution, errors can occur in a CRM solution with GWI. Rather than simply listing individual errors here, we will introduce you to the tools that you can use to analyze any errors and problems that you may encounter.

MapBox log files On the MapBox, you can create the following log files and then activate them in the MapBox configuration:

▶ **MapBox Message Dump**
You can store inbound and outbound messages here and then use them later to analyze the data exchange process. Because the data quantities involved can be very large, and performance may suffer

as a result, we recommend that you activate this function in your live system in emergencies only.

▸ **MapBox Statistics**

You can store performance metrics of MapBox processing here. Again, you should not activate this in a live system as a rule.

▸ **MapBox Log Files**

Here, you can set the degree of detail of the internal log file using the configuration menu. The higher the number you set, the more detailed this file will be. The value "4D" is the recommended one.

If you're experiencing performance problems in the data exchange process, you can activate a trace of the internal SyncPoint to analyze it. To do this, open the table maintenance Transaction SM30 and maintain table ISPCFG. If there is no entry for the parameter name TRACE, create a new entry and assign value "X" to the parameter name TRACE in the **Parameter Value** column. The trace information is now updated. Start the ABAP Editor (Transaction SE38) to display the created trace files. Enter "CMW_ISPTRACE_DISPLAY" in the **Program** field and start the program using the F8 key or the **Execute** button.

SyncPoint traces

If you're using the GWA_01 scenario (*public folder replication*), enter "GWA_01" in the **Site Type ID** field in the selection screen (see Figure 5.8) to display information that is relevant only to GWI. You can also select the timeframe of your analysis, and the direction of data transfer using the **Outbound** and **Inbound** radio buttons.

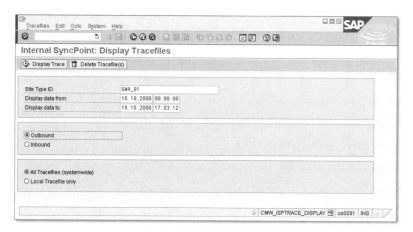

Figure 5.8 Selection Screen for Analyzing ISP Trace Files

Once you have restricted the selection in accordance with your planned analysis, click the **Display Trace** button. A detailed screen opens showing all the relevant information. The trace contains the following information for every message that was exchanged with the MapBox, giving you an initial idea of where the problem is and a starting-point for further analysis:

▶ Start date, start time, and end time

▶ Transaction ID (TID) of the qRFC and the GUID of the job on the MapBox

▶ Return code of the MapBox and of ISP processing

▶ Duration of ISP processing without MapBox, and duration of MapBox processing

PLIF traces Besides a full trace of the internal SyncPoint, you can also activate an explicit trace of the payload interface if you think that there are problems with this component. To do this, open the table maintenance Transaction SM30 and set the PIF_TRACE parameter in Table ISPCFG to "X".

Then, open Transaction SE38 to analyze the trace. Enter the report "CMW_PIFTRACE_DISPLAY" in the **Program** field and execute it using the F8 key. You can now restrict the time period of the analysis in the selection screen (see Figure 5.9). You then have the option to use the **Display Trace** button to display the required trace data or use the **Delete Trace File(s)** button to delete it.

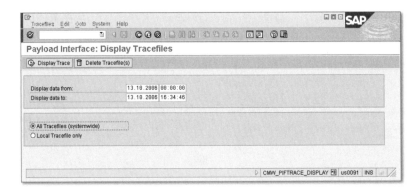

Figure 5.9 Selection Options for PLIF Traces

Figure 5.10 shows an example of a trace file. The start date and start time of the data exchange process are shown in the first column, and the second column shows which function was executed. The **I/O** column specifies whether the call was an inbound (IN) or an outbound (OUT) one, and the last column provides details on the various function calls, such as the parameters transferred.

Figure 5.10 also shows how payload sessions can be controlled using the QLOGON and QLOGOFF methods (**Function** column), and how, during this kind of session, the method GETMSG is used to obtain information about filled queues from _ISP_QFILLED using the corresponding session ID. The ERROR parameter can be used to obtain the relevant error codes of individual sessions and methods.

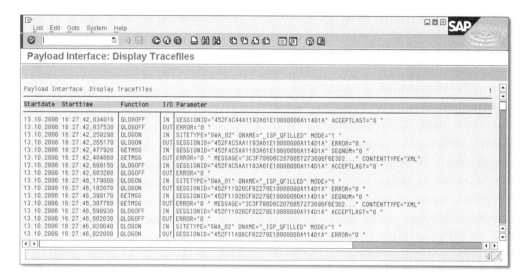

Figure 5.10 Display of PLIF Trace File

Having already introduced you to the individual areas of Middleware in the previous chapters, we will now provide you with an example of how these different areas interact during an exchange of objects.

6 Exchanging Customer-Specific Data

In the example described in this chapter, which concludes the introductory part of this book, the company BodeGolzeSchröder Inc. intends to implement a CRM system. In its existing SAP R/3 system, the company uses a proprietary application to service its authors. The SAP Customer Relationship Management (SAP CRM) system is supposed to extend that application. In the R/3 system, the relevant data is stored in Table ZBUCH.

Field Name	Key Field	Data Element	Description
MANDT	Yes	MANDT	Client
Autor	Yes	Text_30	Author
Buchtitel	No	Text_30	Book Title

Table 6.1 Structure of Table ZBUCH in SAP R/3

Table ZBUCH contains information about authors and book titles (see Table 6.1) and is now supposed to be replicated through SAP CRM Middleware to the mobile clients of field sales representatives via the path shown in Figure 6.1. In addition to the appropriate sBDoc and mBDoc definitions, you'll also need an appropriate flow context as well as the corresponding adapters.

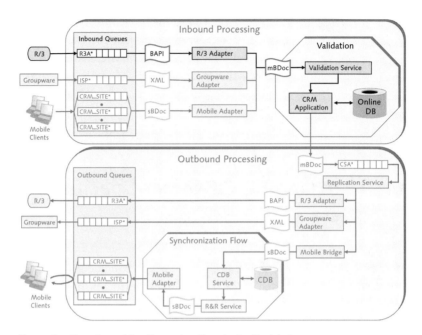

Figure 6.1 Overview of the Messaging Flow to Be Modeled

[»] This section describes only the Middleware-specific customizations and modeling steps in order to clarify the underlying basic principles; the actual programming process and the application logic are not within the scope of this book and are therefore described in a very simplified manner. For example, in real life, the author would be identified by a unique number based on which the table would be linked to detailed data about the author, such as an address, and so on.

In order to implement the exchange of data between SAP R/3 to the mobile clients through SAP CRM Middleware, the modeling and process steps listed below must be carried out, which we'll describe in the following sections:

1. Making the object and extraction module known in SAP R/3

2. Creating a corresponding database table in the CRM system

3. Modeling a new mBDoc type

4. Maintaining the flow

5. Creating a new adapter object and generating the services

6.1 Customizations Required in SAP R/3 to Enable the Import of Custom Data

To enable the download of data from the R/3 system, the data must first be extracted. For this purpose, we need an extraction module that carries out the following tasks:

Creating an adapter object

1. Extract data (if necessary, filtered data) from Table ZBUCH.

2. Transfer this data to the BAPIMTCS structure.

3. Fill the header structure, BAPICRMDH2.

4. Call function module CRS_SEND_TO_SERVER for the actual data transfer.

Appendix D.1 contains a commented code listing for extraction purposes for this type of extractor. Moreover, Appendix D.2 contains an explicit mapping module to map the book data to the BAPIMTCS container, which is called by the extractor.

Once you have created the extraction module, you must make known within the R/3 system that the CRM system requires the book data and is supposed to use the extraction module to extract the required data. The table that must be maintained for this purpose is Table CRMSUBTAB (see Chapter 2, *Inbound Processing and Validation*). This table is read by function module CRS_FIRST_DOWNLOAD_TRIGGER in order to identify the extraction module that is appropriate for this object. Start the table maintenance Transaction SM30 and enter CRMSUBTAB in the **Table/View** field. Then click the **Maintain** button to go to the maintenance screen of this table. In this table, the relevant function module for the extraction is defined on the basis of the object name and object class, which are both transferred from the CRM system. In order to store the extraction module for our planned adapter object ZMADP_BUCH of object class ZBUCH_CLASS, click the **New Entries** button and create the data displayed in Figure 6.2.

Maintaining the adapter object

To be able to carry out a corresponding delta load, we need another function module, which can take into account data that has already been sent.

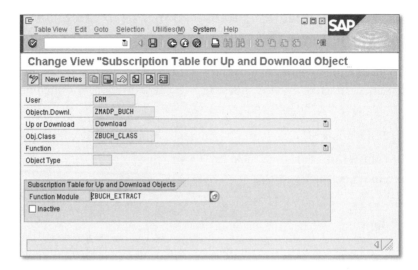

Figure 6.2 Activating the New Extraction Module in Table CRMSUBTAB

This step concludes the development process in the R/3 system, and we can continue by implementing the necessary customizations in the CRM system.

6.2 Customizations Required in SAP CRM to Enable the Import of Data from SAP R/3

6.2.1 Creating a CRM Online Table

To be able to store the data in the online database in the CRM system, we need a database table that has the relevant structure so that it can store the data, which originates from the R/3 system. You can generate the table in the CRM system by using the DDIC maintenance Transaction SE11. Assign the name ZCRMBUCH to the new table. To create the table, start the transaction by entering the transaction code, enter the name "ZCRMBUCH" in the **Database Table** field, and click the **Create** button. Then enter a short appropriate description in the relevant field, for instance "Information about authors and books." Use the F4 help to select **A – Application Table (Master and Transaction Data)** as the delivery class. Then go to the **Fields** tab and enter the fields listed in Table 6.2.

Field Name	Key	Data Element	Description
MANDT	Yes	MANDT	Client
Autor	Yes	Text_30	Author
Buchtitel	No	Text_30	Book Title

Table 6.2 Structure of Table ZCRMBUCH in CRM Online to Be Used in Middleware

Once you have entered the fields, you must specify the technical properties of the table. Select "USER" as the **Data class** and the smallest **Size category**, 0 (0 to 4,800 entries, see Figure 6.3). Save the technical properties and return to the **Fields** tab by pressing F3. Then save the table and activate it. Table ZCRMBUCH has now been created and you can exit Transaction SE11.

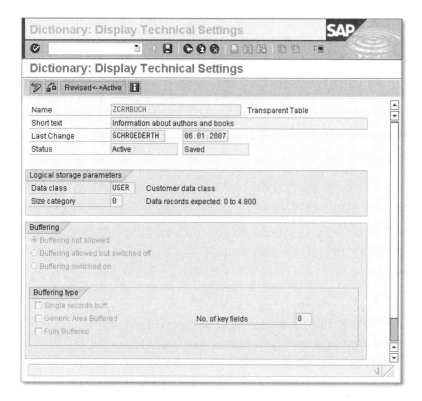

Figure 6.3 Technical Properties of Table ZCRMBUCH

6.2.2 Creating the mBDoc Type

Now that you have created the database table, you must generate the mBDoc type that is supposed to be used for populating the table with data from the R/3 system. Because the extension part must be present in the database in order to model the remaining parts of the mBDoc, we should start with this part. As described in Chapter 4, *BDoc Modeling and Storage*, the extension part of an mBDoc is a complex database structure. For this reason, we must first create several simple structures in the database and then combine these structures to form the extension part of the mBDoc type. The first structure to be created is the one that contains the task type of the BDoc, that is, information about whether the data is supposed to be used for generating new data (**Insert**), for updating existing data (**Update**), or for deleting data (**Delete**) in the BDoc. To create this control segment in the extension part, you must start Transaction SE11, enter "ZMBUCH_KONTROLL" in the **Data Type** field, and click the **Create** button. The system then displays a popup window in which you should select the **Structure** entry. Enter a descriptive name as the short description, for example, "Control segment for root of mBDoc". Then, you must create the components of the structure. Here, you only need one component for saving the task. Therefore, you should enter the name TASK in the **Component** field and assign **Component Type** CHAR1 to this component. Then save the structure and activate it. The first structure has now been created successfully, and you can exit the dynpro by pressing the F3 key.

Next, we need a structure for transferring the actual application data, which is stored in the extension part of an mBDoc (see Chapter 4, *BDoc Modeling and Storage*). For this purpose, enter the name ZMBUCH_DATEN in the **Data Type** field in the initial screen of Transaction SE11 and click the **Create** button. Again, select the **Structure** type in the popup window that appears. Once you are in the actual dynpro, enter "Data within root segment" as the description. After that, you can create the components of this structure. Table 6.3 provides a list of the components of this data structure.

Component	Component Type	Description
GUID	SMO_GUID	GUID
Autor	TEXT_30	Author
Buchtitel	TEXT_30	Book Title

Table 6.3 Components of the Root Data Segment

After you enter the components, you must save and activate the structure. In the next step, we want to create the checkbox structure, which contains information about which fields should be taken into account by the data structure. Assign the name ZMBUCH_DATAX to the checkbox structure. The components are the same as the ones shown in Table 6.3, with the exception of the GUID component, which is not required here. The type of all components is BAPIUP-DATE (see Figure 6.4). After entering the components, you must save and activate this structure as well.

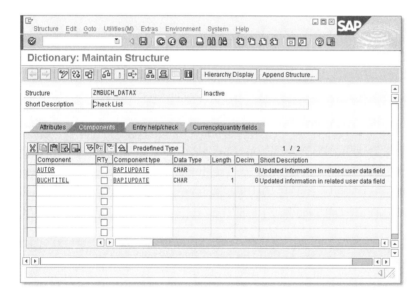

Figure 6.4 Checkbox Structure for the Data Structure

The next step in the creation of the extension part consists of combining the structures we created thus far into the actual root segment. To do that, start Transaction SE11 once again, enter ZMBUCH_ROOT as the name in the **Data Type** field, and click the **Create** button. Again, you must select the **Structure** type in the popup window that appears and press Enter. Enter "root structure" as a description for the structure in the next Dynpro. Then, enter the structures you just generated as components. Create the following components, as shown in Figure 6.5: CONTROL, DATA, and DATAX.

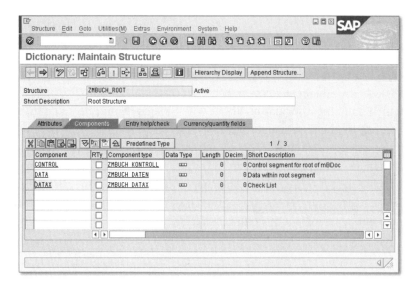

Figure 6.5 Root Segment of the Extension Part

Because it is planned to process multiple instances of the same BDoc type, we must now create a table type that contains the line type ZMBUCH_ROOT we just created. For this purpose, enter the name ZMBUCH_ROOT_TAB in the **Data Type** field in the initial screen of Transaction SE11 and click the **Create** button. Then select **Table Type** in the popup window that displays next. Once you're in the main screen of Transaction SE11, enter ZMBUCH_ROOT in the **Line Type** field contained in the **Line Type** tab (see Figure 6.6). Then save the table type and activate it.

Generating the actual extension part At this stage, all the required structures and table types have been generated so that you can now continue with the last part of this step and generate the actual extension part in the database. We'll use Transaction SE11 once again to do that. Enter the name ZMBUCH_ EXTENSION in the **Data Type** field in the initial screen and click the **Create button**. Select **Structure** in the popup window that appears and confirm your selection. Then enter "Extension for mBDoc ZMBUCH" as the name of this structure. The extension part contains only the ZMBUCH_ROOT component with component type ZMBUCH_ROOT_TAB (see Figure 6.7).

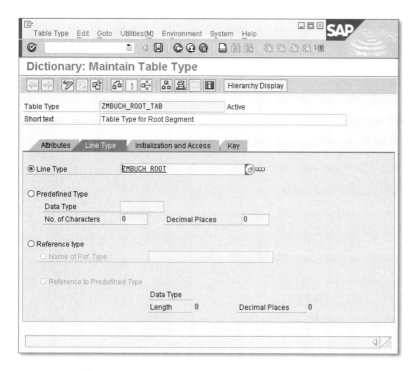

Figure 6.6 Table Type for the Created Root Segment

Once you have created this component, save and activate the structure ZMBUCH_EXTENSION. This completes the creation of the extension part and we can now create the BDoc type and the classic part of the mBDoc.

To create the actual mBDoc type, start the BDoc Modeler (Transaction SBDM). If the popup window for selecting the BDoc type appears, you should click **Execute**. Then click the **Create** button. In the right-hand part of the screen, you will now find the **BDoc Overview** tab. Enter ZMBDOC_BUCH as the name and "mBDoc for book information" as a short description. Then select the **Message Exchange** class. In order to assign the extension part you just created, you must enter the DDIC structure ZMBUCH_EXTENSION in the **Related Data Type** field of the **General Data** section and save the BDoc type. Once you have saved the BDoc type, you must create the classic part (see Chapter 4, *BDoc Modeling and Storage*).

Creating the classic part

177

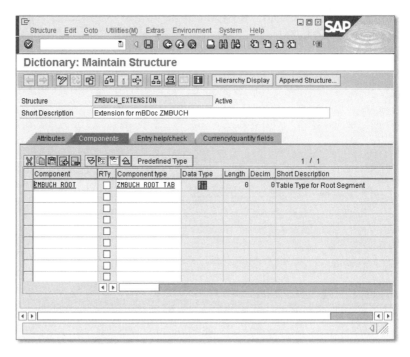

Figure 6.7 Completed Extension Part for mBDoc ZMBUCH

To do that, select the ZMBDOC_BUCH type in the list of BDocs shown in the left-hand area of the screen and click the **Create Segment** button or press the F7 function key. Then go to the **Segment Overview** and enter the name ZBUCH_ROOT and the description "Root segment" in the **Segment Name** field. Although the segment name doesn't necessarily has to be in the customer namespace, we recommend that you use a name that begins with the letter "Z" in order to differentiate the segment from standard segments. Save the segment and go to the **Segment Fields** tab. The first thing we need here is a GUID, which is to be used as a key. For this purpose, enter GUID as a field name and SMO_GUID as a data element in the first line. Then, enter "Author" as the name and "Text_30" as the data element in the second line. Save the segment fields and activate the new BDoc type. The activation causes all necessary modules to be generated. Figure 6.8 shows the completed BDoc type.

This completes the creation of the mBDoc type. However, to be able to use the BDoc, we still need to maintain the flow and the adapter objects so that we can load the data from the R/3 system. Moreover, we have to ensure that the relevant information will actually be sent to the mobile clients of the field sales representatives once it is available in the CRM system.

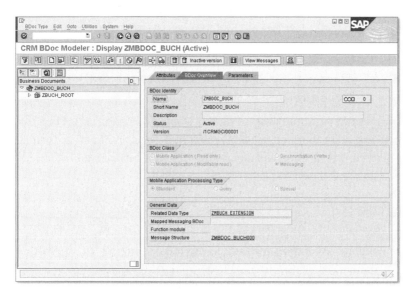

Figure 6.8 Completed mBDoc ZMBDOC_BUCH

6.2.3 Maintaining the Flow

The validation process is responsible for checking the logical correctness of the data, for returning corresponding status information to the messaging flow, and for saving the data in the corresponding application tables, provided the data is accurate (see Chapter 2, *Inbound Processing and Validation*). Because at this stage, we want to describe only the basic concept, you should also refer to Appendix D.4, which contains a validation module as an example. This validation module updates all changes to the data without carrying out any further detailed checks.

Validation

Once you have created the validation module, you can enter it in the flow context. To do that, you should either call the table maintenance Transaction SM30 or Transaction SMW3FDIF to generate an entry in Table SMW3BDOCIF, which should contain the values listed in Table 6.4. Enter the name of the validation module you use as the validation function. In our example, that's function module ZMBUCH_VALIDATION, which is described in Appendix D.

Field name	Value
BDOC TYPE	ZMBDOC_BUCH
Validation function	ZMBUCH_VALIDATION

Table 6.4 Entries in Table SMW3BDOCIF

6.2.4 Mapping the BAPI Container into the mBDoc Structure

In the CRM system, inbound data is available in the BAPIMTCS format and must therefore be converted into our specific BDoc format. For this purpose, we need a mapping function module, which should handle the following tasks:

1. Map the BAPIMTCS structure into mBDoc ZMBDOC_BUCH.

2. Populate the classic part of the BAPI for receiver determination.

3. Populate the extension part of the mBDoc type with application data extracted from the BAPIMTCS container in SAP R/3.

4. Populate the message header of the mBDoc.

Appendix D.3 contains a simple, commented mapping module for your reference.

Making the mappimg known

Now that the mapping module has been created, the CRM-system must be made aware of it. This is similar to maintaining the extraction modules in SAP R/3. To make the mapping known to the CRM system, you must maintain the adapter objects. Because both the flow and the BDoc type have already been defined completely, you can now extend the R/3 adapter (see Section 2.4.2) by this new type in order to be able to process the data that has been extracted from the R/3 system in the CRM system. To create adapter object ZMADP_BUCH of object class ZBUCH_CLASS, start the adapter object maintenance Transaction R3AC3 via **Architecture and Technology · Middleware · Data Exchange · Object Management · Customizing Objects** and click the **Create Object** button. Because we want to exchange data about books through mBDoc ZMBDOC_BUCH, you should enter ZMADP_BUCH as the object name and "mBDoc adapter object book" as the description. Since we already defined the BDoc earlier in this chapter (see Section 6.3.2), you can now enter BDoc ZMBDOC_BUCH in the **Linked BDoc Type** field via the F4 help. After that, you must define the block size, which provides information about the maximum number of objects that may be transported within a BDoc. For our example, you should choose a block size of 200 (for more details on how you can optimally determine the block size, please refer to Section 10.2.1).

Finally, you must specify the flow context. You can use the F4 help again to do that. Go to the **Initial Flow Contexts** tab – provided it isn't active yet – and select **R/3** as the source system via the F4 help. Then go to the **Tables/Structures** tab in order to enter the source from which the data is supposed to be imported. As the source table, enter the name of the table in the R/3 system. In our example, that's ZBUCH. Then go to the **Mapping Modules: R/3 to CRM** tab. Here, you must enter the name of the mapping module you created earlier; for example, ZM_MAP_BAPIMTCS_TO_ZMBDOC_BUCH (see Appendix D, Section D.3). Then, you must change the object class in order to make your object a business object of class ZBUCH_CLASS. To do that, click the **Assign Object Class** button in the **Object Class** field. Then select the **New Object Class** field in the popup window that appears and enter ZBUCH_CLASS (see Figure 6.9). Press enter and confirm the creation of the new class in the popup that appears.

Flow context

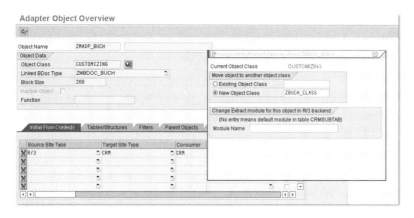

Figure 6.9 Creating a New Object Class

You have now returned to the main screen of Transaction R3AC3, where you must save the new adapter object. Another popup window displays in which you must confirm whether this information should be included in a transport request, which you would normally answer in the affirmative. However, since we're describing a simplified example here, please answer "No." Our object is now a business adapter object and you can find it in Transaction R3AC1 (see Figure 6.10).

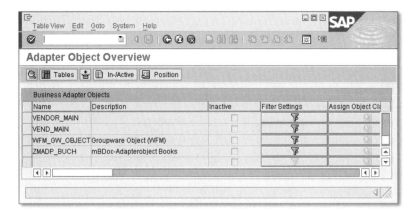

Figure 6.10 Completed Business Adapter Object in R3AC1

Generating the services

The required objects have been created. However, you now need to generate the runtime environment, that is, the coding for the required services. To do that, call Transaction SMOGGEN (see Figure 6.11), go to the **Object Categories** section, and select **BDoc types** ❶. Then, enter the BDoc ZMBDOC_BUCH in the **Available Objects** field ❷. Click **Execute** ❸ (or press F8) to start generating the required function modules.

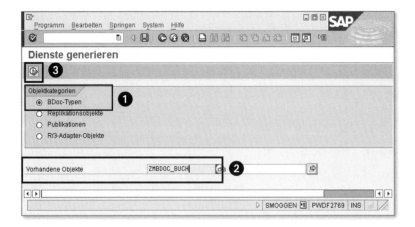

Figure 6.11 Generating the Required Services

6.3 Loading Data from the R/3 System

Once you have generated the services, you have completed all the steps that are necessary to load data from Table ZBUCH in the R/3 system into Table ZCRMBUCH in the CRM system. Start the initial load via Transaction R3AS by entering ZMADP_BUCH in the **Load Object** field, the site name of the R/3 system (in this case, M50_800) as the **Source Site (Sender)**, and the destination "CRM" as the **Destination Site (Receiver)** (see Figure 6.12). Lastly, press F8.

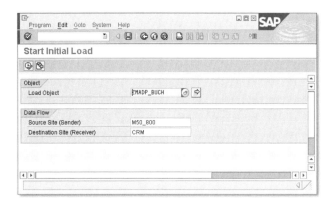

Figure 6.12 Starting the Initial Load

Transaction R3AM1 enables you to monitor the initial load process. Once the initial load has finished, the data is made available for further processing in Table ZCRMBUCH (see Figure 6.13).

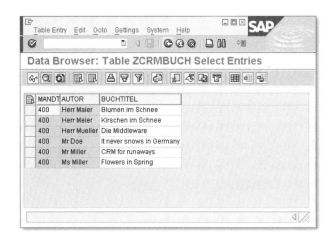

Figure 6.13 Data in the CRM System Is Available for Further Processing

Part II
Performance Optimization in
SAP CRM Middleware

This chapter provides detailed information about the nature and possible effects of a mass change. In addition, it contains a brief outlook on the contents of Part II of this book.

7 Introduction to Performance Optimization

The first part of this book described how data flows through Middleware. Part II focuses on optimizing the Middleware. This part does not describe how you can install an SAP CRM system and which configuration options are available to you. Instead, it assumes that an SAP CRM system has already been installed and gone live, or is at least about to go live.

If configured and monitored properly, SAP CRM Middleware usually does its job without any problems. However, performance problems often occur when the load on the CRM system increases significantly in a short timeframe and the CRM system is not prepared to handle that large a load. In that case, parameter settings that have proven themselves in normal operations suddenly appear as suboptimal and may even cause considerable problems. There are some areas in SAP CRM Middleware that are usually very sensitive when a sudden load increase occurs. The following sections describe these areas, as well as possible problems and proposed solutions.

You'll probably ask yourself now why the load in your CRM system should suddenly increase significantly, although the number of users remains constant and no additional CRM scenarios are implemented or new functions used. In over 95 % of all installations, the SAP CRM system is not implemented as a standalone system, but as part of a system landscape (see Figure 7.1). A CRM system almost always has a backend system (in the SAP world, that's an R/3 or ECC system). Moreover, there are permanent connections to other external systems (SAP BW, SAP XI, Groupware Servers, etc.) through which data is exchanged continuously, as well as interfaces to non-SAP systems

The CRM system within the system landscape

187

through which data is loaded into the CRM system on a more or less regular basis (i.e., flat file interfaces, IDocs/ALE, etc.).

If large quantities of data are generated or updated in a system of the system landscape, it may happen that this data also arrives in the CRM system where it can generate a pretty high load in a relatively short period of time. Even in the CRM system itself, customizations in the replication model or in territory management may modify large data quantities in a short timeframe. From hereon, we'll refer to the processing of large data quantities as *mass changes*, irrespective of whether the data has been received through an interface or generated within the CRM system.

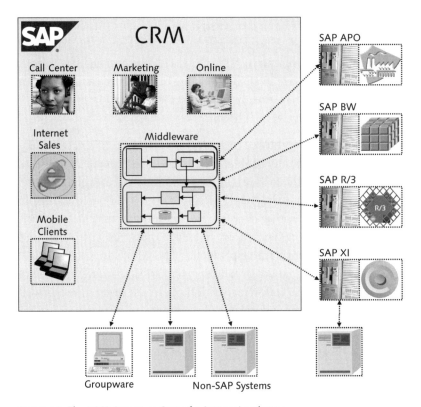

Figure 7.1 The CRM System as Part of a System Landscape

Mass changes In this context, the question arises as to what is the minimum number of data records that allows us to speak of a mass change. At what point exactly does a "major data change" become a "mass change"?

In fact, there is no general answer to that question. Depending on the maximum load for which the CRM system has been configured (i.e., what kind of resources it contains and how it has been set up), a change of several thousands of data records may already be considered to be a mass change. Alternatively, in large SAP systems containing multiple application servers, it may be that several tens of thousands of data records can be processed in parallel to regular operations without encountering any problems. It is not the absolute number that's the determining factor here, but rather the increase of the data quantity during a mass change in comparison to a load peak during normal operations.

Having said this, you should not get the impression that mass changes always involve problems. That's definitely not the case. There are many factors that play a role here. For example, the sizing of the system hardware is very important. Has the hardware been designed in such a way that it can handle load peaks, or do load peaks not occur at all because the hardware was sized correspondingly large?[1]

Our experience has shown that mass changes are often the cause of significant performance problems in CRM systems that are otherwise stable. This is reason enough for us to take a look at the phenomenon of mass changes.

In the following example, we'll define what a mass change is, including the impact it may have if the CRM system hasn't been configured appropriately and the users (and administrators) aren't prepared.

Example

The company Fax&Copy&Print (F&C&P)[2] is a national wholesaler that sells faxes, photo copiers and printers to retailers and major customers. Customers are regularly visited by the sales representatives of F&C&P. In addition, customers can order goods and services by phone or buy them in a business-to-business (B2B) web store where they can also query the status of a purchase order.

---

1 The hardware of your CRM system should be sized in such a way that load peaks can be easily absorbed during normal operations.

2 The name of the company as well as the products and services it sells are fictitious, and any resemblance with existing companies is purely coincidental and not intended.

The services sold by F&C&P comprise regular maintenance work and repairs. In total, F&C&P employs 50 service technicians, 100 field sales representatives, and 20 call center agents. The call center agents not only receive calls, but also inform customers proactively about special offers and actions with regard to office supplies, such as toner cartridges, paper, and so on. The call center works from 7:30 am until 8 pm. During peak hours (from 8 am until 10 am and from 2 pm until 4 pm), 7 agents work concurrently.

The service technicians and field sales representatives use mobile clients. Every day between 8 am and 8.30 am, the technicians retrieve their service orders for the current day and send their service confirmations to the CRM Server every afternoon from 5 pm on. Many field sales representatives don't synchronize their data as regularly with the CRM Server as the service technicians. On average, they execute ConnTrans once in every two days.

F&C&P runs an SAP CRM 4.0 system (Support Package 07) with an application and a database server. All logistics and invoicing processes are carried out in a connected R/3 system. The business partners (BP) can be maintained in both the SAP CRM and R/3 systems. Figure 7.2 illustrates the business process of maintaining business partners.

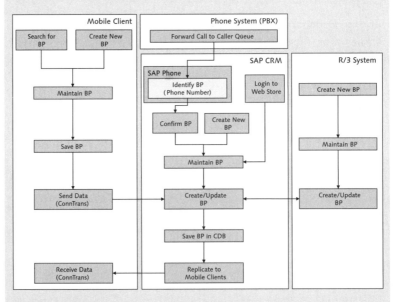

Figure 7.2 Business Process "Business Partner Maintenance"

To improve its customer services, F&C&P decided to extend the customer master in the R/3 and CRM systems by an additional field. The field was filled with data in the R/3 system via a report. After 1,000 data records, the report ran a COMMIT WORK so that blocks were created, which consisted of 1,000 data records each. In total, the report updated 140,000 business partners.

The report run without a problem in the R/3 system and filled the new field in the customer master with data. At the same time, 140 BAPIs were generated in the background, each of which contained 1,000 data records. These BAPIs were transferred to the CRM system. This process created 140 R3AD_BUPA inbound queues in the CRM system. To process the queues, the inbound queue scheduler had to use all the work processes that were available. Because the BAPIs were rather large (1,000 data records each), the processing of every individual BAPI took a little more time so that the work processes couldn't be released quickly. Consequently, all work processes were busy after a short period of time, which led to a CPU bottleneck and another prolongation of the processing times.

Inbound queue processing

The long response times made it virtually impossible for the call center agents and the web store customers to use the CRM system. Consequently, the IT department of F&C&P was notified about this problem.

After being validated, each business partner was written to a separate CSABUPA queue. A BAPI containing 1,000 data records generated 1,000 CSA queues. After the first 15 R3AD_BUPA queue entries had been updated, the system already contained 15,000 CSABUPA queues, which had to be processed concurrently with the R3AD queues. Although a single CSA queue could be processed quickly, the number of inbound queues increased rapidly because more CSA queues were generated than could be processed.

Thus, the entire CRM system focused only on processing the inbound queues (R3AD and CSA), and the CPU load reached almost 100%. From the point of view of the CRM users, this situation came close to a system standstill. The system administrators also had huge problems when trying to analyze the system as they, too, had to cope with the extremely long response times.

System standstill

Due to the increasing number of inbound queues, the performance of the inbound queue scheduler decreased continually. Although a system standstill could be avoided, the scheduler took increasingly more time to assign a work process to one of the tens of thousands of inbound queues. Due to the slow assignment of inbound queues, not all of the work processes could be assigned by the inbound queue scheduler so that the work processes were ultimately assigned to other users again. Pleased by the improving system response times, all users immediately began to process their tasks that had been put on hold. Within a short period of time, the resulting extraordinarily high number of parallel accesses to the system generated a resource bottleneck so that the response times became longer once again.

Stopping inbound
queues

To get the crisis under control, the system administrator deregistered all R3AD queues and therefore interrupted the processing of data from the R/3 system. His intention was to avoid the creation of even more CSA queues. After that, the system administrator inserted stop entries into the existing R3AD_BUPA queues and re-registered the R3AD queues. As a result, the data that was continuously received from the R/3 system during normal operations could be processed normally again (with the exception of changes to business partners, which were written to the queues that had been stopped). Only the business partners that had been updated during the mass change in the R/3 system remained unchanged and stayed in the inbound queues. The inbound queue scheduler then processed the CSA queues one after the other. Due to the decreasing number of queues to be processed, the performance of the scheduler improved again so that the assignment of queues to work processes became faster. After several hours, all inbound queues were completely processed (except the R/3 business partner queues containing the stop entries). During that time, the load on the CRM Server was so high that normal work was not possible.

Once the CSA queues had been processed, things returned to normal. The system administrator began to remove the stop entries one after the other (and to re-insert them again, if necessary) so that the R3AD_BUPA queues could be processed in a controlled manner and the number of resulting CSA queues was kept at a manageable level. Although this procedure caused the update of mass changes to take more time, the online users could carry on with their work without any problem. Most of the mobile client users were not affected at all by the high system load. Only those who had tried to exchange data with the CRM Server during the period of extreme load complained about transfer cancellations or prolonged transfer times.

Outbound queues

However, once the majority of data contained in the CSA queues had been processed, the situation of the mobile client users deteriorated. For each business partner record in the CSA queues, a CUST_HIERARCHY sBDoc and a CAPGEN_OBJ_WRITE sBDoc were generated in the mobile bridge. Whereas at F&C&P, the CAPGEN_OBJ_WRITE BDocs were replicated intelligently (each customer was assigned to exactly one field sales representive), the CUST_HIERARCHY BDocs were replicated in a bulk process (each field sales representative received each BDoc). Correspondingly, after the mass change, each field sales representative received 140,000 CUST_HIERARCHY BDocs and 1,400 CAPGEN_OBJ_WRITE BDocs.

Once the mass change had been completely updated in the CRM Server, the 100 outbound queues of the field sales representatives contained a total of more than 14 million entries. The situation of the 50 service technicians wasn't any better. Business partners were not assigned permanently to them. The service technicians only receive a business partner along with a service order. For this reason, the number of business partners that were written to the outbound queues of service technicians was relatively small. However, the service technicians also received the CUST_HIERARCHY BDoc so that each of their outbound queues contained 140,000 entries as well. In total, the outbound queues of the CRM system contained more than 21 million entries.

The duration of a data transfer between a mobile client and the CRM Server primarily depends on the quantity of data to be transferred. However, if the number of entries contained in the outbound queues exceeds a certain amount, the time required for the data transfer increases exponentially so that even the transfer of small data quantities suddenly takes longer than usual. This situation occurred at F&C&P. Neither had the system been designed for handling more than 21 million entries in the outbound queues; nor had it been optimized for such a large quantity of data.

For the service technicians, this meant that instead of the data transfers taking only five minutes in the morning, they got stuck. Even aborting the communication process in the mobile clients and restarting the application didn't help. Because the 50 service technicians depended on their daily service orders, they started calling the call center. As a temporary solution, the service orders were transmitted over the phone. At the same time, the system administrator was notified about this situation. In order to reduce the number of entries in the outbound queues to a manageable level, the system administrator asked the mobile client users via phone and email to connect to the CRM Server and retrieve their data. The mobile client users were informed about the fact that due to the current situation the data transfer would take several hours. During the course of the day, 100 mobile client users dialed in one after the other to download the data. Because of the long transfer times, the number of work processes that were blocked by ConnTrans increased to such a degree that other users were no longer able to use these work processes and the response times deteriorated again. For this reason, the system administrator decided to abort the ConnTrans processes and to shut down the CommStation in order to avoid any further data transfers. After that, the response times on the CRM Server returned to normal again. As an additional measure, the system administrator began to delete the outbound queues via a report. After that, he had to perform AC extracts for all objects related to all field sales representatives in order to ensure that all the sales representatives had actually received all the data in the mobile clients.

ConnTrans times

> It took more than a day until the outbound queues had been deleted and the AC extracts had been performed and retrieved. During that time, the field sales representatives were able to use their mobile client application, but they couldn't exchange data with the CRM Server.

Critical areas in the Middleware

There are three critical areas in SAP CRM Middleware during mass processing (see also Figure 7.3):

- Inbound queue processing
- Replication & Realignment/replication model
- Outbound queue processing

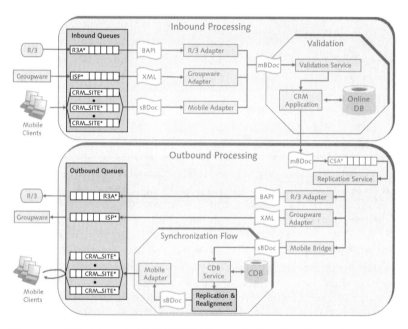

Figure 7.3 Critical Areas in SAP CRM Middleware During Mass Change Processing

This doesn't mean, however, that these areas always cause problems. For example, F&C&P didn't have any problems with Replication & Realignment, because no distribution-relevant fields were changed and the receiver lists of sBDocs were determined on the basis of lookup tables. In other cases, you won't see any problems regarding the outbound queues or the replication model. However, if problems do occur, they are very likely to occur in one of the above areas. For this reason, the following chapters focus on these components of SAP CRM Middleware. Based on a number of examples, we'll describe the problems that may occur repeatedly in this context. We encountered most of the examples described here or similar ones during our work at SAP Support. However, what is most important here is to understand that the problems could have been avoided if the CRM system had been optimized and monitored appropriately. We hope that the descriptions and recommendations provided in this part of the book will help you to avoid the occurrence of similar problems in your company.

In addition to the primary topic of mass changes, we'll also discuss general options for optimizing CRM Middleware that are not related to mass changes.

Data sent to CRM is usually written into the inbound queues first and then further processed by CRM Middleware. It is not surprising, therefore, that inbound queues are the first place in CRM Middleware where optimization can begin.

8 Inbound Queues

If we consider the different systems that can be connected to CRM, the SAP R/3 system in particular is the one that can cause problems for CRM due to its large quantities of data. If you change a business object in R/3, the change is transferred directly to CRM and saved in an inbound queue. The inbound queue scheduler takes the data from the queue and transfers it to the R/3 Adapter (see Figure 8.1).

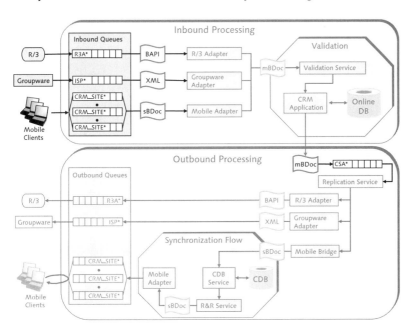

Figure 8.1 Inbound Queues in CRM Middleware

This delta supply of data works well in normal operations. However, if a connected system sends a large quantity of data faster than CRM can process it, the data accumulates in the inbound queue, and the corresponding repercussions, as was explained with examples in Chapter 7, *Introduction to Performance Optimization*, can occur if settings are incorrect. Therefore, the objective should be to optimize the inbound queue processing as much as possible.

All queues in CRM Middleware are based on *Remote Function Calls* (RFCs). RFC is therefore critically important for processing in Middleware. Inbound and outbound queues are implemented using *qRFC* (queued RFC), although Replication & Realignment queues are based on *tRFC* (transactional RFC) rather than qRFC. It is also important to note that, in addition to R3A*, ISP* and CRM_SITE* inbound queues, CSA* queues are also implemented as inbound queues as of CRM Release 4.0. Figure 8.2 shows CRM Middleware from the perspective of RFC. For all inbound queues, there is only one inbound queue scheduler.

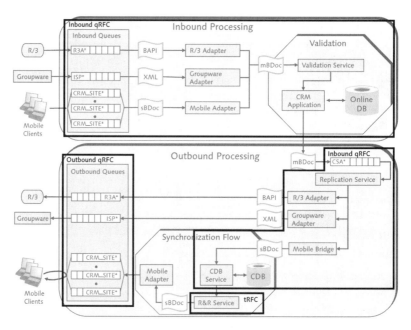

Figure 8.2 RFC in CRM Middleware

Chapter 2, *Inbound Processing and Validation*, contains a detailed description of inbound queues and qRFC.

Different reasons can account for why inbound queues are processed slowly:

Causes of problems

- ▶ So many inbound queues are created that the inbound queue scheduler experiences problems in processing these queues (see Section 8.1).

- ▶ Only a few queues are created, however, these contain a very high number of data records and the available resources in CRM cannot be used effectively (see Section 8.2).

- ▶ All the CRM system's work processes are occupied by the inbound queue processing and a resource bottleneck occurs, which slows down the processing (see Section 8.3).

- ▶ The inbound processing of individual data records is slow (see Section 8.4).

- ▶ Dependencies exist between inbound queues (see Section 8.5).

In the following sections, we will describe the different causes of problems for inbound queue processing and introduce possible solutions.

8.1 The Number of Inbound Queues Is Too High

The inbound queue scheduler ensures that the inbound queues are processed in parallel. To do this, it occupies all work processes available to it. However, the increasing number of queues impairs the performance of the scheduler. The deterioration in performance is clearly noticeable after 10,000 inbound queues. At worst, the performance is impaired to such a degree that it takes longer to assign the next queue entry to a free work process than it takes to post the entry itself. From a performance point of view, this means that the inbound queues are actually processed sequentially, in other words, they are no longer processed in parallel, and the available hardware resources are not used (see example below). The only way to prevent this is to limit the number of inbound queues in CRM.

> **Example**
>
> The company, BodeGolzeSchröder Inc. (hereafter abbreviated to "BGS"), has 2.7 million customers worldwide, 500,000 of which are in Germany and are serviced by 500 field sales representatives. BGS performs a realignment in R/3 once a year. The sales territories of the field sales representatives are reassigned during this realignment. This reorganization does not affect 40% of customers (200,000), since they have traditionally been serviced by the same field sales representative for years and the goal here is to retain this established customer relationship. The remaining 60% are assigned the new sales areas.[1] BGS has developed two reports for this purpose. The Z_DELETE_ASSIGNMENT report deletes the assigned employee responsible for a customer, and the Z_CALCULATE_NEW_ASSIGNMENT report uses a range of criteria to calculate which employee will be responsible for the customer in future. Reports Z_DELETE_ASSIGNMENT and Z_CALCULATE_NEW_ASSIGNMENT change 300,000 data records each. Due to the delta supply of data, 300,000 inbound queues with two entries each are generated in CRM. In addition to the day-to-day activities, CRM Middleware must also process the 600,000 BUPA_REL data records. In BGS's CRM system, the R/3 Adapter and validation usually need two seconds to process a BUPA_REL BDoc. Due to the extremely high number of inbound queues, the inbound queue scheduler needs 2.2 seconds to assign a queue entry to a work process. This results in an estimated inbound processing duration of 600,000 × 2.2 = 1.32 million seconds (which is equivalent to 15 days, 6 hours).[2]

Solution approaches

There are three approaches that you can adopt to reduce the number of inbound queues:

- Reduce the single records in R/3
- Change the naming for queues
- Use R/3 parameter CRM_MAX_QUEUE_NUMBER_DELTA (which ultimately also affects the naming of queues)

Reducing single records

The first approach involves reducing the single records generated by R/3. The company BGS (from our example) has this option. You could change the reports in R/3 to the effect that the COMMIT WORK is executed only after n data records, not after every single data record, and n objects are written into a BUPA_REL BAPI. If we pick 500 as the number to represent n, for example, the Z_DELETE_

---

1 In most cases, the result is the same as before, whereby the field sales representative retains most of his customers.
2 The impact of daily activities and the duration of outbound processing were not included in this estimate.

ASSIGNMENT report would only create 600, rather than 300,000, inbound queues. Unfortunately, this option is not always available. The other factor to bear in mind with this solution is that many (500) CSA queue entries can be generated from one R3A queue entry. Since CSA queues are also inbound queues in terms of CRM Middleware, they also "overload" the inbound queue scheduler.

The second approach consists of limiting the number of inbound queues by changing the *naming for queues*. R/3 queues for the delta supply of data in CRM have the following names by default: R3AD_ <object part><object ID>. There is one entry in the CRMQNAMES table for each object type. The "object part" element of the queue name is located in the QOBJPART field, and the BAPIFLD field indicates which field is used to fill the "object ID". Figure 8.3 shows the entry for the BUPA_REL object. The R/3 outbound queue (and the CRM inbound queue) would have the queue name R3AD_ BUPA12345 for the object 12345. Chapter 2, *Inbound Processing and Validation*, provides a detailed description of the naming conventions for the different inbound queues for delta loads, initial loads, and so on (R3AD*, R3AI*, etc.).

Changing the naming for queues

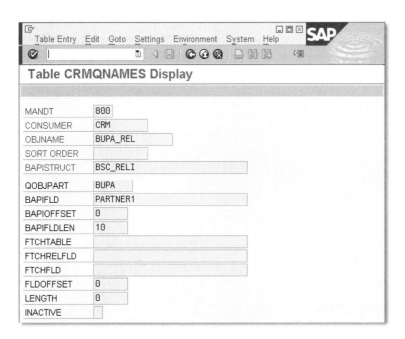

Figure 8.3 R3AD Queue Naming; Table CRMQNAMES in SAP R/3 (Transaction SE16)

By changing the naming for queues, several business partners are written into the same queue, rather than each business partner being written into its own queue. You control the maximum number of queues that can be generated and which object instances are written into a particular queue by determining which and how many positions from the object ID are important for the queue name. You use the LENGTH field to control the number of relevant positions for naming queues and the FLDOFFSET field to select the position.

For example, if the LENGTH field has the value 1 and FLDOFFSET has the value 9, this means that all object instances that have the same number on the tenth position are written into the same queue. You can therefore create a maximum of 10 queues.

The queue name is determined by the first object ID, for which a queue is generated, and does not change again until the queue has been processed completely (and disappears). The left-hand column of the table in the example below contains the R/3 object ID of the business partner. The same business partners are used in all four examples, but the values differ for the LENGTH and FLDOFFSET fields. The right-hand column of the table contains the name of the inbound queue, into which the business partner is written. As you can see from this example, the number of queues depends on the field values and IDs of the business partners.

Example

1. Setting: Standard Naming
   Result: The six customers are written into six queues.

R/3 Customer Number	CRM Queue Name
0000054601	R3AD_CUSTOME0000054601
0000034541	R3AD_CUSTOME0000034541
0000099421	R3AD_CUSTOME0000099421
0000028421	R3AD_CUSTOME0000028421
0000028422	R3AD_CUSTOME0000028422
0000067822	R3AD_CUSTOME0000067822

2. Setting: FLDOFFSET = 9 and LENGTH = 1

   Result: The six customers are written into two queues.

R/3 Customer Number	CRM Queue Name
0000054601	R3AD_CUSTOME0000054601
0000034541	
0000099421	
0000028421	
0000028422	R3AD_CUSTOME0000028422
0000067822	

3. Setting: FLDOFFSET = 8 and LENGTH = 2

   Result: The six customers are written into four queues.

R/3 Customer Number	CRM Queue Name
0000054601	R3AD_CUSTOME0000054601
0000034541	R3AD_CUSTOME0000034541
0000099421	R3AD_CUSTOME0000099421
0000028421	
0000028422	R3AD_CUSTOME0000028422
0000067822	

4. Setting: FLDOFFSET = 6 and LENGTH = 2

   Result: The six customers are written into five queues.

R/3 Customer Number	CRM Queue Name
0000054601	R3AD_CUSTOME0000054601
0000034541	R3AD_CUSTOME0000034541
0000099421	R3AD_CUSTOME0000099421
0000028421	R3AD_CUSTOME0000028421
0000028422	
0000067822	R3AD_CUSTOME0000067822

Proceed as follows to change the naming for queues (see Figure 8.3):

1. In the CRMQNAMES table *in R/3*, find the entry with the object name OBJNAME, for which you want to change the queue naming (Transaction SE16, or alternatively, Transaction SM30).

2. Enter the corresponding values for the **Field Offset** (FLDOFFSET) and **Field Length** (LENGTH) parameters.

3. Make sure that the total of the two values does not exceed the maximum length of the object ID. The maximum length of the object ID is specified in the BAPIFLDLEN field.

CSA queues

Proceed as follows to change the naming for CSA queues (see Figure 8.4):

1. In the SMOFQFIND table *in CRM*, find the entry with the object name in the **BDoc Type** column, for which you want to change the queue naming (Transaction SM30, or alternatively, Transaction SE16).

2. Enter the values for the **Field Offset** (corresponds to FLDOFFSET) and **Internal Length** (corresponds to LENGTH) parameters.

3. The entries for all objects written into the same queue must be changed; in other words, all entries for which the values in the fields **Queue Object Part** and **Segment Field** are the same.

[»]

Note that you may only change the queue naming if the queues are empty.

Using the CRM_
MAX_QUEUE_
NUMBER_DELTA
parameter

The third approach for reducing the number of inbound queues requires using the CRM_MAX_QUEUE_NUMBER_DELTA parameter. This parameter is maintained in the CRMPAROLTP and determines how many queues are created, irrespective of the settings in the CRMQNAMES table. If the parameter is set, the ASCII values of the last three positions of the queue name are combined and calculated modulo CRM_MAX_QUEUE_NUMBER_DELTA. The result is a number that is lower than 1,000 and smaller than CRM_MAX_QUEUE_NUMBER_DELTA. The new queue name is created based on this number.

You can maintain the number of queues differently for each object type.[3]

---

3 As of PI_BASIS 2006.1, or if you have implemented SAP Note 944633.

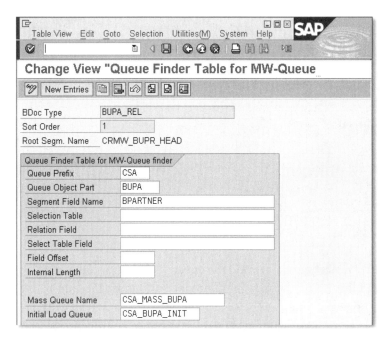

Figure 8.4 CSA Queue Naming; Table SMOFQFIND in CRM (Transaction SM30)

Proceed as follows to limit the number of R3AD queues (see Figure 8.5):

(margin: Limiting R3AD queues)

1. Create a new data record for the CRMPAROLTP table *in R/3* (Transaction SM30).

2. Enter the value "CRM_MAX_QUEUE_NUMBER_DELTA" in the **Parameter name** (PARNAME) field.

3. Enter the name of the object type in the **Param. Name 2** (PARNAME2) field.

4. Enter the name for your CRM system in the **User** (CONSUMER) field.

5. Enter the number of queues in the **Param. Value** (PARVAL1) field.

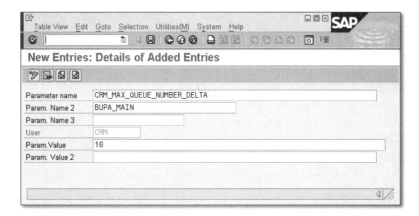

Figure 8.5 Table CRMPAROLTP in SAP R/3

Advantages and disadvantages

When you change the naming for queues, you can use the LENGTH field to determine the maximum number of queues that can be created, however, you cannot determine how many are actually created. The maximum number of queues is not only influenced by the value of the LENGTH field, but also by the type of object ID. Table 8.1 illustrates this dependency. However, it also shows that you can only limit the maximum number of queues in very granular steps. You cannot limit the maximum number of queues to 25, for example.

Type of Object ID	Value of LENGTH	Max. Number of Queues
Numeric	1	10
	2	100
	3	1,000
Alphanumeric	1	36
	2	1,296
	3	46,656

Table 8.1 Maximum Numbers of Inbound Queues Depending on the Type of Object ID and the LENGTH Parameter

The actual number of queues is influenced to a certain extent by the value of the FLDOFFSET field. Depending on the selection and status of the number ranges, certain positions in the object ID have the same value for all instances, whereas, for others, all values are found.

In contrast to changing the queue name, you can limit the maximum number of queues exactly by using the CRM_MAX_QUEUE_NUMBER_DELTA parameter. The type of object ID is not important in this case. Difficulties only occur if the last three positions of the ID are not distributed equally. This problem does not occur when you use the standard naming function (unless there are fewer than 1,000 objects). However, if you have implemented your own rules when assigning IDs, you may not be able to use the parameter as shown in the BGS example.

> **Example**
>
> To be able to identify a customer's country of origin immediately based on the customer number, all customer numbers at BGS end with a two-digit country code (external number assignment). When the CRM_MAX_QUEUE_NUMBER_DELTA parameter is used, a maximum of 10 queues are therefore created for the realignment in Germany.

You could say that the CRM_MAX_QUEUE_NUMBER_DELTA parameter is generally better suited to limiting queues than it is to changing the queue naming. To achieve optimum processing, it is worthwhile to distribute the data records across all queues as evenly as possible.

You may only change the queue naming or the CRM_MAX_QUEUE_NUMBER_DELTA parameter if all inbound queues are processed. Otherwise, data inconsistencies may occur between R/3 and CRM, as illustrated in the following example.

Attention

> **Example**
>
> Before you implement the change, all data records relating to customer A are written into queue A. After you make the change, they are saved in queue X. If you implement the change, even though queue A still contains data, two queues will exist for a certain period of time in the system that contain data from customer A. Queue A contains the older data records and queue X contains the newer data records. If queue X is processed before queue A, the newer data records supersede the older data records. Consequently, the newer data records are posted in CRM first and then the values in the older data records overwrite the newer values.

We recommend that you first deregister the outbound queues in R/3 and then wait until the R3AD inbound queues have been processed completely in CRM. Then make the change to the CSA queue naming

Reducing SAP R/3 outbound queues

and register the queues again. You will find it harder to change the naming of R3A queues, because you cannot prevent outbound queues from being created in R/3. You can therefore only implement a change within a maintenance window if no data is created in R/3, which is transferred to CRM.

8.2 The Number of Inbound Queues Is Too Low

In Section 8.1, we described how you could limit the number of inbound queues. We also mentioned that the actual number of inbound queues can be a lot smaller and data records are not necessarily replicated evenly across all queues. The following example highlights the problems that can occur if you limit the number of queues too much.

Example

BGS has decided not to change the report, but instead has chosen to change the queue naming. To avoid overloading the CRM system too much, the value 1 is selected for the LENGTH parameter and the value 7 is chosen for FLDOFFSET. BGS's CRM system consists of an application server and a database server with four CPUs each. There are 20 dialog work processes in each case on both servers. The CRM system should easily be able to process 10 inbound queues in parallel. BGS expects that 10 queues with 72,000 data records each will be created and that the processing will take 40 hours, based on 72,000 * 2 seconds = 144,000 seconds. After the mass change is started, it becomes apparent that the longest of the 10 queues contains 151,200 data records (i.e., 21% of the changed customers have the number 3 as the last number before the country code in their customer number; 14% have the number 8; 10% have the numbers 7 and 5; 9% have the numbers 6 and 9; 8% have the numbers 2 and 4; 7% have the number 0; and 4% have the number 1). The processing for this queue takes 3.5 days, based on 151,200 × 2 seconds = 302,400 seconds.

In some circumstances, you can solve the problem described in the above example by analyzing the customer numbers and choosing the corresponding FLDOFFSET parameter. However, this analysis is very laborious and there is also no guarantee that it gives you an ideal value for FLDOFFSET. Alternatively, the maximum number of inbound queues can further increase. The crucial factor here is to choose the correct balance between the number of inbound queues that is too low and too high.

8.3 Hardware Bottlenecks

In addition to the number of inbound queues, there are other parameters that you must take into account in order to guarantee optimum processing of inbound queues. This is demonstrated in the following example.

Example

For the next test, BGS selects the value 2 for the LENGTH parameter and the value 6 for FLDOFFSET. After the mass change starts, 84 inbound queues, rather than the expected 100, are generated in CRM with an average of 8,500 entries. The inbound queue scheduler uses the available resources to process the queues as quickly as possible, and occupies all dialog work processes. This results in an overload situation (CPU bottleneck). The CRM system is still busy processing only the inbound queues and no other work can be performed with the CRM system (this also applies in particular for the system administrator). The processing time of the individual data records also multiplies due to the CPU bottleneck.

The problems that BGS experienced in the last example were not caused by the number of inbound queues being too high, but due to the fact that the inbound queue scheduler occupied too many dialog work processes of the CRM system. The inbound queue scheduler doesn't have the necessary logic to check how heavily the system is already being utilized and subsequently to decide whether other queue entries can be processed, or whether there should be a break in the processing. All work processes available to the inbound queue scheduler are used for the processing until all inbound queues are empty.

You can only prevent this kind of overloading by limiting the number of dialog work processes that the inbound queue scheduler is allowed to occupy. For this purpose, the inbound queue scheduler is assigned to an *RFC server group*. You create and maintain RFC server groups in Transaction RZ12. Figure 8.6 shows a CRM system with three RFC server groups. The first group (without a name) is the standard group. This group is always used if there is no explicit assign-

RFC server group

ment to a group. The other two groups, **Queue_Scheduler** and **parallel_generators**, were created manually and one instance each was assigned to both groups. In principle, several instances can also be assigned to a group. In such cases, when a user logs on, the instance with the best response times is determined automatically and the user is logged on to this instance.

To create an RFC server group, start Transaction RZ12, and click the **New** button (**Edit · Create assignment menu option**). To display the resource assignment of an instance or to change it, double-click the corresponding row. A **Change Assignment** dialog window appears with the RFC parameter values of the instance.

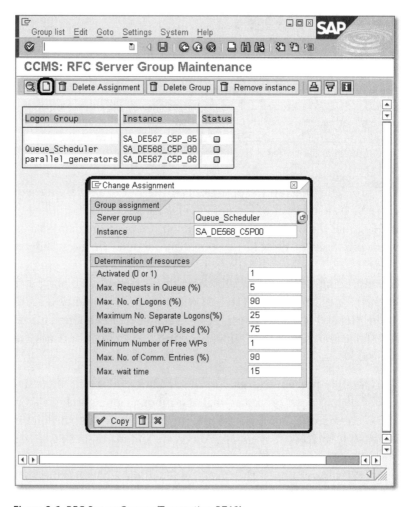

Figure 8.6 RFC Server Groups (Transaction RZ12)

The parameters are used as follows:

▶ **Activated (0 or 1)**
Switch for activating the determination of resources. This should always have the default value 1 (= active).

▶ **Max. Requests in Queue (%)**
Quote for the number of maximum pending requests in the dialog waiting queue of the dispatcher, which is proportionate to the maximum length of the dispatcher request queue. The default value is 5.

▶ **Max. No. of Logons (%)**
This value specifies the maximum percentage of logons allowed to this instance by asynchronous RFCs (the total number of logons is contained in the rdisp/tm_max_no parameter). The remaining percentage continues to be reserved for dialog and HTTP users, i.e., if the number of logons exceeds this value, the caller will not be assigned any resources. The default value is 90.

▶ **Maximum No. Separate Logons (%)**
This value specifies the maximum percentage of logons allowed to this instance by asynchronous RFCs of a user (the total number of logons is contained in the rdisp/tm_max_no parameter). If the number of separate logons exceeds this value, the user is not assigned any further resources. Ideally, this value should not be greater than the **Max. No. of Logons (%)** parameter. The default value is 25.

▶ **Max. Number of WPs Used (%)**
Quote for the number of dialog work processes that a user is allowed to use. If the number of dialog work processes used exceeds this value, the caller is not assigned any further dialog work processes. This quote prevents all dialog work processes from being occupied by a user's RFCs. The default value is 75.

The system doesn't check the user name, which means that, if a user logs on to the system several times, each logon is viewed as a separate user, even though the user name is the same.

▶ **Minimum Number of Free WPs**
Quote for the number of dialog work processes that must be reserved for other users. If the number of free dialog work processes is less than the number specified in the quote, the caller is not assigned any dialog work processes. The default value is 1.

The value must always be smaller than the number of dialog work processes (rdisp/wp_no_dia parameter); otherwise, an RFC request cannot be processed.

▶ **Max. No. of Comm. Entries (%)**
Quote for the maximum number of communication entries of an instance that may be used by parallel RFCs (the total value of the communication entries is contained in the rdisp/max_comm_ entries parameter). If the number of entries used exceeds this value, the caller is not assigned any resources. The default value is 90.

▶ **Max. wait time**
Maximum number in seconds that a work process can "remain in idle mode" if it doesn't receive any resources after the load on the system has been checked. The actual wait time is determined from the available resources. The fewer resources available, the longer the wait time.

Profile parameters of RFC server group

All settings that you implement in Transaction RZ12 are immediately active, however, they are only saved up until the next time when you restart the instance. After you restart the instance, the settings are lost and the old values are active again. To save the values permanently, you must save them as profile parameters. Table 8.2 contains the names of the profile parameters for the individual values in Transaction RZ12.

RZ12	Profile Pparameters
Activated (0 or 1)	rdisp/rfc_use_quotas
Max. Requests in Queue (%)	rdisp/rfc_max_queue
Max. No. of Logons (%)	rdisp/rfc_max_login
Maximum No. of Separate Logons (%)	rdisp/rfc_max_own_login
Max. Number of WPs Used (%)	rdisp/rfc_max_own_used_wp
Minimum Number of Free WPs	rdisp/rfc_min_wait_dia_wp
Max. No. of Comm. Entries (%)	rdisp/rfc_max_comm_entries
Max. wait time	rdisp/rfc_max_wait_time

Table 8.2 Names of Profile Parameters

You assign the inbound queue scheduler to an RFC server group in Transaction SMQR. You select the menu option **Edit · Change AS group and enter the name of the** RFC server group.

Figure 8.7 shows that the **Name of AS Group (DEFAULT = All)** parameter no longer has the "DEFAULT" value; it now has the "Queue_Scheduler" value instead.

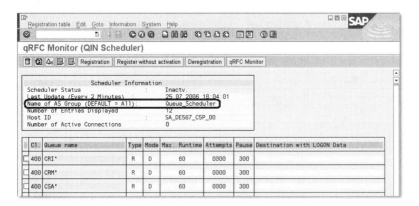

Figure 8.7 Assigning the RFC Server Group (Transaction SMQR)

The optimum setup of RFC server groups depends on the available hardware, volume of data and scenarios used. If you use a pure mobile sales scenario, online or Internet sales users must not be considered when the system is being optimized. In this case, almost all work processes can be made available to the RFC. In all other cases, you must limit the resources for the RFC in such a way that the users will still be able to continue using the system, even if the RFC load is high. If the CRM system has more than one application server, you may find it useful to set up the RFC server groups in such a way that the RFC processing is restricted to the resources of one application server, while the online users use a different application server. By adopting this approach, you can ensure that the users and the RFC will not disturb one another. This holds true especially if data is transferred from the backend, or from/to the mobile clients and the CRM application is used intensively (i.e., both scenarios occur concurrently). The disadvantage of this setup is that the RFC is restricted to one server if the RFC load is high (e.g., if you implement a mass change), even though resources are available on another server (e.g., during the night).

If there is only one application server, it is critical that you optimize the parameters of the RFC server group. The distribution of resources should reflect the actual load distribution — RFC load versus online load — in each case.

To prevent the inbound queue scheduler from using all work processes of the CRM system, you must set the **Max. Number of WPs Used (%)** and **Minimum Number of Free WPs** parameters correctly. The **Minimum Number of Free WPs** parameter determines how many work processes are available for the RFC and the **Max. Number of WPs Used (%)** parameter specifies how many work processes *one* RFC user is allowed to use.

If the system has sufficient dialog work processes, the **Minimum Number of Free WPs** parameter should have the value 3, rather than the default value 1. This ensures that you can still log on to this instance through the SAPGUI, even if the load on the system is very high. This recommendation applies only to a pure mobile sales scenario or a pure RFC instance. In all other cases, the value should be greater, and should also be based on the number of simultaneously active ("concurrent") online users.

When determining the **Max. Number of WPs Used (%)** parameter, remember that the RFC is used not only by the inbound queue scheduler, but by other users as well (replication & realignment, outbound queue scheduler, external systems, and especially mobile clients through the DCOM station/.NET Connector). If you select a value that is too high, although the inbound queues will be processed quickly, the data will accumulate in other areas of the CRM Middleware because resources will not be available there. You can only achieve an optimum processing speed if all the system's components have sufficient resources. We discuss these dependencies in the CRM Middleware in more detail in Chapter 13, *Performing Optimized Mass Changes*.

Detailed documentation about configuring the system resources for parallel RFCs, tRFCs, and qRFCs is available under *SAP NetWeaver* in the SAP Help Portal (*http://help.sap.com*). Click **Search Documentation**. As Search string, enter "Configuration of System Resources for Parallel RFCs tRFC qRFC". Choose **SAP NetWeaver** and the release and language that you want, and click **Search**.

8.4 Performance Analysis for Processing Single Records

SAP provides an entire range of statistical information and trace options for a performance analysis. Some of these are listed in Table 8.3.

Transaction	Description
ST03N	Workload Monitor
STAD	Statistical Records
ST12	Single Transaction Trace
SE30	Runtime Analysis (ABAP Trace)
ST04	Database Performance Analysis
DB02	Database Performance: Tables and Indices
ST10	Table Call Statistics
ST05	Performance Analysis (SQL Trace)
SQLR	SQL Trace Interpreter
SMWMFLOW	Message Flow Statistics
SMWT	Middleware Trace

Table 8.3 Performance Analysis Transactions

Except for the *Message Flow Statistics* (Transaction SMWMFLOW) and the *Middleware Trace* (Transaction SMWT), which we'll discuss in further detail, the analysis transactions are "standard" (i.e., not CRM-specific transactions that are found in every SAP system). Detailed descriptions about these transactions and the most suitable way that you can use them are already available; therefore, we don't want to repeat them here.[4]

Analysis transactions

However, we would like to point out how the performance analysis of CRM Middleware differs from the performance analysis in other SAP systems. The user who executes a transaction often acts as a *filter* for the performance analysis, in order to find the correct statistical data records or trace a particular action in the system. The "user" is not always identified very easily in CRM Middleware. For example,

---

4 We recommend that you refer to the book, *SAP Performance Optimization Guide: Analyzing and Tuning SAP Systems*, by Thomas Schneider, published by SAP PRESS (4th edition, 2005).

you will only be able to clearly establish which user is processing an inbound queue if a *logical destination* has been maintained. Otherwise, the queue processing is performed under the user ID that is currently processing a registered queue (this does not have to be the same queue).

Therefore, a queue entry is not necessarily processed further by the user ID that has written it into the queue; instead, it can be processed using a different user ID. If both of these users have different rights, a user with insufficient rights may try to process the queue entries of another user. The resulting errors are very difficult to analyze because, generally, they rarely occur and can seldom be reproduced.

8.4.1 Logical Destinations

We therefore urgently recommend that you create logical destinations for all inbound queues. There is little effort required, but the benefits are great. You must perform the following steps to create a logical destination:

1. For each queue, you should create one user, whose ID is used to process the queue, for example, *R3A_Inbound* for the R3A* queues. Start Transaction SU01, click the **New** button and create a user of the type "communication".

2. In Transaction SM59, check whether it has an internal connection of the type "NONE" and note the name of this connection.

3. Create a new internal connection in Transaction SM59. Select **Connection Type** "L" and enter the name of the internal connection "NONE" from Step 2 into the **Reference Entry** field on the **Technical Settings** tab (see Figure 8.8). Go to the **Logon & Security** tab and enter the user's logon information from Step 1 here (see Figure 8.9).

4. In Transaction SMQR, you can now assign the internal connection to the corresponding queue (see Figure 8.10).

   ▸ Select the corresponding queue.

   ▸ Click the **Registration** button.

   ▸ In the **Queue Registration** dialog box, enter the ID of the internal connection from Step 3 into the **USERDEST** field.

   ▸ Confirm your entries.

Figure 8.11 shows that the logical destination R3A_INBOUND is now assigned to all queues that start with the prefix "R3A".

Repeat these steps until you have assigned a logical destination (and therefore a separate user) to all inbound queues in Transaction SMQR. You can now see directly from the process overview (Transaction SM50) which work processes are working on particular inbound queues. The user also proves to be helpful in other transactions. For example, when analyzing BDoc errors (Transaction SMW01), you can use the user ID as a filter in the **User (Creator)** field if you want to select the corresponding mBDocs.

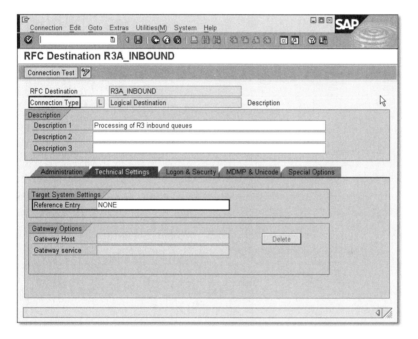

Figure 8.8 Creating a New Internal Connection of Type "L" (Transaction SM59)

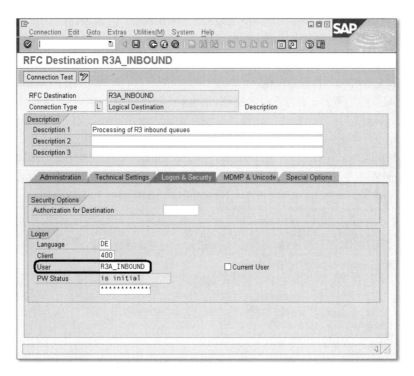

Figure 8.9 Assigning a User to the New Connection (Transaction SM59)

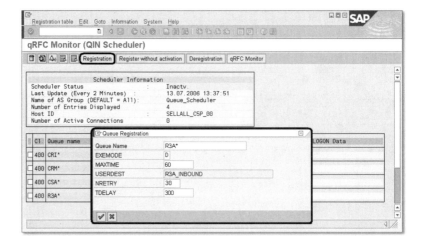

Figure 8.10 Entering a Logical Destination (Transaction SMQR)

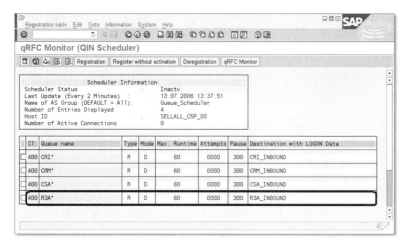

Figure 8.11 R3A Queue with Logical Destination (Transaction SMQR)

8.4.2 Message Flow Statistics

Message flow statistics are CRM-specific statistics that can be very helpful when analyzing performance. You can access the message flow statistics by using following specified path in the SAP Easy Access menu:

Architecture and Technology • Middleware • Monitoring • Message Flow • Display Message Flow Statistics

Alternatively, you can also use Transaction SMWMFLOW. Figure 8.12 shows the transaction's start-up window. You can choose between different statistics: the **Message / Service Kernel Application Statistics** and the **Message / Site / Queue Statistics**.

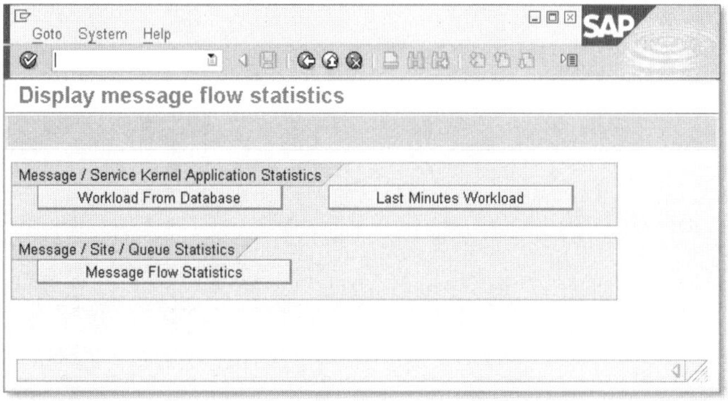

Figure 8.12 Start-Up Window of Transaction SMWMFLOW

The writing of statistics can be switched on and off. Therefore, prior to a performance analysis, you should check to ensure that the statistics are written. First, select **Goto · Activate statistics** from the menu.

In the next window that opens, you can switch the kernel application statistics and site/queue statistics on and off independently of each other (see Figure 8.13):

▶ **Message / Service Kernel Application Statistics**
When you click the **Kernel application statistics** button, the window that you see in Figure 8.14 opens. To ensure that the statistics are written for the CRM Middleware, you should mark the checkbox in the **Middleware Message Hub Statistic** row in the **active** column. To make sure that the kernel statistics are also actually activated, you must have already scheduled the SAP_COLLECTOR_FOR_PERFMONITOR background job.

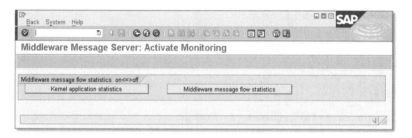

Figure 8.13 Activating Statistics

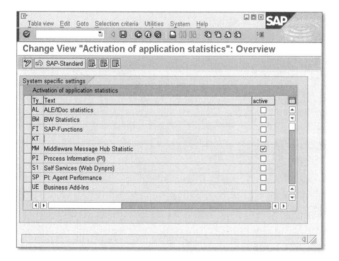

Figure 8.14 Activating Kernel Application Statistics

▶ **Message / Site / Queue Statistics**

When you click the **Middleware message flow statistics** button (see Figure 8.13), the window that you see in Figure 8.15 opens. Both the **Monitoring Message Flow** and the **Collector** should be switched on for an analysis.

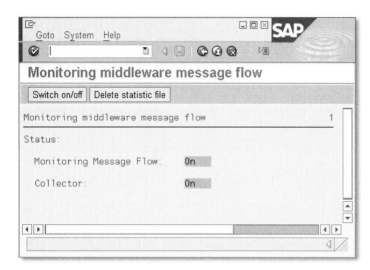

Figure 8.15 Switching Site/Queue Statistics On

Workload Statistics

To display the *workload statistics*, click one of the two buttons **Workload From Database** or **Last Minutes Workload** in Transaction SMWMFLOW (see Figure 8.12).

When you click the **Last Minutes Workload** button, the current load of the last x minutes of the CRM instance on which you are working is displayed. You can define how big "x" is yourself.

Last minutes

When you click the **Workload From Database** button, "historical" data is displayed. You can display statistics of one instance or all instances and choose between different time intervals.

Historical data

In both cases, the layout of the results window is identical. You receive data about the number of BDocs per type that were processed in the time period, as well as data about the processing time, CPU time, wait time, database time and the number of Kbytes requested. You also receive additional information about the total time and the average time for all time data (see Figure 8.16). Since the values in milliseconds are used for the internal calculation, but the total time is specified in seconds, this may lead to rounding variances. This occurs in particular with relatively small values or with few statistics records.

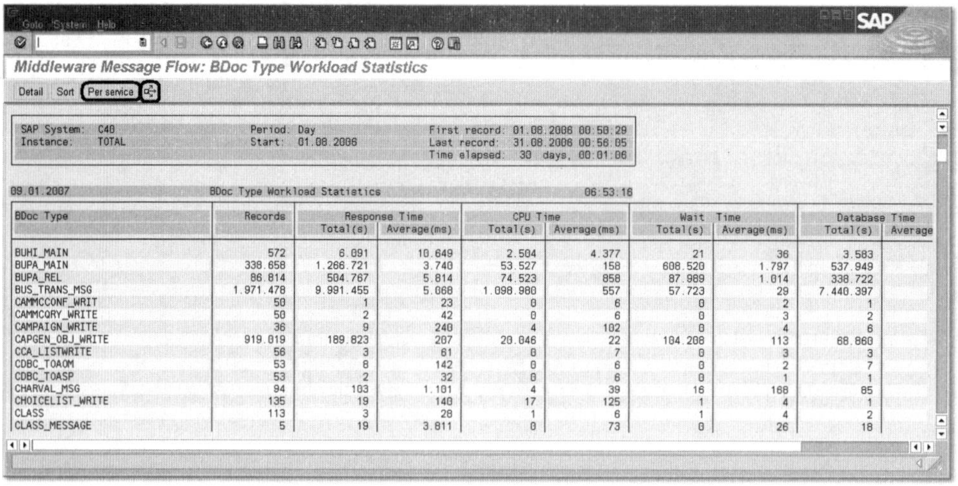

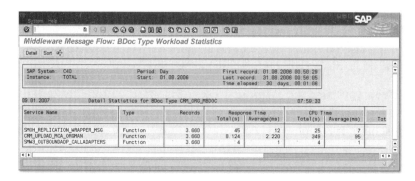

Figure 8.16 Workload Statistics (Transaction SMWMFLOW)

Workload statistics
"per service"

You can receive additional detailed information about the processing times of a particular BDoc type by selecting a row and clicking the **Per service** button. The services that were called for processing a BDoc type are then listed, and the response time, CPU time, wait time, and database time are specified for each service (see Figure 8.17).

Figure 8.17 Workload Statistics Per Service (Transaction SMWMFLOW)

BDoc
type hierarchy

You can obtain information about the *BDoc type hierarchy* by selecting a BDoc type and clicking the **where-used list** button to the right of the **Per service** button (see Figure 8.16). Figure 8.18 shows an example of the BUS_TRANS_MSG BDoc type. Information about the different times that were required for processing a BDoc or a service is also displayed. You will also receive a range of information about the generated BDocs.

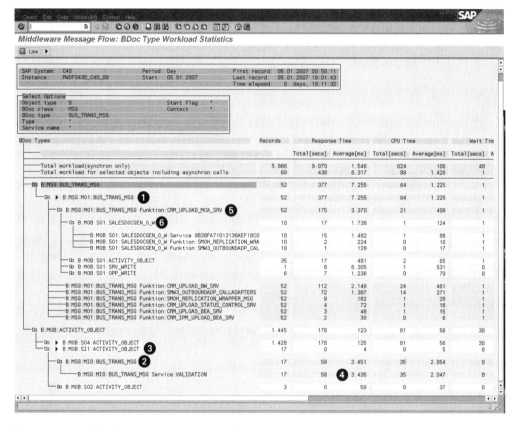

Figure 8.18 Workload Statistics — BDoc Hierarchy (Transaction SMWMFLOW)

In row ❶, you can see that 52 mBDocs of the BUS_TRANS_MSG type were generated with the *M01* flow context. In addition to these 52 mBDocs, another 17 BUS_TRANS_MSG mBDocs were generated with the *MI0* flow context (see row ❷). Only the VALIDATION service was called for these 17 BDocs. You can identify the relevant predecessor and successor BDocs based on the tree structure. A total of 17 ACTIVITY_OBJECT sBDocs were processed with the *SI1* flow context (see row ❸) and the 17 BUS_TRANS_MSG mBDocs were generated as a result. From a business point of view, this means that 17 activities were transferred from mobile clients to the CRM Server during the day and validated there. The validation took 3.435 ms on average for each mBDoc (see row ❹).

The 52 BUS_TRANS_MSG mBDocs with the *MO1* flow context do not have a predecessor BDoc. This means that the objects were created in CRM Online itself and were not sent from SAP R/3 or a mobile client. The average response time of 7.255 ms (see row ❶) for a BUS_TRANS_MSG mBDoc is only provisionally significant, since a BUS_TRANS_MSG mBDoc can contain different business objects, the processing of which has different degrees of complexity. Underneath row ❶, you can see the services and functions that were called when the BUS_TRANS_MSG mBDocs were being processed. (Note that the sequence in the tree structure does not correspond to the actual sequence. The actual sequence is contained in Transaction SMO8FD.)

Row ❺ contains the processing times of the *Outbound Flow Service for Mobile Clients* (CRM_UPLOAD_MCA_SRV function module). In the mobile scenario, the mBDoc is mapped to one or more sBDocs. Here, you receive information about which sBDocs were generated when the 52 BUS_TRANS_MSGs were processed. You can subsequently also tell, from the names of the sBDocs, which business objects are "hiding" in the 52 BUS_TRANS_MSG mBDocs. When you open the tree under row ❺, you see that the 52 BUS_TRANS_MSG mBDocs contain 10 orders (SALESDOCGEN_O_W sBDoc), 35 activities (ACTIVITY_OBJECT sBDoc), one service order (SRV_WRITE sBDoc), and six opportunities (OPP_WRITE sBDoc). When you open the tree structure under these SO1 BDocs (e.g., SALESDOCGEN_O_W in row ❻), you receive information about the different services and functions that were called when the sBDocs were being processed.

Summary If the processing times of an object are not good enough, the statistical data in Transaction SMWMFLOW enables you to analyze exactly which service or function and area (database, CPU) is slow. Based on this information, you can then use a SQL or ABAP trace to determine the database statement or coding segment where time is being lost.

Message Flow Statistics

To display the *message flow statistics*, click the **Message Flow Statistics** button in Transaction SMWMFLOW (see Figure 8.12). Due to the decoupling of the inbound and outbound processing, the processes may run on different instances. The statistics for the inbound and outbound processing are therefore listed separately. Within the inbound or outbound processing, you can display the total load (**Total**) or the load distribution across the individual instances. You can also select a time interval (day or week). Figure 8.19 shows an example of message flow statistics. The system in this example has over five instances (us0091_Q5C_91 to us4399_Q5C_91) and daily statistics from January 01, 2007 to January 10, 2007.

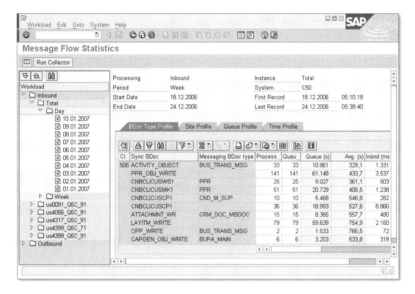

Figure 8.19 Message Flow Statistics (Transaction SMWMFLOW)

The different queue and processing times are displayed on the right-hand side of the window. Depending on which tab you select, the figures for each BDoc type, site, or queue are summarized. In the **Time Profile** tab, you will find information about how many BDocs were processed in a particular period and how long the processing took. If you select a day as the time interval, the **Single Records** tab will also be displayed. The data for each BDoc is listed here individually.

To make it easier for you to understand the data, we have provided a list of the column headers on the **BDoc Type Profile** tab and their descriptions in Table 8.4 (inbound processing) and Table 8.5 (outbound processing). In Figure 8.20 (inbound processing) and Figure

8.21 (outbound processing), we have illustrated where the times are measured within the Middleware.

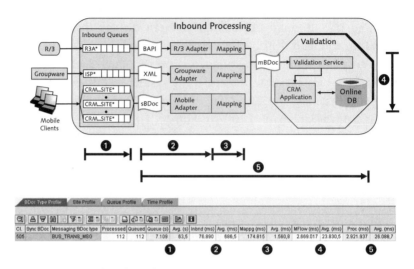

Figure 8.20 Times for Inbound Processing (Transaction SMWMFLOW)

Times for inbound processing

Column title	Description
Synch BDoc	Name of synchronization BDoc type
Messaging BDoc type	Name of messaging BDoc type
Processed	Number of BDocs of this type processed in total
Queued	Number of BDocs of this type in the inbound queues
Queue(s)	Total wait time in seconds in the inbound queues
Avg. (s)	Average wait time in seconds in the inbound queues
Inbnd. (ms)	Total processing time in milliseconds in the inbound adapter
Avg. (ms)	Average processing time in milliseconds in the inbound adapter
Mappg. (ms)	Total processing time in milliseconds for mapping the BDocs
Avg. (ms)	Average processing time in milliseconds for mapping the BDocs
Mflow. (ms)	Total processing time in milliseconds in the message flow
Avg. (ms)	Average processing time in milliseconds in the message flow

Table 8.4 Descriptions of Columns in Inbound Processing (Transaction SMWMFLOW)

Column title	Description
Proc. (ms)	Total processing time in milliseconds (without the wait time in the inbound queue)
Avg. (ms)	Average processing time in milliseconds (without the wait time in the inbound queue)

Table 8.4 Descriptions of Columns in Inbound Processing (Transaction SMWM-FLOW) (cont.)

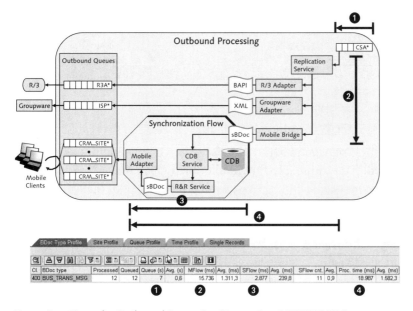

Figure 8.21 Times for Outbound Processing (Transaction SMWMFLOW)

Column title	Description	
BDoc type	Name of BDoc type	Times for outbound processing
Processed	Number of BDocs of this type processed in total	
Queued	Number of BDocs of this type in the inbound queues	
Queue(s)	Total wait time in seconds in the inbound queues	
Avg. (s)	Average wait time in seconds in the inbound queues	
MFlow. (ms)	Total processing time in milliseconds in the message flow	
Avg. (ms)	Average time in milliseconds in the message flow	

Table 8.5 Descriptions of Columns in Outbound Processing (Transaction SMWMFLOW)

Column title	Description
SFlow. (ms)	Total processing time in milliseconds in the synchronization flow
Avg. (ms)	Average time in milliseconds in the synchronization flow
SFlow. cnt.	Number of BDocs of this type in the synchronization flow
Avg.	Number of BDocs in the synchronization flow divided by the number of processed BDocs
Proc. time (ms)	Total processing time in milliseconds (without the wait time in the inbound queue)
Avg. (ms)	Average time in milliseconds (without the wait time in the inbound queue)

Table 8.5 Descriptions of Columns in Outbound Processing (Transaction SMWM-FLOW) (cont.)

8.4.3 CRM Middleware Trace

Setting trace levels

The *CRM Middleware Trace* enables you to obtain additional information that is written into the Middleware during processing. The CRM system not only allows you to switch the writing of the Middleware trace on and off, it also enables you to define the area where the trace is written and its granularity. For example, you can specify that the trace is restricted to errors and warnings in the message flow (**Trace level: Warning**), whereas you want all information (**Trace level: Detail Level 2**) to be written during the generation (see Figure 8.22). To maintain a trace level, go to **Architecture and Technology · Middleware · Monitoring · Message Flow · Set up Middleware Trace** from the SAP Easy Access menu or by using Transaction SMWTAD.

Trace levels

The following trace levels are available:

▶ **Level 0: Error**
Only serious errors are reported.

▶ **Level 1: Warnings**
Only situations that can lead to an error are reported.

▶ **Level 2: Service Flow**
A note is made of all services that are processed in the Middleware.

▶ **Level 3: Detail Level 1**
Additional information is written about the executed programs and modules.

▶ **Level 4: Detail Level 2**

Program-specific information is written.

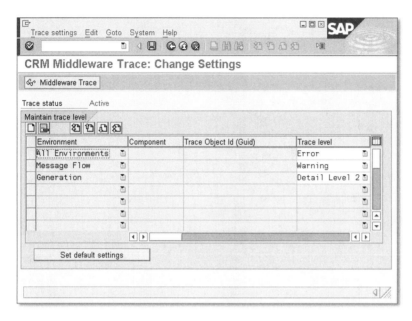

Figure 8.22 Settings for Middleware Trace (Transaction SMWTAD)

The standard setting in the live system is Level 1. Levels 3 and 4 are intended for developers.

For performance and disk space reasons, you should delete old traces on a regular basis. SAP provides the SMO6_REORG2 report for reorganization purposes, which you can also use (among other things) to delete traces.

Chapter 12, *Reorganization*, contains information about this report, and reorganization in general.

You can access the trace itself by using the following path in the SAP Easy Access menu:

Displaying a trace

Architecture and Technology · Middleware · Monitoring · Message Flow · Display Middleware Trace

Alternatively, you can also use Transaction SMWT. Figure 8.23 shows the selection screen that appears when you start the transaction.

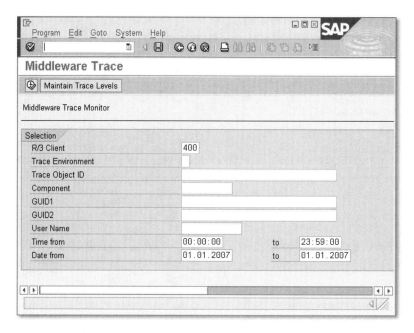

Figure 8.23 Selection Screen for Middleware Trace (Transaction SMWT)

In accordance with the selection criteria you enter, a list of the available traces in the system is displayed. You can display the trace by double-clicking the corresponding row (see Figure 8.24).

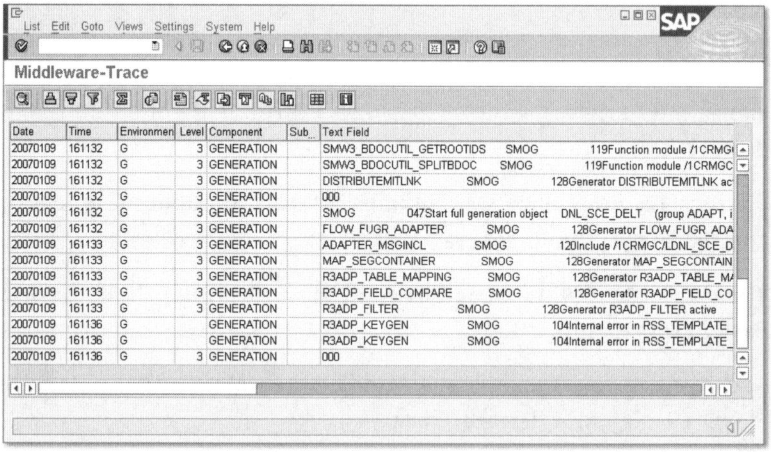

Figure 8.24 Middleware Trace

The trace itself contains a range of information: in addition to the **Date**, **Time**, **Environment and t**race level (**Level**), the **Text Field** and **Trace GUID** in particular are displayed. **Text Field** contains the trace message (maximum of 250 characters) and **Trace GUID** contains the GUID of the trace object. If you're searching for the trace messages for a particular BDoc, for example, you can search according to the GUID of the BDoc in the **Trace GUID field**. Alternatively, you can enter the BDoc GUID as your selection criterion in the **GUID1** field; only the traces that contain messages for the BDoc will subsequently be displayed (see Figure 8.23). In the case of BDocs in particular, you can also jump directly to the trace from Transaction SMW01.

To do this, select the BDoc in Transaction SMW01 and click the **Middleware Trace** button, which is highlighted (see Figure 8.25).

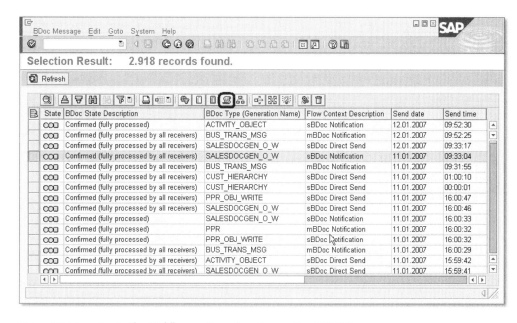

Figure 8.25 Jumping to the Middleware Trace from Transaction SMW01

8.5 Dependencies Between Inbound Queues

You cannot always process CSA inbound queues in parallel on an unrestricted basis. Dependencies may occur between individual queues for some object types, which means that the processing for a queue must wait until one or more entries of another queue are processed. The following example illustrates this problem, based on a download of business partner relationships from SAP R/3.

Example

A request for all business partner relationships is started in a CRM system. The number of R3AR_BUPA* queues is limited to three and there is no limit on the number of CSABUPA* queues. A BUPA_REL BDoc from R/3 contains all relationships of a business partner (to simplify matters, let's assume that all business partners have four relationships). If an RFC record is being processed in a R3AR queue, the individual relationships are written into different CSA queues (depending on the business partner GUID in the relationship). Therefore, this results in five CSA queue entries (and consequently the corresponding CSA queues), even though only one mBDoc is generated. If the mBDoc is being processed, you see in Transaction SMQ2 that the five queues have the *running* status; while in Transaction SM50, you see that only one work process is busy.

The BDoc can only be processed if all CSA queue entries are in the first position of the queue in question, since otherwise, the queue entries would be superseded.

If the number of CSA queues is not restricted, they usually have one entry. Two or more entries will only appear in a CSABUPA queue if two business partners have a relationship to one another or to a common third party. Figure 8.26 shows that both business partners 1111 and 2222 have a relationship to business partner 4112. If both entries in the R3AR_BUPA1111 and R3AR_BUPA2222 queues are processed, two entries are written into the CSABUPA4112 queue. Only one entry is written into all other CSABUPA* queues. The BUPA_REL BDocs in the CSA queues for business partners GP1111 and GP3333 can be processed immediately and in parallel, since the relevant entries are situated in the first position in the CSA queues. The BUPA_REL BDoc for business partner GP2222 cannot be processed immediately, because the GP2222-GP4112 relationship is not in the first position in the CSABUPA4112 queue. All queues that have a business partner relationship to GP2222 as the first entry (CSABUPA412*) get the *waiting* status, since they can only be processed after the GP1111-GP4112 business partner relationship has been processed in the CSABUPA4112 queue.

If there is no limit to the number of CSA queues (as described in the example), situations only rarely occur where queues have to wait for each other, or so many queues are created that this does not affect the processing speed. It is a different situation if the number of CSA queues has been severely limited. The CSA queues generally have more entries and the number of queues waiting for each other increases, as explained in the following example.

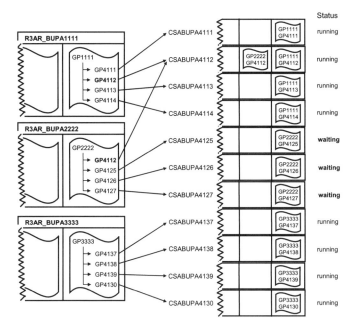

Figure 8.26 Dependencies Between CSA Queue Entries

Example

The prerequisites in this example correspond to those from the last example, however, the only difference in this case is that the number of CSABUPA* queues has been limited to 10.

Figure 8.27 shows that the relationship between GP2222 and GP4127 and the relationship between GP3333 and GP4137 are written into the same queue due to the different queue naming.

Consequently, the BUPA_REL BDoc of business partner 3333 can only be processed if the GP2222-GP4127 entry of queue CSABUPA4127 (i.e., the BUPA_REL BDoc of business partner 2222) has been processed. However, this entry can only be processed if the first entry GP1111-GP4112 of queue CSABUPA4112 (i.e., the BUPA_REL BDoc of business partner 1111) has been processed. In other words, this means that the BUPA_REL BDocs are processed sequentially, even though 10 CSA queues exist.

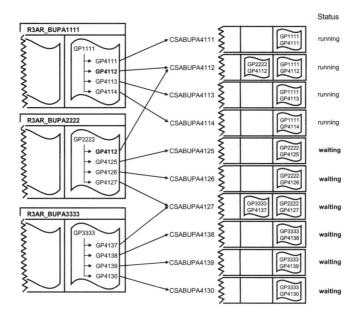

Figure 8.27 Dependencies with Limited Number of CSA Queues

A widely used term in the CRM world is R&R or Replication & Realignment. Because R&R often constitutes a bottleneck in the CRM system, it is worth describing this concept. In this chapter, we will focus on optimization options for the R&R process and the replication model.

9 Replication Model and R&R

The acronym *R&R* actually stands for two different processes: the calculation of possible new receivers of data (*realignment*) and the identification of already known receivers, that is, of specific mobile clients (*replication*), if the data has already been replicated. The main purpose of these two processes is to determine all relevant receivers of a message and to ensure that the data is made available to these receivers. The following sections describe how the system can distinguish between these processes. If you know the details involved in these processes, you can optimize the overall process regarding different situations in everyday CRM operations. Figure 9.1 shows that the Replication & Realignment (R&R) service is integrated in the synchronization flow and that it is responsible for providing the data in the outbound queues through the mobile adapter.

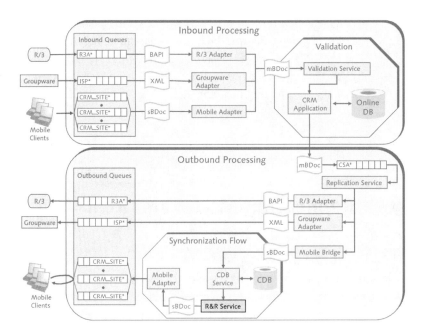

Figure 9.1 Integration of R&R in the Middleware Flow

9.1 Basic Principles

Call the queue monitor, SMOHQUEUE, in order to monitor the data distribution process carried out by the R&R service. You can find this transaction in the SAP Easy Access menu by selecting the following path: **Architecture and Technology • Middleware • Monitoring • Queues • Monitor R&R Queues**. You will see that this distribution process can involve up to five different queues (Figure 9.2).

For a better understanding of the different optimization options, it is useful to take a closer look at how these queues are used and how they interact. Chapter 3, *Outbound Processing*, contains a detailed description of the queue processing process.

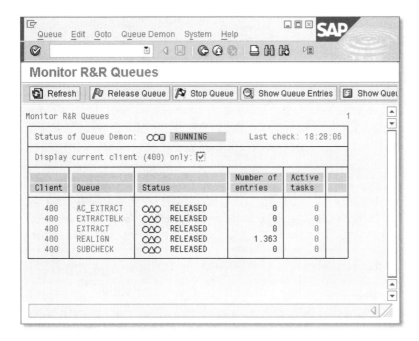

Figure 9.2 R&R Queue Monitor

The individual R&R queues are as follows:

Meaning of the queues

▶ **SUBCHECK**
This queue is used if a mobile client (in the administration console) is assigned a subscription or had one withdrawn, either directly or when a subscription check job is triggered.

▶ **REALIGN**
During the processing of this queue, the receivers of the data are determined.

▶ **EXTRACT**
This queue will contain the data after the receivers have been determined.

▶ **EXTRACTBLK**
This queue is used for bulk objects.

▶ **AC_EXTRACT**
This queue is used during an AC extraction that is carried out via the administration console.

If a business object is created or modified in the application and intelligent replication (see Figure 9.3) is used, a BDoc is transferred

Intelligent replication

to the *replication wrapper* after a successful validation process. This BDoc contains *send bits* indicating in which fields of the business object values have been changed. Within the replication wrapper, a check is carried out to determine whether the data change also involved fields that are relevant for the replication process, that is, fields that are directly used to determine receivers. If the contents of a single replication-relevant field have changed, the receivers of the modified object must be determined again.

Example

Company BGS assigns business partners to its field sales representatives via ZIP codes. Now one of the business partners moves to a different location. If this move requires the ZIP code to be changed in the business partner maintenance, the CRM system has to check whether this business partner must be assigned to a different field sales representative. If only the contents of other fields have changed for this business partner, such as the phone number, however, the change affects only those field sales representatives of BGS who have already been assigned this business partner. In that case, the receivers of the message don't need to be redetermined.

For this reason, if replication-relevant data is changed, the replication wrapper first transfers the object to that part of the replication service, which is responsible for determining the receivers. In other words, the BDoc is first written to the realignment queue. If, on the other hand, only the data that is not replication-relevant is modified, then the receivers are already known and the data can directly be written into the outbound queue of the receiver on the basis of the lookup table, thereby skipping all other steps. This means, however, that the load on the CRM system is smaller if the receivers are already known and don't need to be determined.

Bulk replication If a business object is replicated in a bulk, all instances of this type are sent to all subscribing receivers. Therefore, bulk-replicated objects don't involve any realignment process, which may be a way to reduce the system load. In the bulk lookup table SMOHLUBULK, the system only checks which sites are supposed to receive this BDoc through a publication and whether the **Extracted** field contains the value "T" (= TRUE). Then, the BDoc is generated, including the corresponding list of receivers, and written to the outbound queues. This process is illustrated in Figure 9.4.

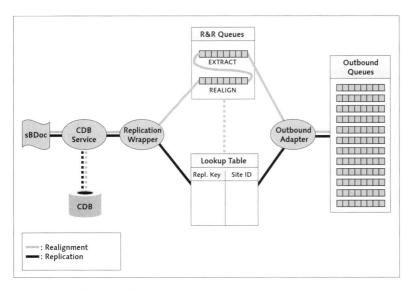

Figure 9.3 Intelligent Replications

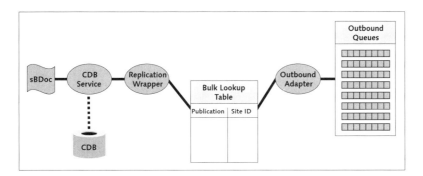

Figure 9.4 Bulk Replications

9.2 Optimizing the Replication Model

As described in Section 9.1, the load generated in the system is smaller, if the receivers of the data to be replicated don't need to be determined. Thus, you can substantially reduce the system load by optimizing the replication model with regard to the bulk replication and intelligent replication of business objects. Furthermore, an optimization of the data model to reduce the data load can also have a significant impact on system performance. You should note that the smaller the quantity of data that is sent to the different sites, the smaller the number of entries to be processed in the outbound queues. In general, a smaller number of entries means that smaller data quantities must be retrieved and processed by the ConnTrans service. This results in shorter ConnTrans processing times and often increases user satisfaction.

Consideration For this reason, the first thing that you need to do is to optimize the replication model. An optimization of the replication model must always take into account two conflicting requirements: On the one hand, there is the desire to replicate as little data as possible in order to keep the network load and table size of outbound queues small. On the other hand, there is the goal to keep the load on the server, which as caused by Middleware processes such as the realignment service, as small as possible, too. In order to carry out as few realignment calculations as possible, the receiver determination should be performed frequently, if that's feasible. For this reason, you should first define the data basis on which you want to base the receiver determination in your company. We recommend that you choose data that doesn't change often. Moreover, you should determine the number of sites to which a given data record would be sent in the context of intelligent replication. If the instances of a business object type are sent to most of your sites, you should consider distributing this object type in a bulk replication process. In case of a bulk replication, it may happen that an object is sent to more sites than necessary, but the workload placed on the Middleware will be reduced. Prior to reconfiguring the replication model, you should carefully consider whether a reduced workload on the Middleware justifies the increased resource consumption caused by a larger quantity of data that needs to be replicated through the network. The following sections describe the analysis and optimization of some typical cases.

Bulk publications An initial, fast way to optimize the replication model is to check whether the bulk publications contain objects that aren't needed for the current business process. It often happens that a (required) bulk publication, such as Customizing data, also contains replication objects that aren't needed (e.g., Customizing tables for applications that aren't used). If you discover that a bulk publication contains both required and (currently) non-required objects, you should transfer the non-required objects to a separate publication.

A common reason for excessive data distribution is using intelligent replication without defining any filter criteria. To determine whether that's the case in your system as well, you must call Transaction SMOECK. You can find this transaction in the SAP Easy Access menu by selecting the following menu path: **Architecture and Technology • Middleware • Development • Checks**. Then enter the value "PUBL" in the **Object Type** field and click the **Execute** button or press F8. In the results screen, double-click the **Publications** line to go to the detail screen. The section **Intelligent publication without criteria fields will be treated as bulk** has a list of all intelligent replication objects for which no filter was defined (see Figure 9.5).

Filter criteria

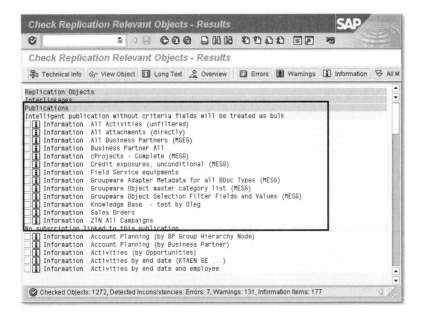

Figure 9.5 Intelligent Publications without Filter Criteria

If you don't want to set any filter criteria, you should always set the object in question to bulk replication; otherwise, the receivers will always be the same as those in a bulk replication, although the realignment service is carried out. In other words, all sites that have been assigned this subscription will receive this data. Because objects that are replicated in a bulk replication don't comprise any distribution-relevant fields, the realignment service won't be carried out here (see Figure 9.4).

To be able to decide whether or not an object should switched from intelligent replication to bulk replication, you should clarify the following issues regarding the objects in question:

▶ Does a current or planned business transaction exist as a basis of the existing modeling (e.g., managers who are supposed to receive all data from their employees)? If you answer Yes to this question, you should first consider the importance of this business transaction and whether there is a more efficient way to model it. If a different way of modeling is not possible, you should keep the existing one.

▶ How many sites is the object currently sent to on average? If an object is already being sent to the majority of sites, you should consider switching it to bulk replication.

▶ What additional load (e.g., network load, additional entries in the outbound queue) would a switch to bulk replication generate? In this analysis, you should also consider the distribution of dependent objects that may exist, because you can't define any dependencies for bulk replications (i.e., the dependent objects would also have to be switched to bulk replication).

SAP provides various tools for this analysis in the context of the *Business Process Performance Optimization Service for xMSA* service. You will find more detailed information about this service in the SAP Service Marketplace at *http://service.sap.com/bppo*.

Example 1

At BGS, activities are replicated intelligently on the basis of sales organizations. In an analysis, the company discovers that all activities are replicated to 100 % of all sites, because there is only one organization that currently uses Mobile Sales. If, instead of this, the object is replicated as a bulk object, the necessity of carrying out a realignment can be eliminated and the efforts involved in maintaining the lookup tables can be reduced. However, since the company plans to roll out the application in additional sales organizations, BGS decides to continue using intelligent replication.

Example 2

At BGS, 5,000 products are replicated on the basis of intelligent subscriptions. An analysis of the replication model shows that due to the different mapping criteria most of the products (95 %) are sent to many different sites (on average, to 96 % of the existing 500 sites).

Because the reception of product masters at so many different sites is required, BGS considers switching the distribution process to bulk replication. This means that 100 % of the sites will receive all products, but again, the realignment as well as the maintenance of lookup tables can be eliminated so that the overall system load will be reduced. Consequently, the company decides to change the distribution of products. After this change in distribution of products, an average of 96 % of the sites receive only 250 products more than before (i.e., they now receive 5,000 products instead of 4,750). If, on the other hand, 500,000 products were replicated, most of the sites would receive 25,000 products more than they used to, which would certainly not go unnoticed by the individual users, and the ConnTrans times would increase as well.

If your analysis has shown that you should switch an object from intelligent replication to bulk replication to reduce the load generated on the CRM Server by the Middleware, you should first determine all the sites that subscribe to the replication object. Then, you should stop the processing of messages on the server by deregistering all CSA queues in Transaction SMQR (see Figure 9.6). This way, you can ensure that no additional data is written to the R&R queues.

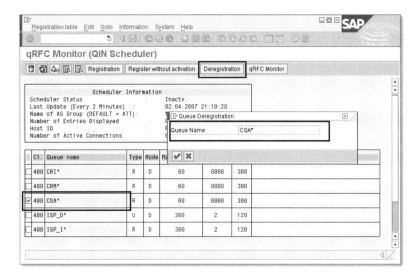

Figure 9.6 Deregistering All CSA Queues

Once all messages in the R&R queues have been processed (which can be checked in Transaction SMOHQUEUE), you must delete the existing site mappings and subscriptions for all clients in the administration console by using Transaction SMOEAC.

[»] Deleting the subscription assignments for the mobile clients requires the removal of subscribed objects from the mobile clients. For this reason, deletion messages are generated in this step. The number of deletion messages corresponds to the number of object instances on a client and can therefore also cause performance problems.

Once you have deleted the subscriptions, you must delete the corresponding publication in the administration console as well. Then, you can use the same transaction to delete the relevant intelligent replication object because all dependent objects have been removed. Next, you should create the replication object as a bulk replication object in the administration console. As soon as the replication object exists, you must also create the publication object. Having created the objects, you must start the necessary Middleware creations via Transaction SMOGGEN (see Figure 9.7). In Transaction SMOGGEN, you must first select object category **Replication Objects** and enter the replication object you just created in the **Available Objects** field. Then start the generation process by clicking on the **Execute** button. Once the objects have been generated, select the **Publications** radio button and enter the publication you created previously into the **Available Objects** field. Then start the generation process by clicking the **Execute** button again. After that, you can create the required bulk subscriptions in the administration console.

Deactivating sites
In order to avoid flooding the outbound queues with data at the time of mapping these subscriptions, you can deactivate the sites. When a site is deactivated, the realignment service is carried out as usual, that is, the lookup tables are updated, but no BDocs are written to the outbound queues. At the same time, the Middleware memorizes the replication objects, for which the lookup tables were updated and no BDocs were generated yet.

Once you reactivate the site, the Middleware triggers an AC extract for each of these replication objects. Because of that, AC extracts are generated during the activation of the sites instead of individual messages.

[!] In this context, the system generates a complete extract for *all* instances of the object, even if the lookup tables were updated only for one instance. Therefore, you should identify other object types prior to the deactivation, which might be modified through online activities, such as a call center that's operated concurrently.

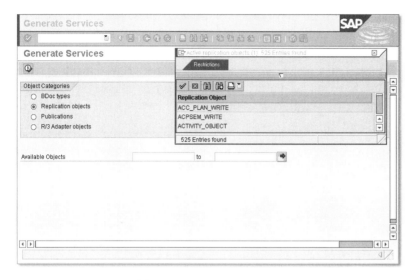

Figure 9.7 Generating Middleware Services

You can deactivate sites through the administration console (Transaction SMOEAC). To do that, you must first select the relevant site. In change mode, you can then uncheck the **Active** field so that the **Activation Status** changes from *Active* to *Deactivated* (see Figure 9.8).

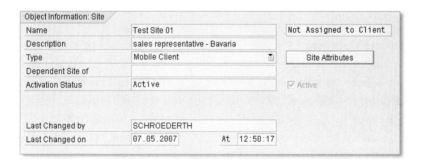

Figure 9.8 Activating and Deactivating Sites

Even if a site is deactivated, the mobile client user can still use the mobile application and transfer data to the CRM Server. In that case, the data is updated (usually in the CRM system) and replicated to other sites. However, the site itself will no longer receive any data (this includes both confirmations for data that has been sent by the site itself, and data from other users).

If many sites, perhaps even hundreds of sites, should or must be deactivated, using Transaction SMOEAC can be very tedious and extremely time-consuming. At the other end of the spectrum, a simple report that merely activates or deactivates a selected subset of all sites is also not useful, as the following example of BGS demonstrates.

Example

Out of the 500 field sales representatives of BGS, 15 employees are absent for a longer period of time (vacation, sick leave, etc.) and do not execute any ConnTrans operation. In order to reduce the workload on the CRM system, the corresponding sites have been deactivated. In the run-up to the mass change, all sites of the field sales representatives are supposed to be deactivated. After the mass change, all sites are supposed to be reactivated with the exception of the ones that had already been deacivated previously. What BGS needs is a report that enables the company to deactivate a subset of all sites and that memorizes which sites had already been deactivated before. Those sites are then supposed to be reactivated at a later stage.

To resolve this problem, SAP developed the SMOE_BULK_SITE_ACTIVATION report that enables mass deactivation and mass activation of sites. To be able to use this report, you must implement SAP Note 828890.

On the **Deactivate Sites** tab, this report enables you to select sites according to the **Site ID** or **Site Name** (see Figure 9.9). Then, the subset is assigned a **Deactivation ID** and a description (**Comment**). After clicking the **Execute** (F8) button, a popup window opens in which the report tells you how many sites will be deactivated by the selection and it allows you to view a list of those sites affected by this deactivation.

The **Activate Sites** tab provides a list of all active deactivation IDs (see Figure 9.10). In addition, it contains information concerning which users have deactivated the subset and when. If you select a line and click **Execute**, the corresponding site will be reactivated. A popup window then tells you how many sites were activated and how many extracts were started. The selected entry will be removed from the list.

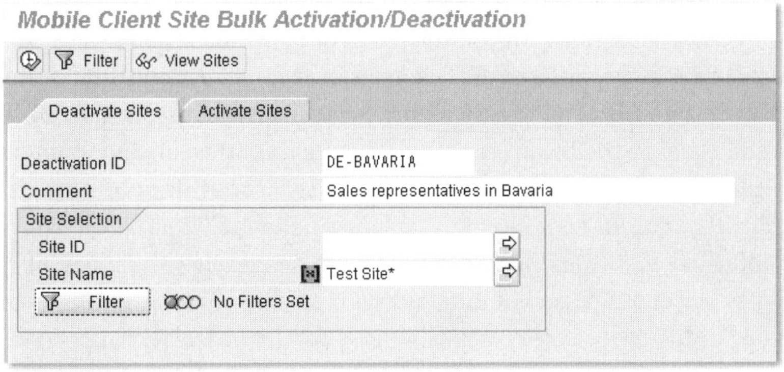

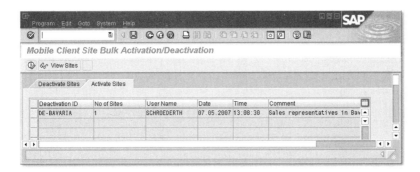

Figure 9.9 Mass Deactivation of Sites

Figure 9.10 Mass Activation of Mobile Sites

Once the sites have been deactivated, you can create the relevant subscriptions on each system and client. Then you must assign the new subscriptions to the sites you had previously listed on a piece of paper.

Next, you can activate the message processing process again.

As described above, when you remove the assignment between a subscription and a mobile client, the system generates a deletion message. If each mobile client that had been assigned the subscription, prior to the change from intelligent replication to bulk replication, is assigned the bulk subscription after the change, you will avoid creating a deletion message. For this purpose, you must deactivate the sites before deleting the mapping and also stop the sub-check queue. After that, you can proceed in the aforementioned manner.

Avoiding deletion messages

247

Sliding window

Oftentimes, specific data is of interest to a field sales representative only for a certain period of time. To avoid large data quantities, particularly with regard to major changes in regional assignments or the initial data load to a mobile client, we recommend inserting an additional field in the business object. This field must be included in the replication model as filter criteria, and is set at specific points in time via a report. This new filter ensures that individual application data is replicated to the mobile clients of field sales representatives only within a certain period of time, which is referred to as a "sliding window". This procedure is typically used for activities and opportunities.

Example

At BGS, each of the 500 field sales representatives is assigned 100 customers based on the ZIP codes. On average, every sales representative visits his customers once in every two weeks. These visits are scheduled in advance in the system via activities, and then are evaluated online in the CRM system. After the first year, each field sales representative had stored 3,000 activities (100 customers x 60 weeks/biweekly visits)[1] on the mobile client. At the end of that year, BGS decided to reorganize the regional mappings so as to optimize its business. During this reorganization, approximately 50% of all mappings between field sales representatives and customers were changed. As a result, a total of 1,500,000 activity BDocs were written to the outbund queue (750,000 deletions and 750,000 new creations), which had a significant impact on live operations. Because only future activities and those of the two months prior to the reorganization were relevant to the sales representatives, BGS included a replication-relevant filter criteria in the replication model, which was set for this specific period of time via a customer-specific report. Consequently, during the next reorganization of regions, there were only eight activities per customer that were relevant. This meant that in a reorganization, which had the same exact scope as the previous one, the fact that an additional filter was set reduced the load in the outbound queues from 1,500,000 entries for activities to 4,000 entries ((8 deletion messages + 8 new creations) * 500 customers * 50%) so that the second reassignment of regions at BGS didn't have a significant impact on the field sales representatives or online users.

Interlinkages

Another frequent example of high system load caused by an inappropriately configured replication process is the creation of very high data quantities due to dependent objects and interlinkages, particularly if these interlinkages generate recursions.

---

1 Fifty-two weeks of the current year plus the subsequent eight weeks.

248

In addition to the complete master data of customers that is assigned to the respective field sales representatives, BGS intends to make available the complete master data of business partners that is included in the orders of the assigned sold-to parties on the mobile clients as well. For this purpose, the administrator enters a setting in the administration console that ensures that these partners follow the orders. Unfortunately, another setting in the administration console ensures that the orders follow the business partners as well (so that the orders of assigned sold-to parties are also available on the mobile clients). Consequently, all orders that contain the other business partners are also sent to the mobile clients. As a result, new partners are added based on these orders so that the complete master data must be sent for these new partners, and so on (see Figure 9.11).

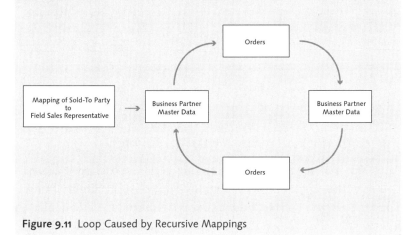

Figure 9.11 Loop Caused by Recursive Mappings

To determine to what data quantities are generated, you must first check which dependent objects and interlinkages were defined for each replication object. After that, you should clarify the following aspects for each of these objects:

▶ Are the dependent objects really needed by all parent objects? If not, find out whether or not these objects can be replicated directly; whether you can reduce the number by using intelligent dependencies; or whether you can entirely forego a replication.

▶ Are these child objects simply dependent or intelligently dependent? In case of a simple dependent replication, you may be able to reduce the data volume by implementing an intelligent replication.

> ▶ Can the dependent objects replicate independently, that is, without any direct dependencies to the parent objects. If so, could you use a more selective publication?

In particular, you should check if recursive bidirectional interlinkages exist. To do that, start the administration console and select the "Interlinkage" value in the **Object Type** field. Then check whether interlinkages exist in which the leading and following objects are identical and whether these interlinkages are displayed multiple times. If that is the case, double-click on these entries to enter the detail view. If the destination and relation fields are interchanged in the two interlinkages, this is referred to as a recursion.

To identify bidirectional interlinkages, you must start the data browser (Transaction SE16). Enter SMOHILTP in the **Table Name** field. Table SMOHILTP contains the definition of replication-relevant interlinkages. Press **Enter**. The system opens a selection screen. Enter the industry template used in the **INDUSTRY** field, and then enter "X" in input field **SMOACTV**. If you don't exactly know which industry template is used, you can either find it in table field **SMOHPARIND-INDUSTRY**, as shown in Figure 9.12, or, as of SAP CRM 5.0, use Transaction SMOHPARIND to load it directly.

After that, sort the results list according to the timestamp (**ACCDATE** and **ACCTIME** columns), as shown in Figure 9.13. If identical timestamps occur, the **Bidirectional** flag was set during the creation of an interlinkage. This may cause problems especially in cases where the source and destination objects are identical and the relation field can be used in both directions.

Example
BGS wants to also send those business partners to the mobile clients that are related to the assigned business partners through the ZIP code. For this purpose, the company had defined a CA/CAP interlinkage containing a relation field for the relation value (SMOKVBEZ6-RELTYP) in order to be able to receive all other related business partners as well. In addition, the **Bidirectional** flag was set. Ultimately, this resulted in sending almost all of the business partners to the mobile clients, because every time new business partners were added, the system searched for business partners related to the new ones and replicated them, which, in turn, caused the replication of all business partners related to the related business partners, and so on.

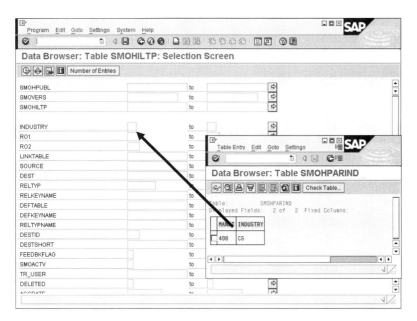

Figure 9.12 Input Screen for Selecting SMOHILTP

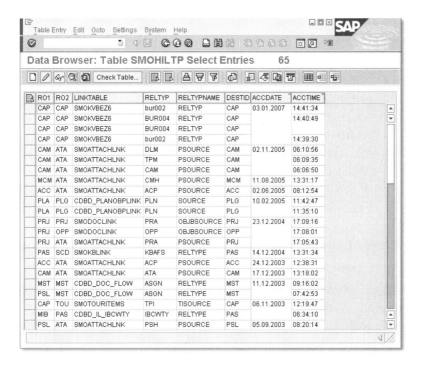

Figure 9.13 Results List Sorted by ACCDATE and ACCTIME

Large lookup tables for intelligently replicated objects As described in Chapter 3, *Outbound Processing*, a lookup table contains the connection between a business object (OBJ_ID field) and a mobile client (SITE_ID field). Therefore, you can calculate the total number of entries in a given lookup table by multiplying the estimated average number of application objects on a client by the total number of mobile clients. If the resulting number is too high (i.e., if it reaches a range of 100 million entries), you should consider using bulk replication. As is the case with each change from intelligent replication to bulk replication, you should consider the pros and cons, because a poor performance with regard to accessing lookup tables may actually reduce or compensate for an extremely large number of update processes on the mobile clients in the case of a bulk replication. We can't make any general recommendations here, but when it comes to large lookup tables, you should try to answer the following questions:

▸ Do all sites need the subscription in the way it is currently implemented? If not, do you think you can remove the subscription from some of the sites?

▸ Are you using the most appropriate filter criteria in the subscriptions? Instead of implementing bulk replication, would it be possible to use more selective filter criteria?

▸ What do you think the table size will be after the complete rollout or a couple of years down the road? If you expect the table size to increase considerably, you may think about using bulk replication immediately. In that case, you should, of course, also take into account the increase in the number of data replication processes. If the object becomes extremely large, even the tiny difference of a few percentages between bulk replication and intelligent replication can make a big difference (an increase of 4% of data in relation to an absolute quantity of 20 million objects is certainly different from an increase of 4% with regard to 10,000 objects).

Data collector The CRM Middleware synchronization services write all changes as individual messages directly into the outbound queues of the affected receivers. This produces a high load on the system, especially if many changes must be processed within a short period of time. A typical example of this is the update of business partners or products in the backend. This type of mass update generates high data quantities in the queues, because in individual messages the number of qRFC entries corresponds to the number of data changes multiplied by the average number of receivers. Particularly in installations containing a large number of mobile clients, this scenario may often cause the queues to be flooded with entries, which leads to system bottlenecks during the processing of qRFC (queued RFC) entries on the CRM Server.

To improve this situation, SAP provides the *data collector* and the extraction service as of SAP CRM 5.0. This service collects all data that belongs to a specific object in a temporary storage in order to avoid the direct writing of the data into the outbound queues. The data transfer to the outbound queues is carried out regularly at certain defined intervals and the data is consolidated into bulk messages (i.e., in BDocs that contain multiple change messages). Chapter 10, *Outbound Queues*, has more detailed information on using bulk messages to optimize the Middleware. These measures help to achieve a significant reduction of the data volume in the outbound queues. This is particularly important for object types that are changed frequently.

A possible disadvantage of this method is that the modified data records are no longer immediately available in the outbound queue, since you will have to wait for at least the next extraction job. If you schedule the extraction at an inconvenient time with regard to the usual ConnTrans execution times, a field sales representative might not receive any updated data through ConnTrans. To avoid this potential problem, you should choose a frequency for extraction, which ensures that a sufficient quantity of data is collected in order to achieve a reasonable degree of consolidation and a significant reduction of the system workload, but at the same time provides all employees with all the current data they need.

To keep the effects caused by these processes as small as possible, you should try to synchronize the scheduling of extraction jobs with the typical ConnTrans behavior of the field sales representatives. It usually makes sense to schedule the extraction job in such a way that it is carried out before the users retrieve their data. In addition, you should note that using the data collector and extraction service is optional. You can activate the service for only some of the mobile clients and you can configure it specifically for individual object types by setting up the corresponding publications and subscriptions. For all other mobile clients and object types for which the new service has not been activated, the data distribution process occurs as usual on the basis of the standard mechanisms.

Setting up a data collector

Figure 9.14 illustrates that a data collector represents a specific site type. As with any other site, you can maintain it in the administration console.

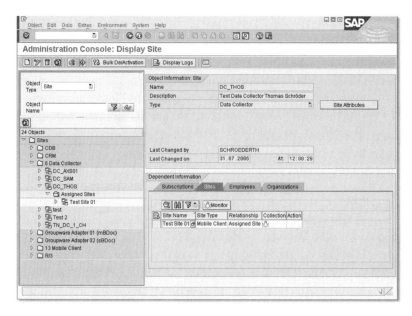

Figure 9.14 Data Collector in SAP CRM 5.0

The specific characteristic of the data collector is that it enables you to map other physical sites of the mobile client type as well, in addition to the subscriptions you're already familiar with from the other site types. In that case, the lookup tables for business objects that have been mapped through subscriptions will contain the site ID of the data collector instead of the usual site IDs of mobile clients. The resolution between the site ID of the data collector and the outbound queue of the physical sites occurs during the course of the extraction job (see Figure 9.15).

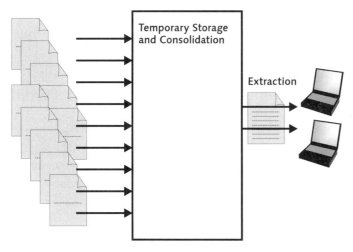

Figure 9.15 Functionality of the Data Collector

To configure a data collector, you must start Transaction SMOEAC and select object type "Site" via the F4 help. Then click the **Create** button. In the **Object Information: Site** section, you must enter a name and description that characterize the data collector. Select **Data Collector** as the type. Then click the **Site Attributes** button to open a detail view in which you can define the periodicity of the extraction job (see Figure 9.16). After that, you can assign the respective mobile clients and subscriptions to the data collector.

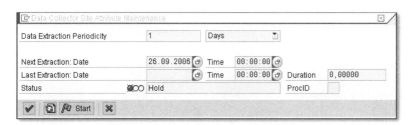

Figure 9.16 Maintaining the Attributes of the Data Collector

Transaction SMOJDC enables you to obtain an overview of data collectors and statistics, as well as details on the duration of individual extractors for data collectors. The initial screen of this transaction provides an overview of the individual collectors including an indication of the times at which the last extraction run occurred and when the next one will start. To view more details on individual actions, click the **LOG** button in Transaction SMOJDC.

Overview of data collectors

9.3   Parallelizing the Queues

To achieve optimal performance for the processing of R&R queues, you should parallelize these queues.

To configure the parallelization of R&R queues, you must start the table maintenance (Transaction SM30). Enter the table name SMOF-PARSFA in the **Table/View** field and click the **Maintain** button. The system provides a list of all entries contained in Table SMOFPARSFA. To filter out the entries that are specific to the R&R service, you must choose **Selection • By Contents** from the menu. In the popup window that displays, select the **Parameter Name** and **Key** fields and press **Enter**. This opens an input screen for both fields with the logical link, AND. In this screen, you must enter the value "RRS_COMMON" for the key (**Key** field), and the value "RRQUEUE_PARALLEL" for the parameter (**Parameter Name** field). Then click the **Execute** button to obtain a selection of relevant rows in the displayed table (see Figure 9.17). Alternatively, you can also maintain the data using mainte-nance Transaction R3AC6.

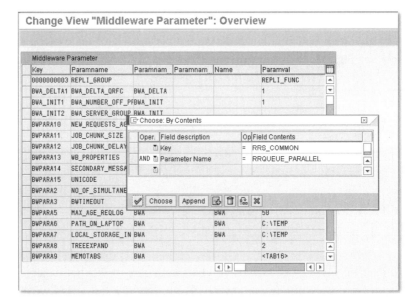

Figure 9.17 Selection of Relevant Entries for Queue Parallelization

If the system doesn't display a new results list, you should click the **New Entries** button to create new entries for the queues you want to parallelize.

In addition to the fields that indicate the parallelization of the R&R service, the **ParamName2** field specifies the various queues described earlier:

▶ AC: AC extract queue

▶ EB: Extract bulk queue

▶ EX: Extract queue

▶ RE: Realignment queue

The parallel processing of queues can be achieved by entering the number of queues to be processed concurrently in the **paramval (Parameter Value)** field.

Once you have changed the parameter, you must stop the queue (status *HOLD*). To do that, click the **Stop Queue** button in Transaction SMOHQUEUE (see Figure 9.18). To restart the queue afterwards, click the **Release Queue** button in the same transaction.

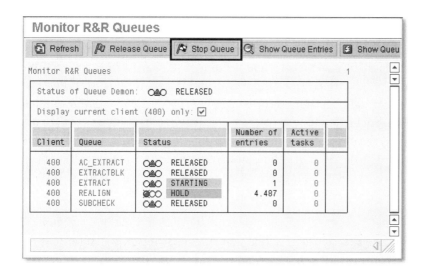

Figure 9.18 Stopping an R&R Queue (Status HOLD)

In addition to using parallelization, you can specify an RFC server group in the **Parameter Value2** field. If an RFC server group has been defined in Transaction RZ12 and assigned via the table field in Table

RFC server group

SMOFPARSFA, the queues will be processed exclusively on these specific application servers. This way, you can reduce the potential impact of parallel operations (for instance in a call center or a web store) caused by the processing of R&R queues to a minimum. If you don't specify any RFC server group, the required work processes are distributed across all application servers.

Degree of parallelization

You should select a number of parallel work processes for processing a queue, which doesn't cause a hardware bottleneck (such as a high CPU load) at peak times on the application servers involved. Moreover, the current project phase should always be taken into consideration. If, for example, it is necessary to load data quickly via an AC extract, because data had been lost or inconsistencies occurred, it is useful to increase the degree of parallelization at this stage of the project compared to normal operations. During an initial rollout, it makes sense to increase the degree of parallelization and, if necessary, to use additional application servers, because usually only a few users work in the system during the rollout phase and no system load is generated by any other administration tasks. Other CRM scenarios that have already gone live should be considered during the distribution of work processes.

In general, you should take into account the required number of dialog work processes for users and other RFC processes. Even though it is possible that the maximum number of work processes available for parallel processing is actually utilized, experience has shown that in normal operations approximately 50 % of the maximum number of available processes are used. For this reason, it makes sense to use a degree of parallelization that is higher than 10 during an initial rollout. The degree of parallelization used for the normal operation of an average system should be below 10, as specified in SAP Note 453882.

Usually, the extract queue is processed faster than the realignment queue. Because the realignment queue is not only responsible for providing data to the extract queue, but also has to generate entries for dependent data in the realignment queue itself, the degree of parallelization used in the realignment queue should be approximately twice as high as that used for the extract queue.

[»] Chapter 14, *A Look Ahead*, describes new ways to optimize the R&R service.

If the degree of parallelization you use is too high, you may encounter a decrease of performance in the database. For this reason, you should carefully monitor the performance of the database if you decide on using a higher degree of parallelization. If you see that bottlenecks occur, you can reduce the number of parallel work processes for queue processing at any time. To do that, stop the queues for which you want to reduce the degree of parallelization in the R&R queue monitor (Transaction SMOHQUEUE), change the parameters in SMOFPARSFA to a lower value, and then release the queues again. After that, the queues will be further processed with the new number of work processes.

Notes on Release Dependencies	[«]

▶ SAP CRM releases up to and including SAP CRM 3.0 have minimum system requirements, such as support package levels and a kernel patch. SAP Note 453882 contains detailed information about these system requirements.

▶ The realignment queue can be parallelized only as of SAP CRM Release 4.0.

9.4 Optimizing the Access Path

As described in detail in Chapter 3, *Outbound Processing*, the following tables are used in the R&R service:

R&R tables

▶ SMOHMSGQ contains all data records of the R&R queues.

▶ SMOHSITEQ is an optional table that contains details about sites for requests.

▶ SMOHMSGST contains the status of individual queues, that is, information as to whether queues have been stopped or are active.

▶ SMOHJOBQ (as of SAP CRM 4.0) contains the job IDs and is used for system monitoring.

The most critical of these tables is Table SMOHMSGQ, as it can become very large and therefore produce very expensive accesses at runtime. To check whether the right access path is used, you must start the database performance monitor (Transaction ST04). Then click the **Detail Analysis Menu** button to go to the detail view. Click the **SQL Request** button in the **Resource consumption by** section to start analyzing the shared cursor cache. In the window that pops up next, you should sort the results list by BUFFER GETS. In order to list only the accesses to Table SMOHMSGQ, which is the one we're interested in, you must press the F8 key or click the **Find Access to Specific Table in SQL Statements** button. Then enter the table name, SMOHMSGQ, in the popup window that appears (see Figure 9.19).

NOTE: The GUI of Transaction ST04 was changed with the newest basis release. You now have to drill down in the left-hand pane to **Performance · SQL Statement Analysis · Shared Cursor Cache** to reach the described functionality.

Select the SQL statement you want to examine closer. Because the SQL statements are sorted by BUFFER GETS, the entries listed at the top of the list are usually the expensive statements.

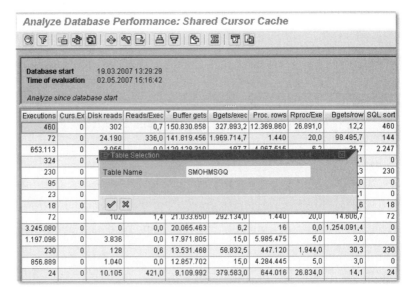

Figure 9.19 Limiting the Results List to Table SMOHMSGQ

[»]   After analyzing the currently expensive statements, you should also take a look at the entries listed further down in the list of SQL statements as they may create a performance issue after future growth of the database tables even if the execution time is currently satisfactory.

Access path   Click the **EXPLAIN** button to view the access path that is being used. We cannot go into greater detail about analyzing an access path, as that would be outside the scope of this book. If you need support or more details regarding access paths, please refer to the respective literature.[2]

Experience has shown that the access path to Table SMOHMSGQ can become rather inconvenient, because the number of table entries changes very often (fragmentation caused by fast and strong table growth and shrinkage). What makes the situation even worse is that the table statistics are often created at a point in time when the table either didn't contain any data or only had a few entries. For this reason, the statistics are not representative, and at peak times (i.e., when an optimal performance of the system would be essential), they provide incorrect access optimizations that are inappropriate for the current situation through the *Cost Base Optimizer* (CBO).

Depending on the cause and the specific situation, there are different options for optimization if your analysis has shown inappropriate accesses for Table SMOHMSGQ.

SAP Note 820231 contains a HINT statement for ORACLE databases for a SQL statement, which is often responsible for expensive executions within the CRM system. If your analysis has shown that only this statement causes problems, you should implement this SAP Note to reduce the database load and to achieve better execution times.

If the analysis shows several points with expensive access to Table SMOHMSGQ due to an inappropriate index selection, you should update the statistics to improve the system performance. To obtain improved statistics, you should stop the queues when a considerable number of queue entries exist. In this context, "considerable" means that the number of entries is identical to the number that occurs during normal operation. By stopping the queues, you can ensure that the statistics to be created are based on a representative distribution of data. If you don't stop the queues, the data distribution could change before the statistics are created so that empty queues might exist, for example. Then, you should generate sound statistics for the tables of the queues that have been stopped.

Updating statistics

Then you should check the results of the optimizer in the database performance monitor in the manner described above. If the access

---

2 Schneider, Thomas: *SAP Performance Optimization. Analyzing and Tuning SAP systems*. 4th Edition. SAP PRESS 2005.

paths you use from now on are better than the previous ones, you should freeze the statistics you just generated. To do that, use Transaction DB21 and open Table DBSTATC. In this table, you must assign the value "I" to the **ACTIVE** field for the entries that correspond to the queue tables. This way you can make sure that during the regular updates of database statistics no statistics will be created when the tables are small or empty.

To be on the safe side, you should export the statistics in order to have optimal statistics available if you overwrite them inadvertently. Please refer to SAP Note 448380 for an exact description of how you can do that.

Index fragmentation
In addition to inappropriate statistics, the fragmentation of indexes during the Replication & Realignment process is another frequent cause of a decreasing data throughput rate. To calculate the index quality, you can use two methods:

1. Calculate the ratio between utilized space and available space (storage quality). You can calculate the utilized space by multiplying the number of index entries by the average length of a data record and then adding 6 bytes for the row ID as well as 1 byte for the selection of a record and for each column of a record per index entry. Moreover, you must add an overhead value for root and branch blocks. Unfortunately, this value cannot be generally quantified. To calculate the available space, you must multiply the utilized index blocks by the block size and then subtract a certain amount of administrative overhead. The storage quality can be calculated, for example, in Transaction DB02.

2. Alternatively, you can calculate the ratio between the number of deleted leaf rows and the total number of leaf rows.

Both methods provide a rough estimate and an indication for an index fragmentation; you should use them with caution when making final decisions.[3] However, in general, optimization measures should be taken if the ratio between utilized and available space is smaller than or equal to 0.5. If the ratio ranges between 0.5 and 0.8, you should consider taking optimization measures in individual situ-

---

3 If you're interested in finding out more about determining the index fragmentation, you can find comprehensive information in SAP Note 771929. This SAP Note also contains additional details on how you can create new indexes.

ations, if performance problems occur. In that case, you can use Report RSANAORA in Transaction SE38 to specifically rebuild the index or use the **Coalesce** command in Transaction DB02. To do that, start Transaction DB02 and click the **Detailed analysis** button. Then, enter the value "SMOHMSGQ*" in the popup window that appears to obtain details on the indexes and tables in question. Place the cursor on one of the index rows (rows containing SMOHMSG~Q or SMOHMSG~OPT in the **Object** column) and click the **Detailed analysis** button to display the details about the index in question. You can then start the process by selecting **Alter Index · Coalesce** from the menu (see Figure 9.20).

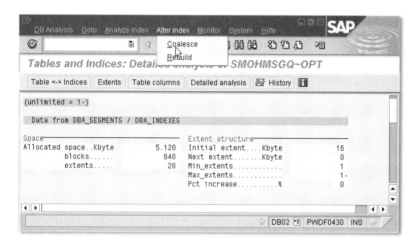

Figure 9.20 Starting Coalesce for Index SMOHMSGQ~OPT

Example

The system administrator at BGS created statistics for all tables prior to the rollout. Because no mobile client was active at that point in time, the tables used in the R&R service are very small (empty). Consequently, the *Cost Base Optimizer* (CBO) recommends carrying out a full table scan. After rolling out the mobile clients for all 500 employees, load is generated on the system, and the employees are busy receiving and sending data. However, the number of complaints about an ever slower system is increasing. After running an analysis, the system administrator discovers that the now inappropriate access path (full table scan) to the very large qRFC and R&R table causes this situation. This can be significantly improved by generating new statistics for these tables as they enable the access via an appropriate index.

9.5   Special Optimization Options in R&R

Internal
optimization of the
R&R service

CRM Middleware also provides various options for optimizing the initial load of data to mobile clients. In addition to the options for parallelization and access optimization described in the previous sections, you can also utilize the internal processes that occur between R&R queues. By utilizing these relationships, you may be able to reduce the number of data records to be transferred through the R&R queues, especially if some mobile clients are assigned identical data. The reason for this is that the realignment service recognizes and aggregates identical object entries in the queues. This way, the quantity of data to be processed can be reduced and the processing of individual data records is faster because multiple updates of lookup tables can be combined instead of updating lookup tables individually.

Combining
messages

Moreover, you can combine multiple messages in a BDoc instead of using single messages.

To take advantage of this internal optimization measure, you must generate the sites in a deactivated state. Then, prior to mapping the subscriptions, you must set the SUBCHECK queue in to the *HOLD* status in Transaction SMOHQUEUE to ensure that no data is made available to the realignment service. Next, you must assign the subscriptions to the new sites in the administration console (Transaction SMOEAC). In this context, it is important that you map individual subscriptions to multiple mobile clients. This way you can make sure that entries which contain the same subscription are combined in the SUBCHECK queue. Then you must stop the realignment queue via Transaction SMOHQUEUE and release the SUBCHECK queue. Now you can take advantage of the internal optimization process for identical business objects within the realignment queue. The REALIGN queue that was generated contains only one entry for business objects that are concurrently used by mobile clients due to overlapping filter criteria that are used in the subscriptions. When the REALIGN queue is processed, the lookup tables are simultaneously updated. Because the new sites haven't been updated yet, no extracts are created immediately. The major advantage of that is that single instance messages are no longer transmitted from the REALIGN queue to the EXTRACT queue, which would otherwise cause many small BDoc messages to be created. Once the entries in the realignment queue have been processed, you can activate the sites.

Example

At BGS, every 20 field sales representatives are assigned a manager who also receives the data of the employees assigned to him on his laptop computer. On average, each field sales representative is assigned 100 customers. Therefore, each manager is assigned a total of 2,000 customers. From an organizational point of view, the rollout can be carried out in such a way that the overlapping subscriptions are assigned to both the managers' laptop computers and the sales people's laptop computers at the same time. Alternatively, the computers of the managers can be provided with the data at a different time. In the latter case, the assignments between customers and mobile clients would have to be newly determined in the R&R service, whereas in the former case, the calculation can be carried out along with the data assigned to the salespeople's computers. Since this reduces the number of mapping calculations in the R&R service by a total of 50,000 for customers only, the project team decides not to set up the managers' laptop computers separately, but along with the computers of the respective sales representatives.

9.6   Mass Changes

If a mass change needs to be carried out, the respective sites must be deactivated *prior to* the mass change. After the mass change, you must reactivate the sites, and an AC extract starts automatically for all objects that were changed. The AC extract then writes bulk BDocs to the outbound queues. Unfortunately, however, there's a problem with this process. If during the mass change an object is changed that is not involved in the mass change process, the Middleware memorizes this as well and starts an AC extract for that replication object, too.

Optimizing mass changes

Example

BGS deactivates the 500 mobile clients of the field sales representatives. After that, conditions are downloaded from the R/3 system to the CRM system. During this download, an employee changes a product in the R/3 system and a call center employee creates a new customer. Both objects are replicated to the mobile clients. Products and CUST_HIERARCHY are replicated in a bulk process while the business partner is replicated using intelligent replication (to five mobile clients in this case). After the successful completion of the download, the 500 sites are reactivated. As intended, the 500 employees receive all conditions as bulk messages. At the same time, however, the Middleware also starts the AC extracts for products and CUST_HIERARCHY for all 500 mobile clients (and five mobile clients receive additional AC extracts for all business partners). Consequently, the mobile clients receive a multiple of the data quantity they should have originally received, and, depending on the number of customers, products, and the packet size for these objects, they receive even more data than they would have received if the sites had not been deactivated. In a worst-case scenario, the data quantity is identical to that which was involved in an initial load of the objects.

This example demonstrates that you cannot solve the problem by merely deactivating the sites, especially because in a live CRM system a change of objects or the creation of new objects usually involves more than two objects and the effects will consequently be even worse. Therefore, it must be guaranteed that only objects that are part of the mass change are included in the realignment process, and that all other objects are stopped upfront.

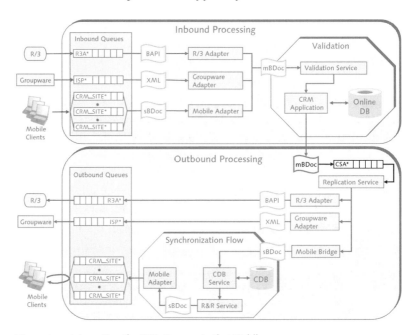

Figure 9.21 Integrating the CSA Queues in the Middleware

Stopping objects   Figure 9.21 illustrates that the CSA queues represent the first stage at which the objects can be stopped before the Replication & Realignment services begin. The easiest way to stop objects at this point in the Middleware is to deregister all CSA queues with the exception of those in which the objects of the mass change are processed. As described in Chapter 2, *Inbound Processing and Validation*, Transaction SMQR enables you to deregister the queues easily.

In summary, the following procedure should be carried out in order to perform mass changes efficiently by deactivating sites:

Procedure for mass changes

1. Deregister all CSA queues; if there are queues that have already been deregistered, note the names of these queues (Transaction SMQR).

2. Wait until the R&R queues are empty (Transaction SMOHQUEUE).

3. Then deactivate the sites that are affected by the mass change (Transaction SMOEAC or Report SMOE_BULK_SITE_ACTIVA-TION).

4. After that, you can register the CSA queues for objects involved in the mass change again.

5. Start the mass change and wait until all BDocs have been updated. During this phase, you must monitor the system (see also Chapter 13, *Performing Optimized Mass Changes*).

6. Then stop the AC_EXTRACT queue in the Replication & Realignment service (Transaction SMOHQUEUE).

7. Because the AC_EXTRACT queue was stopped, you can reactivate the sites you previously deactivated (Transaction SMOEAC or Report SMOE_BULK_SITE_ACTIVATION).

8. Once you have successfully reactivated the sites, you must restart the AC_EXTRACT queue in the Replication & Realignment service (Transaction SMOHQUEUE).

9. Then register all CSA queues with the exception of those queues that had already been deactivated prior to the mass change, and which you noted in Step 1.

Unfortunately, the deregistration of the CSA queues does not only prevent the transfer of BDocs into the R&R service, but also the transfer of this data to any other system, such as SAP R/3. There is no way to avoid this in CRM Middleware. The repercussions of this problem depend on the duration of the mass change and on the business processes that were implemented in the CRM system, which are illustrated by the following two examples.

No transfer to other systems

Examples

▶ Company A uses the Business Partners and Activity Management business processes in a call center and on mobile clients. A reorganization of regions in which the assignments of customers to field sales representatives is newly arranged takes three days.

Despite the mass change of data, the call center employees can carry out their work as usual. Only if they need to arrange short-term meetings for the sales representatives do they have to notify their colleagues by phone, because changes to activities and newly created activities are not transferred to the mobile clients until the mass change has finished. The field sales representatives can use their mobile clients as usual, but they don't receive the data of the past three days.

▶ Like company A, company B also uses the Business Partners and Activity Management business processes in a call center and on mobile clients. But in addition to that, company B operates a web store where customers can order products. A reorganization of regions in which the assignments of customers to field sales representatives is newly arranged takes three days. As with company A, the field sales representatives and the call center employees are not significantly affected by the mass change. However, the situation is different for the customers of company B. Although purchase orders can be accurately created in the CRM system, they are not transferred to the R/3 system; therefore, they aren't processed. Express orders, which are usually delivered within 24 hours, are delayed by several days.

For company A, the impact of the mass change is relatively small, and the deactivation of sites proves to be useful for that company. For company B, the process of deactivating sites, during the deregistration of CSA queues, is not optimal for performing mass changes.

When mobile clients are used, outbound queues represent a neuralgic point in CRM Middleware. Performance problems occur if the queues contain too many entries. This chapter describes a number of measures you can take to get the problem under control.

10   Outbound Queues

After data is updated successfully by the application, it is transferred to outbound processing as a *messaging BDoc* (mBDoc). The replication service determines the recipients, and the corresponding adapter is called for each recipient. If the recipient is an SAP R/3 system, the R/3 outbound adapter converts the mBDoc to a BAPIMTCS data container and transfers the data to SAP R/3 by a *queued RFC* (qRFC). If the recipient is the *Consolidated Data Base* (CDB), the mBDoc is transferred to a mobile bridge. One or more *synchronization BDocs* (sBDocs) are generated from the mBDoc and the synchronization flow is started. At the end of the synchronization flow, the mobile adapter writes the sBDocs as qRFC records into the outbound queues of the mobile clients. The data waits there until the mobile clients establish a connection to the CRM Server using ConnTrans and retrieve the data. After the data is transferred successfully to all recipients, the entries are deleted from the outbound queues. To give you a better overview, Figure 10.1 illustrates the Middleware with the outbound queues once again. Chapter 3, *Outbound Processing*, provides a detailed description of outbound processing.

Outbound processing

Outbound queues are based on the *outbound qRFC with recipient list*. Section 2.3.1 has a detailed description of the qRFC.

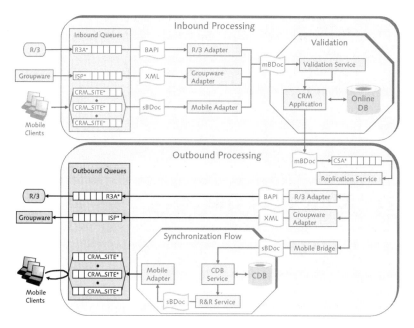

Figure 10.1 Outbound Queues

Benefits

There are plenty of good reasons why SAP has implemented outbound queues with recipient lists using the outbound qRFC:[1]

▶ Loss of data is prevented.
  If an error occurs during data transfer, a rollback is performed and the data record and all subsequent data records remain with the sender, that is, in the CRM outbound queue.

▶ The same data record cannot be transferred twice.

▶ Sets of data cannot supersede each other.

▶ Data is not saved several times; it is only saved once and a recipient list is created.
  If the same data is transferred to several recipients, one data record is written into the TRFCQOUT, ARFCSSTATE, and QREFTID tables for each recipient. However, these entries don't contain the data itself. They simply contain a reference to the

---

1 The qRFC with recipient list is based on the tRFC and "inherits" its characteristics. The benefits mentioned here don't differentiate between whether these are tRFC characteristics that were "inherited" or original characteristics of the qRFC with recipient list.

same data record in the ARFCSDATA table where the data is located. The following example illustrates the benefit offered by the recipient list.

Example

All of BGS's 500 field sales representatives have data about all the company's products on their laptops. Illustrations and technical information about the products have also been transferred to the laptops. This additional information occupies an average of 1MB disk space for each product in the outbound queue.

If BGS creates 10 new products, 10MB disk space will be occupied when the data is in the outbound queues. In terms of disk space, it doesn't really matter if the data is sent to one recipient or to 500 recipients. The only difference is the number of data records in the TRFCQOUT, ARFC-SSTATE, and QREFTID tables, and these don't require much disk space. If there were no recipient lists, the product information would have to be saved separately for each field sales representative. In this case, the ARFCSDATA table would receive 5,000 data records, rather than 10 data records with a volume of 1MB each. Changing 10 products would then result in 5GB of disk space being occupied.

If a field sales representative retrieves his data, the entries in the TRFC-QOUT, ARFCSSTATE, and QREFTID tables will be deleted. The data record in the ARFCSDATA table is only deleted when the last field sales representative has retrieved his data.

The processing speed of the outbound queues reduces significantly the more the number of entries in the outbound qRFC tables increases. Depending on the hardware, database, and configuration you use, there are different thresholds as to when the data retrieval from the outbound queues becomes noticeably slower. We cannot make generalizations in this context. There are CRM systems where a significant deterioration in performance is only noticeable once there are 20 million entries in the outbound queues. Smaller and poorly configured systems with three to four million entries in the outbound queues already experience performance problems when retrieving or writing new entries into the outbound queues. For a mobile client user, the performance will deteriorate to such an extent that a user will have to wait significantly longer until ConnTrans has retrieved his data. In particular, the user will not be able to just quickly synchronize his data in the morning for example.

Processing speed

Rather than being generated during normal operation, millions of entries are usually generated only in the outbound queues when you perform mass changes. The only exceptions in this case are CRM systems with many thousands of mobile clients (that are nevertheless designed and configured for a correspondingly high number of entries in the outbound queues).[2]

Example

Where you have 5,000 mobile clients, for example, a change to 1,000 conditions that are replicated in a bulk process is already sufficient to generate millions of additional entries in the outbound queues. After the change is made, 5,000 outbound queues exist with 1,000 additional entries each. Since the same data records are replicated on all mobile clients, the ARFCSDATA table only receives 1,000 additional data records. However, the TRFCQOUT, ARFCSSTATE, and QREFTID tables each receive five million additional entries.

Many parallel ConnTrans sessions

If there are initially several million entries in the outbound queues, different effects occur that aggravate each other and impair the duration of the ConnTrans. The following basic principle applies: If there is a very high number of entries in the queues, ConnTrans already takes longer because each site must retrieve a particularly large amount of data. This increases the number of parallel ConnTrans sessions. Figure 10.2 illustrates this effect.

In both graphics, 12 users execute ConnTrans. Four users start ConnTrans at 5 pm. Another three users start ConnTrans five minutes later. Two users start ConnTrans another five minutes later, and three users start it at 5:15 pm. The first graphic shows that ConnTrans takes 10 minutes and a maximum of seven parallel ConnTrans sessions are created (between 5:05 and 5:10 pm).

The second graphic illustrates that the duration of ConnTrans increases to 30 minutes due to the high volume of data (much longer ConnTrans times are not unusual if mass changes are involved). As of 5:15 pm, there are 12 parallel ConnTrans sessions.

---

2 The SAP customer with the highest number of mobile clients operates a CRM 4.0 system with more than 8,000 mobile clients.

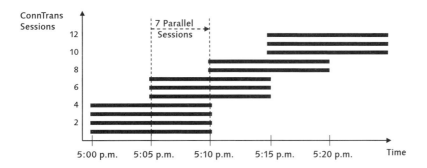

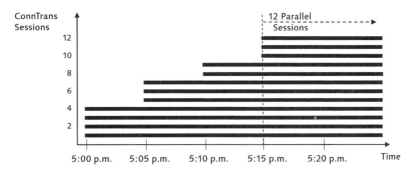

Figure 10.2 Parallel ConnTrans Sessions

Example

At BGS, ConnTrans usually takes 10 minutes and 300 of the 500 employees start ConnTrans between 5 pm and 8 pm. In the case of equal distribution, this results in 17 employees on average executing ConnTrans in parallel. After the price is adjusted, each field sales representative receives 15,000 conditions in addition to the normal data. Even without the particular effects that occur due to the many entries in the outbound queues, the duration of ConnTrans would increase to 45 minutes because of the high volume of data. This in turn increases the number of parallel ConnTrans sessions from 17 to 75.

The increased number of parallel ConnTrans sessions can cause different problems. The CRM Server may not be designed to cope with such a high number of parallel ConnTrans sessions and doesn't have a sufficient number of work processes. A resource conflict occurs with the CRM Online, Internet Sales, and Call Center users. Worst-case scenario is this can lead to a sort of standstill of the CRM system. If the ConnTrans sessions have to wait for a free work process, this

Shortage of work processes

increases the duration of the ConnTrans sessions for the mobile client user.

To retrieve the data from the CRM Server, ConnTrans executes SELECT and DELETE statements on the qRFC tables. This results in a very high database load. The four qRFC tables have millions of entries, from which many thousands of entries are processed, since all ConnTrans sessions simultaneously access the four tables. Due to their size, the qRFC tables are usually not located in the buffer of the database, therefore the data must be read from the *storage subsystem*. This can cause a performance bottleneck in the *disk subsystem* or *Storage Area Network* (SAN). The I/O times increase and that leads to longer ConnTrans times, which further increases parallelism. The performance of the disk subsystem will determine the severity of the effects of the increased database load.

There are two strategies that you can use to address performance problems with outbound queues:

▶ System optimization

▶ Minimization of the number of entries in the outbound queues

10.1 System Optimization

Under the heading *System Optimization*, we have summarized measures that are in the area of Basis/system administration and not in the application.

10.1.1 Optimizing the Disk Subsystem

As we described at the beginning of the chapter, large outbound qRFC tables and parallel ConnTrans sessions result in extreme loads on the database and disk subsystem. Therefore, you must ensure that all *database objects* (table/index area, logs, and dictionaries) are or already have been replicated across all components of the disk subsystem. In particular, the data should be separated from the logs.

Over time, we found again and again that the automatic distribution of database objects that a storage subsystem performs is often not ideal for a CRM system with the mobile sales or mobile service scenario. SAP Support's experience with mobile client installations with high system loads shows that the highest *I/O performance demands* are placed on the following tables and objects:

1. Online redo log files

2. Tables that begin with the following characters (this may also include customer-specific tables)

   ▷ ARFC*

   ▷ TRFC*

   ▷ SMOH*

   ▷ SMW3_BDOC*

3. PSAPROLL

4. PSAPTEMP

Accordingly, access to these database objects should be as efficient as possible. Besides this general recommendation to replicate the database objects, there are several other optimization measures that you can use to improve the performance; however, to discuss these measures in detail would exceed the scope of this book. SAP Support can help you if you require support in this area. As part of its *System Optimization Services*, SAP provides the *Storage Subsystem Optimization Service* for optimizing I/O performance. Information about this service is available in the *SAP Service Marketplace* under the alias *ATG* (Advanced Technology Group), or directly at *http://service.sap.com/atg*. On this web page, click **Storage • Storage Subsystem Optimization** under **Quick Links**.

10.1.2 Index Rebuild

Indexes degenerate rapidly due to the high number of newly created and deleted data records in the outbound qRFC tables (this applies to Oracle, for example, but not to all databases). This can cause a loss in performance when the tables are accessed. We therefore recommend that you regularly rebuild the indexes of the outbound qRFC tables (and inbound qRFC tables also). This includes the following tables:

▶ ARFCSSTATE

▶ ARFCSDATA

▶ TRFCQOUT

▶ TRFCQIN

<table>
<tr><td></td><td>▶ TRFCQSTATE</td></tr>
</table>

▶ TRFCQSTATE

▶ TRFCQDATA

▶ ARFCRSTATE

You should note that it can take several minutes to rebuild an index.

Storage quality

You can tell by the *storage quality* of an index whether the index has degenerated and requires a rebuild.

You will find details about this topic in Chapter 9, *Replication Model and R&R*.

10.1.3 Buffering qRFC Tables

Default pool

To be able to access data in the database, the database blocks must first be read from the disk and written into the *buffer cache* of the database. The blocks of all segments and segment types (tables, indexes, etc.) are normally written into the *default pool* in an Oracle database. If the default pool is filled and more blocks have to be read, blocks that are already buffered are pushed out of the default pool (these are usually blocks that have not been accessed for a long time).

Due to the many accesses to the qRFC tables for very big outbound queues and many parallel ConnTrans sessions, the tables or indexes may be written into the default pool and continuously force other tables (or each other) out of the cache. However, this is not necessarily the case and can only be determined by performing an exact analysis.

KEEP pool (Oracle)

To prevent this from happening, Oracle enables you to create a *KEEP pool*. The KEEP pool is a part of the Oracle buffer cache. The particular tables or indexes to be loaded into the KEEP pool have to be defined.[3] The major advantage of a KEEP pool is that (if it is sufficiently large) it achieves a permanent buffering of the main memory of tables and indexes, since a displacement by blocks of other tables or indexes does not take place. The major disadvantage is the very high requirement for additional main memory in some circumstances. You should therefore use the KEEP pool only if all other tuning measures were performed and were not successful.

---

3 An object can either be loaded into the default pool or the KEEP pool.

Other databases don't have a KEEP pool, but they do provide you with other options to prevent certain tables and indexes from being purged from the buffer. Essentially, you can also increase the normal buffer to such a size that the effect described above does not occur. In particular, you can also consider increasing the buffer temporarily, since the qRFC tables are very large only during a mass change, and not permanently.

10.1.4 RFC Server Groups

You can improve the performance of ConnTrans by optimizing the disk subsystem and, if necessary, buffering the qRFC tables. Nevertheless, there will be more parallel ConnTrans sessions after a mass change than during normal operation. Consequently, more work processes are occupied by the CommStation, and fewer, or no work processes remain for online, call center, and Internet sales users. If the CRM system was configured for this system load as part of the sizing process, no bottlenecks should occur. For cost reasons, however, the CRM system is only rarely configured for occasional mass changes; it is only configured for average loads or a load peak that occurs in normal operation.

You can set up logon groups (Transaction SMLG) to prevent the work processes of all instances from being occupied by the CommStation. However, this option is not available if the CRM system only consists of one instance.

Logon groups

10.2 Minimizing the Number of Outbound BDocs

For each business object changed, created, or deleted in the CRM system, one or more BDocs are generated in the outbound processing, and the corresponding qRFC records are written into the outbound queue. In this chapter, we assume that the replication model has already been optimized (see Chapter 9, *Replication Model and R&R*) and all business objects must be sent to the corresponding recipients because of business requirements. The number of business objects is therefore no longer reducible; however, this doesn't apply to the number of qRFC records that are written into the outbound queues. CRM Middleware provides other optimization options here.

10.2.1 Packaged Messages

As part of the normal delta supply of data for mobile clients, at least one sBDoc is created for each changed business object and written into the outbound queue. However, the Middleware also enables several objects (instances) of the same type to be written into one BDoc (see Figure 10.3). A packaged BDoc is generated. The maximum number of objects that are combined in a packaged BDoc is determined by the *block size*.

Block size The block size is BDoc type (or replication object) specific and is controlled by the MAX_PACKAGE_SIZE parameter in the SMOFPARSFA table. If there is no entry for a BDoc type in the SMOFPARSFA table, CRM Middleware uses the default value when it creates the packaged BDocs. The default value is 50 for all objects; in other words, a BDoc can contain up to 50 object instances of the same type.

Delta Supply

Packaged Messages

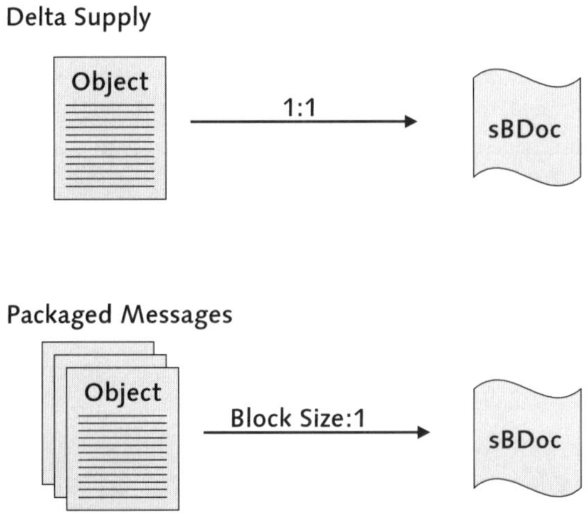

Figure 10.3 Packaged Messages

To change the block size, you must insert a new entry or change the value of the MAX_PACKAGE_SIZE parameter in the SMOFPARSFA table. After you change the parameter, you must stop and restart the AC_EXTRACT queue. To do this, start Transaction SMOHQUEUE (see Figure 10.4), select the AC_EXTRACT queue, and click the **Stop Queue** button. After the status of the AC_EXTRACT queue has changed to *HOLD*, click the **Release Queue** button.

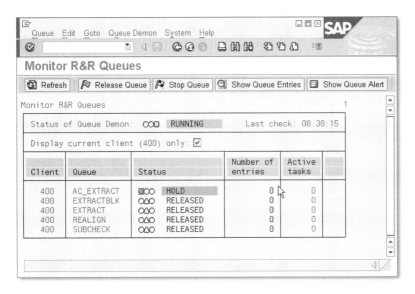

Figure 10.4 AC_EXTRACT Queue (Transaction SMOHQUEUE)

You can maintain the SMOFPARSFA table in Transaction R3AC6. The field names are listed in Table 10.1.

Maintaining block sizes

Field Name in Table SMOFPARSFA	Field Name in Maintenance Transaction R3AC6	Value
PARSFAKEY	Key	RRS_COMMON
PARNAME	Paramname	MAX_PACKAGE_SIZE
PARNAME2	Paramname2	<BDoc type>
PARVAL1	Paramval	<Block size>

Table 10.1 Entering the Block Size in Table SMOFPARSFA

Example

To set the block size for a customer to 100, you insert the following entry into the SMOFPARSFA table:

PARSFAKEY	RRS_COMMON
PARNAME	MAX_PACKAGE_SIZE
PARNAME2	CAPGEN_OBJ_WRITE
PARVAL1	100

The effects of whether objects are packed or written into sBDocs individually are enormous. The example of the annual price change at BGS below demonstrates this convincingly.

> **Example**
>
> As already described, BGS changes 15,000 conditions annually, which are replicated to 500 field sales representatives. This normally generates 7.5 million entries in the outbound queues. However, if the conditions are packed with a block size of 1,000, only 75,000 entries are written into the outbound queues. While 7.5 million entries represent a very big load for the outbound queues, 75,000 entries are negligible.

Optimum block size

This example shows the potential that lies in packing sBDocs. It also illustrates that the bigger the block size you choose, the greater the effect.

[!] *Attention! Here too, there are upper limits*. If the block size you choose is too big, problems will occur both on the CRM Server during the transfer and on the mobile client. In rare cases, timeouts or program terminations may occur on the CRM Server due to an excessively high number of database queries. The performance of the data transfer can deteriorate if the data packages are too big. Very large BDocs can result in a higher paging rate on the mobile client during the data import phase, which consequently increases the duration of ConnTrans.

The best block size depends on the hardware being used and can only be determined by performing tests. Generally speaking, however, you can choose a block size of up to 1,000 and more for the following BDoc types:

- CUST_HIERARCHY
- CRM_DNL_ATTR
- CRM_DNL_ITASSI
- CRM_DNL_STEXT
- CRM_DNL_TJ05
- CRM_DNL_TJ06
- CRM_DNL_TJ07
- DNL_CUST_CAL_C
- DNL_CUST_COUNTR

- DNL_CUST_CURREN

- DNL_CUST_LANGU

- DNL_CUST_UNITS

- DNL_CUST_S_AREA

- DNL_CUST_SYSMSG

- DNL_CUST_SYS_TB

- EXPSELHIER_WRITE

- LAYITM_WRITE

- Simple Z objects

- Conditions

There are also BDoc types for which the default value can already be too big for optimum processing. If BDoc instances with only one object are already very big (e.g., orders with a very high number of items), the BDocs packaged with block size 50 exceed the optimum size for transferring data and the import on the mobile client. In extreme cases, a single-digit block size may be the best choice. Unfortunately, however, such a small block size cannot reduce the number of entries in the outbound queues as effectively.

10.2.2 AC Extract

In CRM 4.0, unfortunately, you cannot determine that certain BDoc types are always packed before they are written into the outbound queues. This was only possible after *data collectors* were introduced in CRM 5.0. In CRM 4.0, packaged BDocs are only created if you execute an *AC extract*.

You can start the AC extract manually in the administration console for one or several replication objects and one or more sites. To do this, click the **Extras • Create Extract** menu option in the administration console (Transaction SMOEAC).

Starting an AC extract

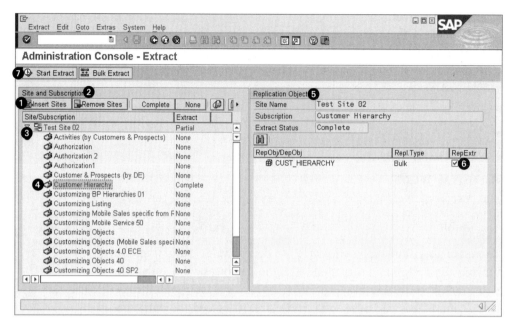

Figure 10.5 Starting the Extract (Transaction SMOEAC)

The first thing you must determine in the **Administration Console –
Extract** screen (see Figure 10.5) is which sites you want an extract to
be generated for. Click the **Insert Sites** button ❶ to do this and select
the corresponding sites. The sites you selected are displayed on the
left part of the screen under **Site/Subscription** ❷. Next, click the
arrow before a site ❸ to display the list of subscriptions. By double-
clicking the required subscription, e.g. Customer Hierarchy ❹ you
display the corresponding replication object and the dependent
objects in the right part of the screen under **Replication Object** ❺.
Select the objects, for which you want an extract to be created ❻.
Repeat this process until all replication objects and dependent
objects are selected for all sites. Now click the **Start Extract button**
❼. A dialog box subsequently opens, informing you that the extract
has started.

The extracts are written into the Replication & Realignment AC_
EXTRACT queue (Transaction SMOHQUEUE). All instances of the
selected objects that the particular site receives are determined there.
They are then combined into packaged BDocs and written into the
corresponding outbound queues as qRFC records.

If you want to extract the same replication objects for several sites, you should use the *bulk extract* function. To do this, click the **Bulk Extract button** (see Figure 10.5). In the dialog box that appears, you can select sites and replication objects using multiple selection fields. When you press the **Start Extract** button, corresponding entries are written into the Replication & Realignment AC_EXTRACT queue.

Bulk extract

An AC extract is only executed automatically by CRM Middleware when a site is activated.

Activating sites

In this case, the Middleware checks whether object instances that the site receives have changed while the site was inactive. If only the value of an object instance has changed, or if a new instance has been created or an existing one deleted, an AC extract is started for the corresponding replication object.

If several AC extracts are started, you can carry out another optimization by stopping the AC_EXTRACT queue in Replication & Realignment (Transaction SMOHQUEUE) beforehand. This accumulates the extracts in the queue and their processing is optimized when you start the queue again.

At this point, we would like to emphasize again that *all instances* are determined for an AC extract and sent to the site. In addition, current state BDocs are sent, rather than delta BDocs. In contrast to a delta BDoc, which only contains the changed fields, a current state BDoc contains all values of the object instance, in the same way that it is saved in the CDB at the time. Therefore, there are fewer BDocs but more object instances (and more data) sent to the mobile client, as illustrated in the following example for BGS.

Example

At BGS, 15,000 conditions were changed (half of all conditions) and this led to 7.5 million entries in the outbound queues. If BGS prevents the BDocs from being written into the outbound queues and instead executes an AC extract, all conditions (not just the changed ones) are extracted. These are 30,000 conditions that are replicated to the 500 employees. The conditions are packed with a block size of 1,000. Therefore, 30 packed BDocs are generated, which are sent to 500 sites. Consequently, 15,000 (30*500) entries are written into the outbound queues.

Although a mobile client receives more instances with an AC extract, the processing on the client itself is faster, because for each BDoc, the

Processing the AC extract on the client

relevant application tables are updated (normal operation) when the delta messages are processed.

Conversely, the AC extract first sends a *ZAP message* (deletion message) that deletes all entries in the corresponding application tables on the mobile client. The sent objects are then written into the database by bulk insert. This is the most efficient procedure for the SQL server on the mobile client. Data cannot be lost with this procedure, since the AC extract sends the *current state* of all object instances of this type to the mobile client. Consequently, the CRM Server and mobile client are synchronized again.

AC extract versus delta supply of data

If you want to replicate data on the mobile clients in an optimum way, you must identify the number of delta messages for which an AC extract is better than the delta supply of data. There is no generally accepted evidence about the break-even point between delta processing and AC extract processing. If you change only a few data records, as you might expect, the processing of these few delta records is faster than the processing of an entire AC extract. Only a test can prove whether the single records or the AC extract are processed faster. However, a general guideline for large packet sizes indicates that you should consider an AC extract if more than 10 % of the instances have been changed.

10.2.3 Strategies for Using the AC Extract

To prevent performance problems from occurring due to millions of entries in the outbound queues, you can use the following strategy.

Prevent the entries from being written into the outbound queues altogether and subsequently start an AC extract that writes packed (and therefore fewer) entries in the outbound queues. You must ensure that the data is posted in the CDB and the lookup tables are updated, regardless of whether any entries are written into the outbound queues.

There are different procedures that you can use to implement this strategy:

▸ Deactivating sites

▸ Manipulating the lookup table

▸ Filtering in the outbound flow

We'll introduce the different approaches in the following sections and also describe the situation in which a particular procedure is best.

Deactivating Sites

As described in detail in Chapter 9, *Replication Model and R&R*, CRM Middleware enables you to deactivate sites (in the administration console, Transaction SMOEAC or Report SMOE_BULK_SITE_ACTI-VATION for mass deactivation and activation).

If you deactivate a site, although the realignment is performed in typical fashion (i.e., the lookup tables are updated), no entries are written into the outbound queues. At the same time, the Middleware notes the lookup tables that were updated for particular replication objects, but for which no entries were created.

If you want to implement a mass change, you must deactivate all affected sites *before* the mass change. After the mass change, you must reactivate the sites and an AC extract is started automatically, which creates packaged sBDocs and writes them into the outbound queues as RFC records. Unfortunately, there is a disadvantage to using this procedure. If, during the mass change, an object is changed that has nothing to do with the mass change, the Middleware also notes this object type and starts an AC extract for this replication object as well. The following example shows the effects that this can have.

Deactivating sites before a mass change

> **Example**
>
> BGS performs the mass change of 15,000 conditions over the weekend to ensure that no processing is carried out on the system during the change. All sites are deactivated and the mass change is started. While the mass change is running, a mobile client user starts ConnTrans and transfers his data to the CRM Server. One of the things that the employee has done is to create a new business partner. This business partner is posted in CRM. The mobile bridge generates a CAPGEN_OBJECT_WRITE BDoc and a CUST_HIERARCHY BDoc. Both are processed by the R&R service, whereby it is established that the business partner must be replicated on 19 other mobile clients. The Middleware therefore notes that an AC extract for CAPGEN_OBJECT_WRITE must be performed for these 19 sites when they are activated again. However, the CUST_HIERACHY is replicated in the bulk process; therefore, the Middleware notes that all sites must get an AC extract of CUST_HIERARCHY.

Since BGS has 2.7 million customers, 2.7 million CUST_HIERARCHY BDocs are each sent to 500 mobile sites. Fortunately, BGS set the MAX_PACKAGE_SIZE parameter for CUST_HIERARCHY from the default setting of 50 to 1,000 so that "only" 1,350,000, rather than 27,000,000, entries are written into the outbound queues.

To prevent objects that are not part of the mass change from slipping into R&R and triggering an AC extract, you need to deregister the CSA queues.

Procedure To deactivate sites for implementing mass changes, proceed as follows:

1. Check the value of the MAX_PACKAGE_SIZE parameter in the SMOFPARSFA table.

2. Deregister all CSA queues; if deregistered queues already exist, note the name of the queues (Transaction SMQR).

3. Wait until the R&R queues are empty (Transaction SMOH-QUEUE).

4. Deactivate the sites affected by the mass change (Transaction SMOEAC or Report SMOE_BULK_SITE_ACTIVATION).

5. Register the CSA queues for the objects affected by the mass change again.

6. Start the mass change and wait until all BDocs have been posted. It is absolutely essential that the system is monitored during this phase (for more information, see also Chapter 13, *Performing Optimized Mass Changes*).

7. Stop the AC_EXTRACT queue in Replication & Realignment (Transaction SMOHQUEUE).

8. Activate the deactivated sites again (Transaction SMOEAC or Report SMOE_BULK_SITE_ACTIVATION).

9. Start the AC_EXTRACT queue in Replication & Realignment again (Transaction SMOHQUEUE).

10. Register all CSA queues up to those queues that were already deregistered before the mass change.

The disadvantage of this procedure is that, by deregistering the CSA queues, no data is sent to any other system, for example, to SAP R/3 or BW. Consequently, the data is not further processed immediately, that is, statistics in BW cannot be updated during the mass change, deliveries in SAP R/3 are delayed, and so on. Depending on the situation, deactivating sites is therefore only a relatively suitable method.

Manipulating the Lookup Table

At this point, we need to remind you briefly of the basic functions of Replication & Realignment in CRM Middleware (a detailed description is provided in Chapter 3 *Outbound Processing*).

Changing an *intelligently replicated* object can trigger a realignment or only a replication.

Intelligently replicated objects

The realignment process is performed if you changed a distribution-relevant field of an object. The object is written into the REALIGN queue. The recipient and the dependent objects are determined and the lookup table is updated. The object is then written into the EXTRACT queue and subsequently written into the relevant outbound queues, and the EXTRACTED field in the lookup table is set to "T" (= TRUE).

If you have not changed a distribution-relevant field, "only" the replication is performed. The lookup table is checked to see to which sites an object must be sent and whether the EXTRACTED field has the value "T". An entry is then written directly into the corresponding outbound queues. If the EXTRACTED field has the value "F" (= FALSE), an entry is written into the EXTRACT queue. Both processes are illustrated in Figure 10.6.

There is no realignment process for bulk-replicated *objects*. Only the SMOHLUBULK bulk lookup table is checked to see which sites receive the BDoc type and whether the EXTRACTED field has the value "T". A qRFC record is then written into the outbound queues. If the EXTRACTED field has the value "F", no entry is written into the outbound queue. This structure is shown in Figure 10.7.

Bulk-replicated objects

If a distribution-relevant field is changed by the mass change, you can prevent entries from being written into the outbound queue by stopping the EXTRACT queue. At this point, the CDB and the lookup tables are already updated. The object instances accumulate in the EXTRACT queue and you can delete them there.

Realignment

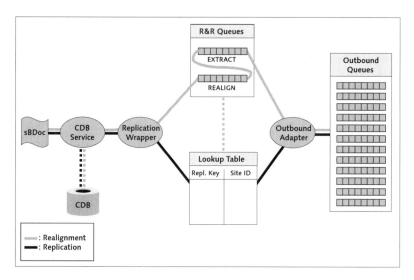

Figure 10.6 Intelligent Distribution

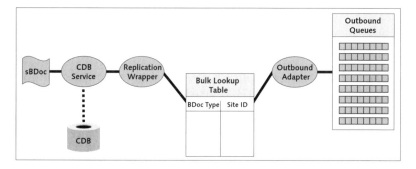

Figure 10.7 Bulk Distribution

However, the EXTRACT queue may also contain object instances that have nothing to do with the mass change. For example, data could have been updated in CRM Online during the mass change or, a mobile client could have transferred data to the CRM Server. If these object instances are processed by the realignment process, they, too, are written into the EXTRACT queue and are placed between the object instances of the mass change.

Therefore, it is important that you don't delete all entries blindly in the EXTRACT queue, but instead delete only those object instances of the type that was changed in the mass change.

To do this, go to Transaction SMOHQUEUE and click the number of entries in the EXTRACT queue. In SAP CRM 5.0, the **queue statistics** are subsequently displayed in a dialog box. Click the **View Queue** button in the dialog box. CRM 4.0 does not have this dialog box and you are taken directly to the queue overview. In the **Filter for message type** field, enter the name of the object type, for example, CAPGEN_OBJ_WRITE, and click the **Refresh** button (see Figure 10.8). Only entries with the CAPGEN_OBJ_WRITE **message type** are now displayed in the list. To display all entries, you may have to increase the number of **Maximum entries to display**. Then, select all entries in the list using the **Select All** button and subsequently delete all selected entries by clicking the **Delete Selected Entries** button. A dialog box opens, prompting you to confirm that you want to delete the entries.

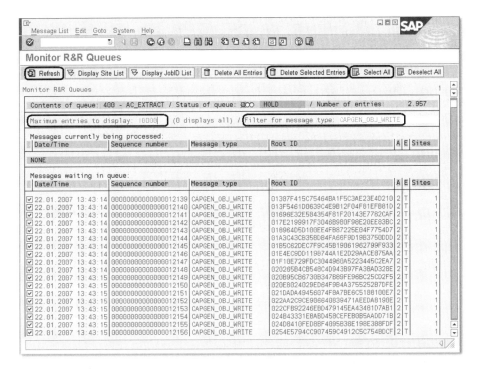

Figure 10.8 Deleting Entries from the EXTRACT Queue

You can only delete the displayed and selected entries in this way.   **[«]**

If you have 10,000 entries of the CAPGEN_OBJ_WRITE message type in the EXTRACT queue, and you have the value 1,000 in the

Maximum entries to display field, only 1,000 entries will be displayed, selected and deleted. In this case, you must repeat the process until you have deleted all entries of this message type.

Attention   As soon as you delete entries from one of the R&R queues, data inconsistencies occur between the CRM Server and the mobile clients. It is *imperative* that you eliminate these inconsistencies.

You can correct these data inconsistencies by starting AC extracts for all deleted BDoc types for all affected sites. If you aren't sure about which sites are affected, execute the AC extracts for all sites. Although this will increase the load for the CRM Server considerably, it is the safer option.

Replication   If a distribution-relevant field has not been changed by the mass change, the replication will be performed. The object is only written into the outbound queues if a corresponding entry was found in the lookup table *and* the EXTRACTED field has the value "T". This process does not have a queue that you can stop. The only remaining option is to manipulate the entries in the corresponding lookup table. If the EXTRACTED field in the lookup table has the value "F" (= FALSE), an entry is written into the EXTRACT queue of R&R. You can stop the EXTRACT queue. Conversely, this means that, if all data records in the EXTRACTED field of the lookup table have the value "F", no entries are written into the outbound queues; they are only written into the EXTRACT queue.

Therefore, you must only change the value of the EXTRACTED field in the relevant lookup table for all affected sites from "T" to "F" using a report. Unfortunately, a report to help you perform this task does not exist in the standard SAP system; therefore, you must create it yourself. When writing the report, you should note that lookup tables could contain many millions of entries. We therefore recommend that you select and change all records in blocks, rather than doing all records at once.

[»]   At this point, you should ensure that absolutely no more BDocs are generated for the dependent objects if the EXTRACTED field is set to "F" in the lookup table of the parent object.

Attention   When you manipulate lookup tables, data inconsistencies can occur between the CRM Server and the mobile clients.

You must correct the lookup tables (and data inconsistencies, if necessary) by performing AC extracts for the replication object (corresponds to the BDoc type) for all affected sites. The following applies for the dependent objects: you either prevent these objects from being run through the Replication & Realignment process (by stopping the corresponding CSA queues), or you must also perform AC extracts for these objects. If only a few dependent objects are changed during the course of the mass change, it is preferable to stop the CSA queues than to extract all objects again. However, if a very high number of dependent objects are changed, it may be better to re-replicate all objects by AC extract. Even if you only manipulate the lookup table for certain sites, stopping the CSA queues results in all sites temporarily not receiving any updates for the dependent objects.

Proceed as follows to manipulate the Replication & Realignment process for performing mass changes: _Procedure_

1. Check the value of the MAX_PACKAGE_SIZE parameter in the SMOFPARSFA table.

2. Change the value of the EXTRACTED field in the corresponding lookup table for all affected sites to "F".

3. Stop the EXTRACT queue (Transaction SMOHQUEUE).

4. Start the mass change and wait until all BDocs are posted. It is absolutely essential that the system is monitored during this phase (for more information, see also Chapter 13, _Performing Optimized Mass Changes_).

5. Delete (only) BDocs of the affected type from the EXTRACT queue (Transaction SMOHQUEUE).

6. Stop the AC_EXTRACT queue in Replication & Realignment (Transaction SMOHQUEUE).

7. Start the AC extract (bulk extract) for the replication object for all mobile sites, for which you manipulated the lookup table, and for which you deleted entries from the EXTRACT queue (Transaction SMOEAC).

8. Start the AC extract for all dependent objects for all mobile sites, for which you manipulated the lookup table.

9. Start the AC_EXTRACT queue in Replication & Realignment again (Transaction SMOHQUEUE).

If you decide to stop the CSA queues, rather than resend all dependent objects by AC extract, do not perform Step 7. Instead, deregister the CSA queues for all dependent objects even *before* you change the lookup tables (as step 0). Do not forget to register the CSA queues again after you have started the AC_EXTRACT queue (Step 9).

Filtering in the Outbound Flow

Another option to prevent data from being written into the outbound queues is to modify the outbound flow. As with all modifications, you should consider the advantages and disadvantages very carefully before you take this action. Changes to the flow are not insignificant and can quickly lead to data inconsistencies if you make a mistake and overlook an exception, for example. If you don't have any experience with these kinds of implementations, you should consult your implementation partner.

When implemented without errors, changing the standard flow also enables you to perform mass changes without RFC records being written into the outbound queues and without you having to stop other queues. The idea here is to maintain all sites that are not intended to receive any BDocs of a certain type in a Z_SITES table first. After the recipient list has been created for a BDoc, a check is carried out to determine whether one of the recipients is also entered in the Z_SITES table. If this is the case, the site(s) will be deleted from the BDoc's recipient list.

New service in the outbound flow

It would be useful to implement a separate service for this function and integrate this service into the outbound flow of the corresponding flow contexts of the relevant BDoc. It is important that the service is integrated into the correct location. The objective is to prevent entries from being written into the outbound queues of specific sites. You are not allowed to change all the other processes in the outbound flow, for example, you must post the data correctly in the CDB and perform the Replication & Realignment, in order to ensure that the lookup tables are maintained accordingly and that the dependent objects are also replicated. You should therefore integrate the new service before the SMW3_OUTBOUNDADP_CALLADAPTERS service (see Figure 10.9).

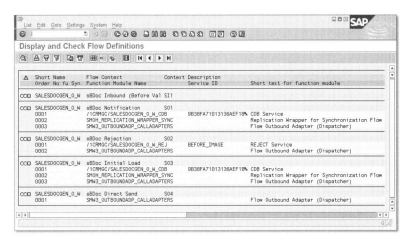

Figure 10.9 Outbound Flow (Transaction SM08FD)

To avoid having to process the source code of the new service completely for each BDoc, you should define a parameter that you can use to deactivate or activate the filter function. At the beginning of the service, you should check whether the parameter is set. If it is not set, the source code of the service should not be processed. This parameter is also beneficial, because you can maintain the sites in the Z_SITES table irrespective of the activation time. However, you should also note that the new service should not only be implemented correctly, but also efficiently, since it is processed millions of times for mass changes in particular. Delays of a few milliseconds quickly add up. Therefore, the Z_SITES table, for example, should be buffered on the application server. We also recommend that you implement a log function so that you can later identify who activated or deactivated the service for particular objects and sites and when this occurred.

You should note that inconsistencies can occur while this function is activated. [«]

The CRM Middleware assumes that certain sites have received data, although this is not the case. It is absolutely essential that you eliminate these inconsistencies by starting an AC extract for the replication object for all affected mobile sites, after you have deactivated the function again using the relevant parameter.

Although the dependent objects are no longer replicated when you manipulate the lookup tables, this is not the case when you use the "filter" service. Dependent objects continue to be written into the outbound queues of the mobile clients. If you manipulate the recipient lists for the business partners, for example, this can result in a mobile client user receiving the activities and orders for a business partner, but not the business partner itself. Because the mobile client application does not perform a validation when posting data, there are no errors and the data records are written into the IDES database on the mobile client. However, if the user accesses the activity and clicks the business partner's hyperlink to display the business partner, an error is displayed because the data record of the business partner does not exist.

Advantages and disadvantages of the procedures

The advantages and disadvantages of the different procedures are summarized once more in Table 10.2.

Procedure	Advantage	Disadvantage
Deactivating sites	No additional developments are necessary. The mass (de)activation is supported by using a report.	All CRM scenarios are temporarily affected indirectly, since all CSA queues must be stopped; in other words, no data is sent from CRM to connected systems.
Manipulating the lookup table	Only the mobile sites don't receive any data temporarily. All other CRM scenarios are available (unless you decide to deregister the CSA queues of the dependent objects).	You must develop and test the report for manipulating the lookup tables. You must start AC extracts for all dependent objects (unless you stop the corresponding CSA queues).
Filtering in the outbound flow	The other CRM scenarios are not affected. Once implemented, it is very easy to use.	The development of the service and "integrating" it into the flow context is not insignificant. You must test the service intensively.

Table 10.2 Advantages and Disadvantages of the Different Procedures

A look ahead

SAP is currently working on an enhancement to the functions of R&R to automate packaging in the standard system. For more information about these and other further developments, see Chapter 14, *A Look Ahead*.

10.2.4 Data Collector

As of CRM 5.0, you can use *data collectors* to minimize (by BDoc type) the number of BDocs that are sent to a site and send them as a packed BDoc. In addition to the increased effort required for setting up and managing the replication model, the price for this optimization are delays when sending the messages. Chapter 9, *Replication Model and R&R*, contains a more detailed description of the data collector.

The data collector reduces the load in the outbound queues and the duration of ConnTrans. You should therefore check for which objects it can be used. It is not well suited as a method for optimizing mass changes. Temporarily switching "normal" subscriptions to data collectors and back would require a high level of administration for intelligently replicated objects, since you would have to create a data collector for each subscription. But, a much worse scenario would be one where the subscriptions are removed from the sites and would then have to be assigned to the data collector. Both actions would lead to a realignment with the result that, in the first step, deletion messages for all instances of the object type would be sent to the mobile client. In the second step, the same object instances would be sent to the data collector (and from there to the assigned sites as a packed BDoc). The load created by this action would probably be higher than the load that would be created by the mass change.

This chapter describes why a data exchange between two systems in XML format may become necessary and which options are available to optimize this type of exchange.

11 XML in Optimization

When data is exchanged between different systems, the internal representation of contents can differ (e.g., Endian and non-Endian), but also the external representation of contents might not be compatible between the systems, for instance, because the two systems use different languages and code pages. If no technical incompatibility exists between the systems (i.e., if the application servers of the backend and of the CRM system are based on the same CPU architecture and use the same code page), the system landscape is referred to as a *homogeneous system landscape*. In contrast to that, system landscapes can also be *inhomogeneous* or *heterogeneous*. Heterogeneous landscapes require special measures, such as operating the systems as Unicode systems or exchanging data in a format that is compatible by definition, such as XML (*Extended Markup Language*).

11.1 Exchanging Data Between SAP R/3 and SAP CRM via XML

To avoid the Endian problem, you can exchange data in XML format between an R/3 system and a CRM system. If and how the exchange of data occurs in this format is controlled via the SEND_XML field in Table CRMRFCPAR in the R/3 system. This field may contain the following values:

► X

All data is always exchanged in XML format. In this case, the backend system generates an XML document based on the outbound data. The generated XML document is then sent to the CRM system where an XML parser converts it back into the original data format. This type of data exchange can be used for both homogeneous and inhomogeneous system landscapes, but it has the disadvantage that the conversion processes require many system resources (high CPU load) and are therefore relatively slow.

▶ **M**
Only certain critical parts of the data flow are exchanged in XML format. Due to the reduced number of conversion processes, the system performance and CPU load are affected to a smaller degree than they are in a pure XML transfer that occurs with setting "X".

▶ **<Blank>**
XML is not used. This is the fastest data transfer mode, but it has the disadvantage that you can't use it in inhomogeneous system landscapes, because of data inconsistencies that may occur in those landscapes.

If your system landscape is inhomogeneous, you should choose the "M" or "X" settings for data exchanges.

If your system is operated with the "<Blank>" value, you must take this into consideration when extending the hardware. If the properties of a server you add deviate from the properties of other servers in your landscape, the system landscape can become inhomogeneous so that the "<Blank>" parameter must be replaced before you activate the new server.

Recommendation: "M"

Because the conversion of data into XML is very time-consuming and, on the other hand, this universal data format is required for an accurate transfer of data in inhomogeneous system landscapes, SAP recommends using the "M" parameter for performance reasons.

Disadvantage

If you operate the system using the "M" parameter in the CRMRFC-PAR-SEND_XML field, a synchronous RFC is carried out during the update of data from the R/3 system to the CRM system in order to query various values and in this way to obtain the DDIC structure of relevant tables in the CRM system, which are needed for the conversion process. If the CRM system is not available, the *synchronous RFC* (sRFC) call (and hence the update task) remains pending until a timeout occurs, which may cause a bottleneck for the update work processes. In the worst case, this bottleneck may lead to a system standstill because all dialog processes are waiting for available update processes. A system operation based on this setting can therefore entail severe problems regarding the conversion of XML data, if the CRM system is temporarily unavailable, for instance, because it was shut down during a maintenance operation.

If this type of situation occurs, you should at least temporarily switch to the "<Blank>" value, if you operate a homogeneous landscape. In a heterogeneous system landscape, on the other hand, you should set the SEND_XML field to "X" in such a situation. Since this setting requires the data to be exchanged in XML format, you cannot completely switch off this format, even if the CRM Server is shut down. Queue entries that are written while the CRM Server is unavailable are processed more slowly due to the additional workload caused by the complete XML conversion. Nevertheless, this is still better than a potential system standstill that can occur if you set the "M" parameter.

After restarting the CRM Server, however, you should set the value back to "M" in order to accelerate the processing of the *queued RFC* (qRFC).

If a complete XML conversion is required, that is, if the SEND_XML field contains the value "X", you can decouple the application transaction from the conversion process to enable faster response times for the users in the R/3 system. You can do that in the following manner: in the **Parameter name** field of Table CRMPAROLTP, you must generate an entry containing the value, "CRM_XML_BACKGROUND_PROCESSING_ON", while the **Param. Value** field must contain the value "X" (see Figure 11.1). However, you should note that these settings generate a higher overall load in the R/3 system, because they involve additional asynchronous steps. Because of the requirement to carry out additional asynchronous steps, end users who want to exchange data between a CRM system and an R/3 system must have the authorization object, S_RFC.

Decoupling the application from the XML conversion

If you operate the CRM system landscape using the "M" value in the CRMRFCPAR-SEND_XML field, you should not use the CRM_XML_BACKGROUND_PROCESSING_ON parameter. The performance increase caused by the optimized conversion processes related to the "M" parameter setting is very high, so that, with regard to system performance, it is relatively useless to decouple the process of generating an XML document from the actual application. In this context, it is much more important to reduce the load that is placed on the

ERP system (i.e., by avoiding using asynchronous steps) than it is to increase the system performance.

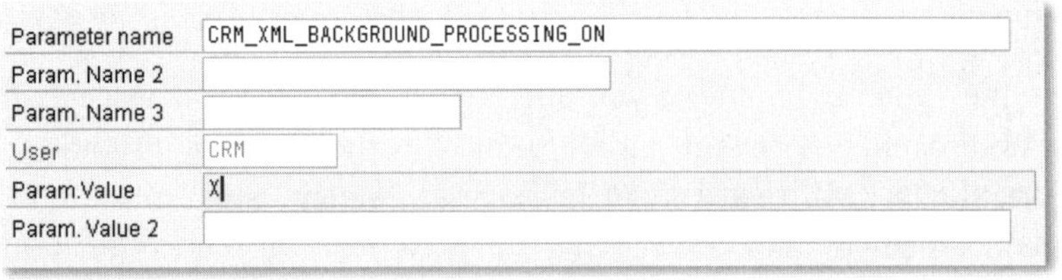

Parameter name	CRM_XML_BACKGROUND_PROCESSING_ON
Param. Name 2	
Param. Name 3	
User	CRM
Param.Value	X
Param. Value 2	

Figure 11.1 Decoupling the Application from the XML Conversion

You can activate the decoupling process depending on the user system. To carry out the activation specifically for a data exchange between an R/3 system and a connected CRM system, you must enter "CRM" as a user in Table CRMPAROLTP.

11.2 Data Exchange Between the CRM Server and a Mobile Client via XML

As of SAP CRM Release 4.0, you can operate your CRM Server using Unicode functionality to exchange data with mobile clients in XML format, irrespective of the language. This is necessary if different code pages are used in the mobile clients (i.e., if the end users speak different languages that cannot be mapped in one common code page). The disadvantage of employing this method is that, due to the insertion of XML tags, transferred strings are significantly longer than the original message. Typically, the length of strings increases by a factor that ranges between 10 and 30. On the one hand, the XML conversion places a significant additional load on the system landscape (similar to the load generated in a data exchange between the server and the backend using the "X" setting in the SEND_XML field of Table CRMRFCPAR, see Section 11.1). On the other hand, the execution time increases during the reception phase, because the quantity of data to be transferred has grown considerably.

Individual code pages for mobile clients

As of SAP CRM 4.0 SP08, you can increase the performance of the data exchange process by assigning individual code pages to the mobile clients via the administration console on the CRM Server. Because in this case, the code page that's used on the client is also known to the server, you can carry out the conversion of UTF-16-encoded double-byte data into the mobile-client-specific data format already on the server. Thus, the data arrives in the old, language-dependent format in the outbound queues and will also be transferred in this format.

This means that while different mobile clients can use different code pages, every individual client can use only one code page. Once a site has been created that is explicitly assigned a specific code page, it can only interpret data relating to the assigned code page.

By default, the new code page functionality uses code page 1100. If you want to use a different code page as the default code page, you can change it in Table SMOFPARSFA. To do that, you must call the maintenance transaction for Middleware parameters in the CRM system, R3AC6, and generate an entry with the value "RRS_COMMON" in the **Key** field and the value "DEFAULT_CODEPAGE" in the **Parameter Name** field, as well as the required code page in the **Parameter Value** field (see Figure 11.2).

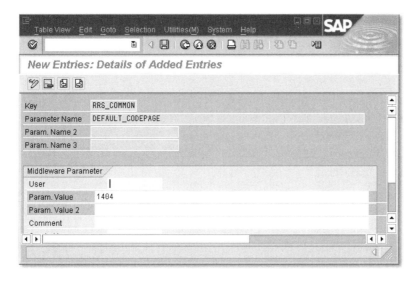

Figure 11.2 Setting a Different Default Code Page in Table SMOFPARSFA

A prerequisite of this functionality, which is provided via SAP Note [«] 873789, is that you must run an SAP CRM 4.0 server with Support Package 08 or higher. If the support package status of your CRM

Server is lower, you must implement SAP Note 903256. As of SAP CRM 4.0 SP10, this functionality is part of the standard version.

The conversion of the data flow into a single-byte representation, which is compatible with the mobile client, is carried out via a qRFC call in the outbound adapter. For this reason, you must maintain the CP_CODEPAGE site in Transaction SM59 if you use this solution to convert the data flow. The site must be specified as a non-Unicode receiver (see Figure 11.3).

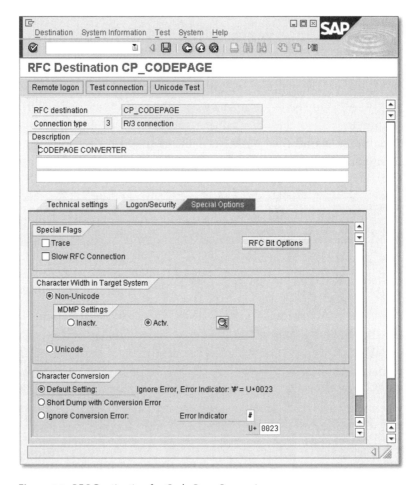

Figure 11.3 RFC Destination for Code Page Conversion

Using the data exchange for existing clients

If you want to use this data exchange functionality for existing clients, you must proceed as follows:

Run ConnTrans to ensure that all data has been retrieved from the outbound queues for the mobile client in question and also, that it has been processed on the mobile client. If the mobile client has sent data to the server, you should execute ConnTrans once again in order to retrieve confirmations that may exist. During the import of the respective SAP Note 873789 or service pack (SP), no data should be exchanged with the mobile clients, in other words, written to the corresponding outbound queues. For this reason, it is useful to deregister the CSA queues.

Call Transaction SMQ1 and check if there is still data for the respective mobile client. If the mobile client hasn't been reset to RFC data transfer, in other words, if the UNICODE_ENABLED flag is still set to 1, you should execute ConnTrans. If, on the other hand, the client has already been reset, you must delete the data from the outbound queue and execute an AC extract, because the data in the outbound queue can no longer be interpreted by the mobile client.

Deleting data in the outbound queues results in inconsistencies that must be eliminated via an AC extract. Therefore, you should by all means carry out the extract in order to avoid inconsistencies; otherwise, the server assumes that the deleted data exists on the mobile client (**Extracted** = "T" flag in the lookup tables).

[!]

To send non-XML messages to an existing mobile client and to assign a fixed code page to that mobile client, you must start the administration console SMOEAC. Then select object type **Site** and click the **Display Objects** button. Expand the mobile client section and double-click the relevant site. The system then displays a detail screen in which you must click the **Site Attributes** button in order to navigate to the attribute maintenance. There you must select the **Send non-XML Messages** radio button. Then enter the code page that can be interpreted and received by the mobile client (see Figure 11.4). Data that is contained in the outbound queue of the corresponding mobile client will be represented on the basis of this code page. If no other code page is maintained as the default value, code page 1100 will be used. Finally, you must save your changes.

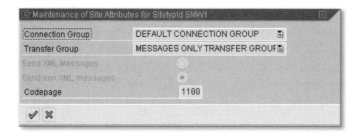

Figure 11.4 Maintaining the Site Attributes of a Mobile Client for Non-XML Messages

Once you have changed the site, start the generation workbench via Transaction GNRWB. Here, you must first select the **Generator group TRANS:BDoc Function Modules ❶**. Then select all BDocs in the **Repository object name** pane by clicking the **Select All** button ❷, and select the generator for the outbound adapters, **FLOW_ OUTBOUND_ADP**, in the **Generator** pane ❸. Finally, you must generate the outbound adapters by clicking the **Generate** button ❹ (see Figure 11.5).

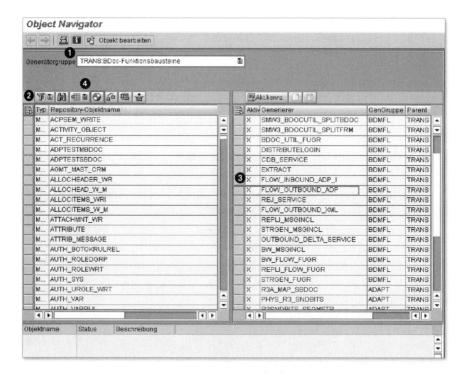

Figure 11.5 Final Steps to be Carried Out in the Generation Workbench

If you want to set up a new site, you can create the mobile client as usual and ensure that the mobile client will not receive data in XML format by activating the **Send non-XML Messages** flag. If you don't set this flag, XML messages will be sent to the mobile client, which the mobile client won't be able to interpret.

At the time of printing this book, the following restrictions existed with regard to optimizing the data exchange between a Unicode server and non-Unicode-enabled mobile clients:

Because both CRM 4.0 Mobile Client and the DCOM connector are not able to process double-byte data, the CRM Server must send single-byte data. For this reason, the CRM Server must know the code page of the client in order to carry out the conversion. The mobile client, in turn, can only use one code page. If different languages are used, the conversion process can only be successful if language-dependent characters are based on the same code page.

With double-byte characters, you may see that character strings get truncated during the dispatch process if the total amount of bytes exceeds the maximum length permitted in the text fields of the outbound adapters.

Starting with CRM 40 SP12, the mobile client is capable of handling double byte language characters and Unicode. Unfortunately, no direct upgrade path exists to move a non-Unicode mobile client below CRM 40 SP 12 to a Unicode client on CRM 40SP12. For a detailed description of how to perform a manual conversion, see SAP Note 1032589. The main reason for not supporting a non-Unicode to Unicode upgrade is that the mobile client database has to be installed afresh with the Unicode code page; and a reload from the CRM Server to the mobile client has to be done (i.e., you cannot upgrade the SQL code page from non-Unicode to Unicode).

Restrictions

[«]

This chapter describes the options provided by reorganizing the Middleware, and which additional measures are necessary to keep the performance of the CRM system at a high level.

12 Reorganization

In the previous chapters, we described which preferences and parameters you can set, and which parameters you can use to optimize the setup of your SAP CRM Middleware considering your intended usage of the system. Apart from setting specific parameters, which you often do only once, everyday maintenance of your Middleware is necessary to achieve long-term optimal throughput. The first section of this chapter describes which maintenance activities are available. The second section of this chapter describes additional parameters, which are directly related to some specific reorganization activities.

12.1 Reorganizing the Middleware

As you have already seen, even processed BDocs are continually stored in the database tables. However, because the data they contain has already been stored in the respective application tables, BDocs should be removed from the system after a certain retention period. Doing so enables you to reduce the size of the database a little and to ensure that the performance of Middleware processes is not unnecessarily impaired by an extensive growth of the BDoc tables. In addition to the actual BDoc data that is stored in tables SMW3_BDOC* and should be reorganized as soon as it becomes obsolete, statistical data such as message flow statistics (Transaction SMWMFLOW; please refer to Chapter 8, *Inbound Queues* for more details), statistics for the data exchange between mobile clients and the CRM Server, and interlinkages between the BDocs are also updated when BDocs are processed. Since these types of data also tend to grow rapidly and can therefore reduce system performance, the data should be cleansed on a regular basis. For this purpose, the SAP CRM system provides the reorganization program SMO6_REORG2 (see Figure 12.1) that can be used to cleanse Middleware-specific data. To be able to carry out this necessary reorganization activity, the program should be scheduled on a regular basis in each client that is used.

[»] Program SMO6_REORG2 was introduced in SAP CRM 4.0 SP6. Before that, SAP provided the SMO6_REORG program, which can still be used. However, make sure you use only one of these programs regularly. If you use SMO6_REORG, you should also schedule the RSRLDREL program for reorganizing the linkage data. As of SAP CRM 5.0, SMO6_REORG2 is the standard program to be used for reorganizing the Middleware.

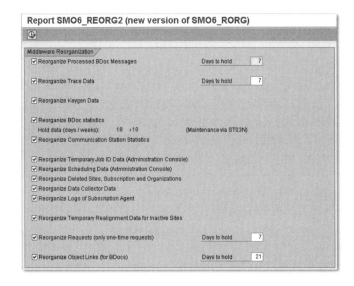

Figure 12.1 Initial Screen of Reorganization Program SMO6_REORG2

Meaning of selections   The selection screen in the program enables you to select individual reorganization steps separately. However, SAP recommends that you select all the steps together (as is predefined in the standard variant, SAP_MW_REORG) and to carry them out on a regular basis. The individual selections have the following descriptions:

▶ **Reorganize Processed BDoc Messages**
   If you select this option, the table entries of all BDoc instances will be deleted whose status is final and whose last change occurred a

longer time ago than the number of days specified in the **Days to hold** field. As a matter of fact, all relevant entries in the following tables will be deleted: SMW3_BDOC, SMW3_BDOC1, SMW3_BDOC2, SMW3_BDOC3, SMW3_BDOC4, SMW3_BDOC5, SMW3_BDOC6, SMW3_BDOC7, and SMW3_BDOCQ.

▶ **Reorganize Trace Data**
This option enables you to delete trace data of the Middleware trace. During Middleware processes, the Middleware trace (see Chapter 8, *Inbound Queues*) writes log entries into Table SMWT_TRC, which can be viewed via Transaction SMWT. Because this table is continually written, the performance of Middleware processes can be negatively affected if you don't reorganize it.

▶ **Reorganize KeyGen Data**
This option allows you to delete temporary, generated key entries from Table SMO9_KYTBL if the respective data record has already been written to the CDB tables that are linked to the sBDoc.

▶ **Reorganize BDoc Statistics**
This option starts the RSMWM_BSTAT_REORG program and deletes entries from Table SMWMBSTAT. As is the case with other statistical data as well, you can control the residence time of the entries via Transaction ST03N. To do that, you must expand the Collector and Performance DB tree, followed by the Performance Database subtree, and then the Monitoring Database subtree. If you double-click the **Reorganization** entry, the system enables you to set the retention periods of statistical data (see Figure 12.2).

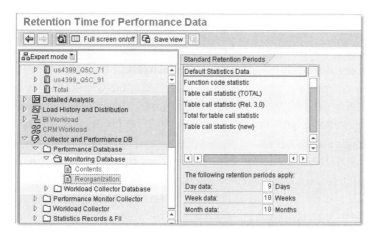

Figure 12.2 Setting Residence Times of Statistical Records

▶ **Reorganize Communication Station Statistics**
This option starts the RSMWM_SESSION_REORG report, which deletes session data of the communication station. This data is displayed in the communication monitor (Transaction SMWM-COMM). Again, you must use Transaction ST03N to set the retention periods of the data, as is the case with BDoc statistics. Here, however, the data is retained for a period of at least seven days. If the value you maintain in Transaction ST03N is smaller than seven days, the program automatically increases it to seven days. The relevant contents of Table SMWMSESSHT (session header data) and Table SMWMSESSIN (session information data) are deleted for sessions that are older than the retention period.

▶ **Reorganize Temporary Job ID Data (Administration Console)**
This option starts Report SMOE_REORG_REPOSITORY, which deletes the entries of Table SMOEJOBID. The temporary jobs to be deleted are actually processes that are carried in conjunction with specific actions in the administration console, such as triggering an AC extract, for example. Once the report is completed, it provides you with a list of individual actions that were carried out (see Figure 12.3). You can control the behavior of the report via two entries in Table SMOFPARSFA, which can be set using Transaction R3AC6. The value assigned to the SMOE key and the parameter name SMOE_REORG_SMOEJOBID_DAYS controls the retention period of the data, whereas the value assigned to the SMOE key and parameter name SMOE_REORG_SMOEJOBID_COMMIT define how many internal records are deleted from the database via a COMMIT. The internal program default values, which can be overruled using this setting, are 1,000 data records for the COMMIT control and 0 days for the data retention period.

▶ **Reorganize Scheduling Data (Administration Console)**
This option starts the SMOE_SCHEDULING_REORG report, which deletes Table SMOESCHED (table responsible for site and subscription substitution rules) as well as the dependent data in tables SMOESJBLOG, SMOESDEST, SMOESRERO, and SMOESTPLNK. Here again, the data retention period is controlled via an entry in Table SMOFPARSFA: The value assigned to the SMOE key and the parameter name SMOE_SCHEDULING_REORG controls the data retention period. However, the value must not be smaller than 10 (days); otherwise, the retention period will be automatically reset to the internal program default value of 100 days.

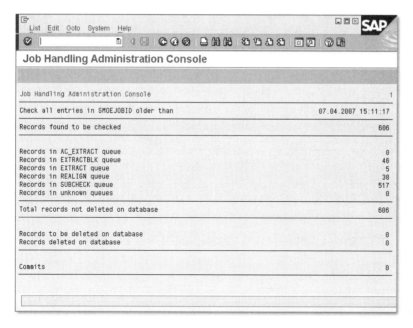

Figure 12.3 Output of Program SMOE_REORG_REPOSITORY

▶ **Reorganize Deleted Sites, Subscriptions, and Organizations**

This option provides a number of reorganization activities or important tables of the Middleware (see Figure 12.4), which can be started using the SMOE_REORG_ADM_OBJECTS report. The internal default retention period is 30 days for the reorganization of Table SMOHGROUP (organization/user group) and the associated link Table SMOHGRPLK. In addition, the table containing the site IDs, SMOHSITEID, is deleted as well, including the dependent data in Table SMOHSUBSIT (site IDs of the subscription) and Table SMOHQTAB (inbound and outbound queues). Additionally, this report cleanses deleted subscriptions from Table SMOHSUBSCR (subscription) as well as from the linked tables SMOHSUBSIT and SMOHVALUES. In contrast to the aforementioned retention period of 30 days, the retention period of Table SMOECK_INDX is fixed to seven days.

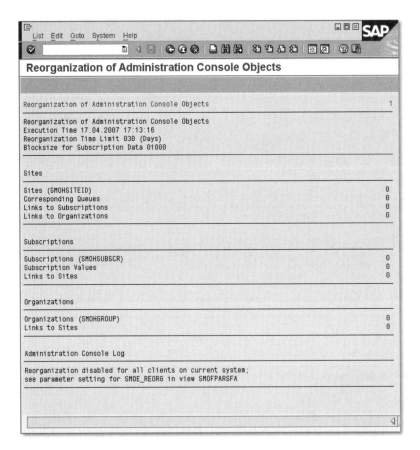

Figure 12.4 Log for the Reorganization of Administration Console Objects

Lastly, this option enables you to reorganize the logs of the administration console that are stored in Table SMOEACLOG. Note that you can switch off this option via an entry in Table SMOFPARSFA (see Figure 12.5). For example, you should deactivate this function in development systems so you can reproduce development-related changes at any time. At this point, you should note that the deactivation always applies to an entire system and that it is client-independent.

▶ **Reorganize Data Collector Data**
As described in Chapter 9, *Replication Model and R&R*, in SAP CRM 5.0 the data collector was introduced to reduce the workload placed on the Middleware. This option reorganizes Table SMOJD-CPROC via the program, SMOJ_REORG_DATA_COLLECTOR. The

table contains temporary information about the extraction runs carried out by the data collector.

▶ **Reorganize Logs of Subscription Agent**

As the name suggests, this option reorganizes the logs of the subscription agent in Table SMOEGENLOG via Report SMOE_ REORG_SUBSCRIPTION_AGENT. The default retention period for this type of data is one day, while 1,000 data record deletions are updated at a time. You can define the retention period via the value field of Table SMOFPARSFA for the SMOE key and parameter name SMOE_REORG_SMOEGENLOG_DAYS.

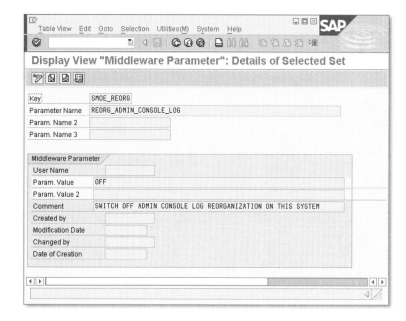

Figure 12.5 Deactivating the Reorganization of the Administration Console Log

▶ **Reorganize Temporary Realignment Data for Inactive Sites**

This option uses Report SMOE_REORG_XRR to delete data only for those sites whose site type does not allow any activation, according to Table SMW1SPRVDR (see Figure 12.6). This condition does not apply to site types contained in the standard SAP version so that, in general, you can use this option only for data of sites that have a custom site type.

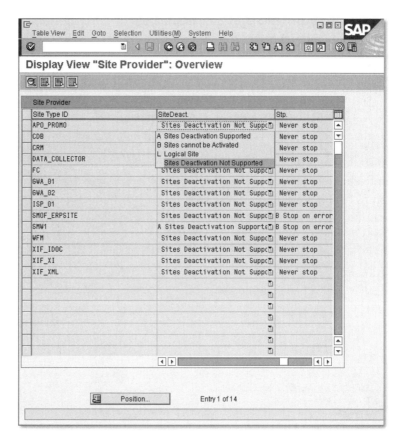

Figure 12.6 Site Types in Table SMW1SPRVDR

▶ **Reorganize Requests (only one-time requests)**
You can set the **one-time** flag in the maintenance transaction for data requests (Transaction R3AR2). In addition, all requests that have been triggered by DIMa (Data Integrity Manager) are automatically one-time requests. This option reorganizes only these one-time data requests using Report SMOF_REORG_REQUESTS.

▶ **Reorganize Object Links (for BDocs)**
This option starts the well-known RSRLDREL and deletes link data. In addition, you can use the parameters of SMOFPARSFA to restrict the writing of link data (see Section 12.2).

Monitor the execution! In addition to scheduling the actual job of reorganizing the Middle-ware data using the options described above, you should also monitor the job through the job log provided in Transaction SM37.

12.2 Avoiding Object Links

In order to enable a fast analysis of BDocs with an error status, object links are created between BDoc messages. These links are displayed in Transaction SMW01 and are used to analyze the relationships between different BDocs. Although you can reorganize these links on a regular basis, as described in Section 12.1, the creation of the links causes a decrease in performance regarding the processing of BDocs. For this reason, the analysis method was changed with the introduction of SAP CRM 4.0 SP09 in such a way that the relationships between BDocs no longer need to be written permanently and can be calculated during the analysis, if needed. In order to deactivate the writing of these links as of SAP CRM 4.0 SP09, you must call Transaction SM30 and create a new entry in Table SMOFPARSFA containing the value FLOW in the key, the value MW_NO_MBDOC_LINKS in the **Paramname** field, and the parameter value X (see Figure 12.7).

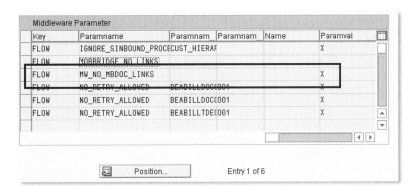

Optimizing BDoc processing

Figure 12.7 Deactivating the Links Between BDocs

In addition to the links that are updated between the mBDocs in the flow, other links are created between synchronous BDoc (sBDoc) messages and the associated messaging BDocs (mBDocs). Since these links can also cause a loss in performance, SAP has made it possible to deactivate the creation of this type of links as well. To do that, you must call the view maintenance Transaction SM30 and maintain an entry in Table SMOFPARSFA containing the value "FLOW" in the key, the value "MOB-BRIDGE_NO_LINKS" in the **Paramname** field, and the parameter value "X".

You can access the new function for calculating the BDoc links in monitoring Transaction SMW01 by selecting a BDoc and clicking the button that is highlighted in Figure 12.8.

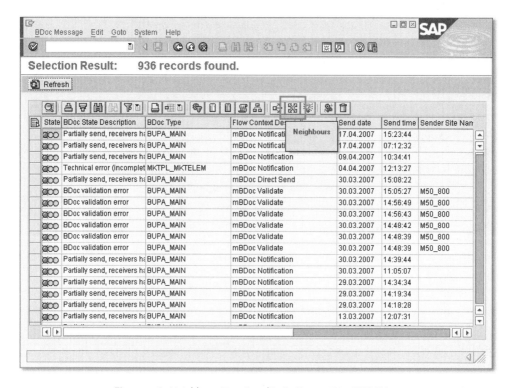

Figure 12.8 Neighbour Functionality in Transaction SMW01

In this chapter, we'll address the question of what you can do to perform mass changes as optimally as possible, that is, what parameters should be adjusted, what preparations should be made, what should be done during the mass changes, and what you can do if something goes wrong.

13   Performing Optimized Mass Changes

In Chapter 7, *Introduction to Performance Optimization*, we showed in detail what we mean by a mass change and what effects it can have. To optimally perform a mass change, it is important, in the first instance, that various parameters be adjusted to the exceptionally high load. If the CRM Middleware is optimally set, all schedulers process the queues with the maximum parallelism and the data is evenly processed; in other words, the number of queues and its entries remain constant within a frame, and the system resources are used to full capacity without being overloaded. If the mass change is not time-critical, we recommend that you set the parameters conservatively, so that you don't use all of the system resources. If the mass change is time-critical, you may need to drive the system closer to the limit. You should note, however, that a system shutdown due to a system overload is very likely to cost you more time than the time lost you would incur by making slightly more conservative settings (aside from the other *side-effects* of a system shutdown).

You should test and optimize these parameter settings for the mass change in the test system.   [«]

During the actual execution in the production system, another factor comes into play, which is difficult to evaluate in the test system, namely the additional load that the users (both online and mobile) and other interfaces generate during the mass change. First, we cannot always know how many users will use the system during a certain period and whether other data will be received and processed, for instance, through IDocs. Secondly, the various users generate different loads. A mobile client who retrieves data generates a very different load on the CRM server than a power user in CRM Online, a customer in a webshop, or a user who is starting a marketing campaign.

If additional or unforeseen loads occur during the mass change, the CRM may no longer have enough reserves left to cope with these loads that haven't been taken into account. Through continuous and timely monitoring of the system, you can identify these critical situations in a reasonable time and take the necessary corrective measures.

We'll discuss all of these aspects — setting the parameters, preparing a mass change, and the system monitoring during the mass change — in this chapter. In the last section of this chapter, we'll look at what to do if something has gone wrong. We'll describe problems that have occurred with mass changes in the past, and what options you have for responding to similar problems should they occur for you.

In this chapter, we'll assume that the mass data comes from an R/3 backend system. Whether the data is generated in R/3 by an SAP or customer-specific report, or is requested by CRM, is immaterial. We will also assume that a functional test has already been performed (i.e., the data transfer and validation are working smoothly).

13.1 Optimal Parallelization of the Middleware

In the CRM Middleware there are a range of parameters you can "play with" to process a mass change as optimally as possible (meaning as quickly as possible). If the R/3 system copies several object instances in a Business Application Programming Interface (BAPI), you can change the number of instances per BAPI (the package size) if required. You can limit the number of R3A and CSA queues in the CRM, and define the maximum number of work processes available to the inbound queue scheduler and the *Replication & Realignment* (R&R). In Figure 13.1, we have flagged the points listed above in the CRM Middleware with a question mark (?). In addition, you have the option to spread the load throughout your server landscape.

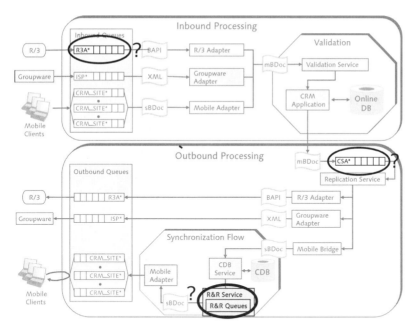

Figure 13.1 Settings for the Optimizations

The optimum setting depends on an entire list of factors. There are **Limiting factors** hard, *limiting factors* such as:

▶ The number of instances

▶ The number of servers

▶ The number of CPUs

▶ The number of work processes

▶ The amount of main memory available

▶ The performance of the database (including the storage subsystem)

There are also *variable factors*, which can change with every mass change. They include:

▶ The object type that is changed

▶ The number of objects to be processed during the mass change

▶ The processing time in the message flow

▶ The load that an object generates in the synchronization flow (whether or not a realignment is performed)

Given the number of factors, you can appreciate that an optimal standard setting is simply not possible. In this book as well, we won't be able to give you the specific optimal parameter setting for your next mass change in your current situation in your system.

However, we will put you in a position where you will be able to determine the global setting for your system yourself. You must then test the settings and correct them as required. If the hardware of your test system is different from the hardware of your production system, you can't really test the settings for the optimal mass change processing. You have no option other than to extrapolate the results of your tests and to make corrections in the course of the mass change. In Sections 13.1.1 and 13.1.2, we'll ask some fundamental questions (i.e., both in relation to points concerning the data to be changed, and about the CRM system itself). The answers to these questions have direct implications for the settings in the CRM system. When taken together, we end up with a kind of checklist that you should run through prior to a mass change, with a series of answers serving as the common denominator for all of your mass changes.

13.1.1 Key Considerations for the Data

The answers to the different questions will help you with the global setting and the further optimization:

1. Are the objects being packed in R/3 (i.e., are several object instances being copied in a BAPI that is sent from R/3 to CRM)?

Packed objects are
transferred

If the objects are packed in R/3, you should strictly limit the number of R3A queues for these objects; otherwise, in a short space of time a very large number of objects will be written into the CSA queues or many CSA queues will be created (unless the object type is mass processing-enabled and is not isolated in the validation). Alternatively, it is possible to drastically limit the number of work processes that the R3A queues process in parallel, but this would simultaneously limit the number of work processes working on the CSA queues.

The optimal number of R3A queues depends on the packing factor and on the question of how quickly your system processes the CSA queues. With a packing factor of 100, the processing of an

R3A entry generates 100 CSA queue entries. To prevent objects accumulating in the CSA queues, 100 CSA queue entries must therefore be processed at the same speed at which a single R3A queue entry is processed. If the processing of a packed entry takes 10 times as long as the processing for a single object, then theoretically you need 10 work processes that process the CSA queues in parallel. In practice, the number will be a little higher, because the scheduler also needs time to assign a queue to a work process. For five R3A queues, 50 to 60 work processes would therefore be required to process the CSA queues. You should run a test with one queue, and determine the average processing time for R3A queues and CSA queues. To do this, you can use the workload statistic (Transaction SMWMFLOW), or a SQL or ABAP trace (Transaction ST05 or SE30 or ST12). Nevertheless, the simplest method is to clock the time required to process x objects, and divide the result by x. You can base your calculations on the values you determine.

If the objects are not packed in R/3, you should allow for a higher number of R3A queues. Generally, it makes sense to limit the system to a maximum of 100 queues (or a maximum of 1,000 queues in very large systems). Once again, in this case, you should determine the average processing times for the R3A and CSA queues. Ideally, the ratio of the processing times should correspond to the ratio of the queues (or the number of work processes that process these queues). If the queues first exist in the system, there is no way to define how many R3A queues and CSA queues will be processed in parallel (you only have this option for the R&R queues). You can only limit, through the RFC server group, the maximum number of work processes the inbound queue scheduler may occupy. This means that you can only define how many work processes the R3A and CSA queues process together.

Objects are not transferred in packed form

As a general rule: If you receive individual messages from the R/3 system during the mass change, it is very important that you restrict the number of R3A queues.

[«]

Otherwise, many thousands of inbound queues may result, and you will encounter the problems we described in detail in Section 8.1.

If you have implemented the mobile sales scenario, questions also arise relating to the synchronization flow:

2. Is a realignment performed for the objects?

   A realignment is only performed for intelligently replicated objects, and only if a distribution-relevant field is changed (or a new object is created or an object is deleted). If in doubt, you should run a test with a small number of object instances. Ensure that your test quantity is as representative as possible. Otherwise, the test results will induce you to make the wrong conclusions.

   If the objects don't trigger a realignment, you don't need to worry about the parallel processing of the R&R queues and can leave the values unchanged.

If a realignment is triggered, subsequent questions arise:

3. How many objects are written into the REALIGN queue (all objects or only some) and how many dependent objects follow the original objects (and must also be processed by the R&R queues)?

   Note that the number of objects that must be processed in the R&R can be many times higher than the number of objects that are loaded from R/3. If a very large number of objects must be processed in the R&R, you must decide whether the CRM system can cope with such a large number of entries in the outbound queues. If you're not sure, you should run a test with a small number of object instances.

[»]   Here again, you must ensure that your test quantity is as representative as possible. Otherwise, the test results will induce you to make the wrong conclusions.

4. What measures will you take to prevent the outbound queues from being flooded with BDocs (details on this topic can be found in Chapter 10, *Outbound Queues*)? Do you plan, for example, to stop the EXTRACT queue, delete the corresponding entries, and perform an AC extract for the affected mobile sites or deactivate the sites?

   If so, you don't need to be concerned with the parallel processing of the EXTRACT queue.

5. For the right settings, we must also clarify the question of priorities: Is it more important that all data is available as quickly as possible in the CRM Online (and the mobile clients get the data with a delay), or do the mobile clients have to be supplied with the data as quickly as possible?

In the first case, you can set the parallel processing of the R&R queues low in the first phase of the mass processing and make the system resources available for processing the R3A and CSA queues. Once the inbound queues are processed, you can then massively increase the parallel processing of the R&R and process the entries there.

In the second case, you must allow for a high parallel processing of the R&R queues from the beginning and achieve a balance between the inbound queue processing and the R&R.

It is not so difficult to set this balance if there are no dependent objects. For instance, if you load conditions from R/3 into the CRM, there are no dependent objects; therefore, the number of objects that must be processed in the REALIGN and the EXTRACT queue corresponds to no more than the number of loaded objects. Next you must determine how long the average processing takes for an object in the REALIGN and the EXTRACT queue. Using this value, and knowing how long the processing of a CSA queue entry takes, you can easily calculate the parallelism with which the R&R queues must be processed. Let's assume, for example, that the processing of an object in the CSA queue takes 200ms, in the REALIGN queue 300ms, and in the EXTRACT queue 150ms, and that the CSA queues are processed in parallel 10 times. The REALIGN queue would then have to be processed 15 times (formula: (queue number/CSA duration) * REALIGN duration => (10/200)*300) and the EXTRACT queue eight times in parallel (if you don't stop the EXTRACT queue).

There are no dependent objects

If there are dependent objects, it is disproportionately more difficult to set the equation. Let's assume, for example, that you load business partners from R/3 into CRM and that a realignment must be performed for the business partners. The business partner is followed by contact persons, activities, and sales documents. To be able to calculate the parallelism, you must now determine how many object instances, on average, follow a business partner. Finally, you must determine how long is the processing duration

There are dependent objects

of the various objects. The REALIGN duration from the above formula corresponds to the processing duration (PD) of the business partner + l*PD of the contact person + n*PD of the activity + m*PD of the sales document, where l, n, and m are the number of contact persons, activities, and sales documents that follow the business partner. The processing duration in the R&R can easily be determined by running a few tests; the number of dependent documents, on the other hand, can only be determined using tests with great difficulty. Frequently, the number of dependent objects will differ considerably from one business partner to another, and it is therefore misleading to draw conclusions from a small number of business partners for tens of thousands.

13.1.2 Basic CRM System Considerations

The questions in the last section pertain to the data of the mass change; the following questions deal with the CRM system:

1. Does the mass change have to be performed concurrently with normal production operation, or is the system blocked?

   If the CRM is blocked for all users and interfaces to other systems, all system resources are available to you for the mass processing. Even the repercussions of a backlog in the system — in other words, the queues are not evenly processed and entries pile up in the CSA or R&R queues — are minor.

   If the CRM is used productively in parallel by online users (and/or interfaces are open), a backlog should be prevented at all costs. Otherwise, the data being processed by the online users will queue up. It cannot be processed further in real time (e.g., in the R/3 backend), nor is it available to all CRM users (e.g., mobile client users).

In the event of concurrent use by other users, the question arises:

2. Do you have several instances?

   If you do, you can use the RFC server groups and login groups to separate the online users and the CRM Middleware processing. In this way, the users won't suffer, or will suffer less, from the mass processing (unless the database performance grinds to a halt under the heavy load). When assigning the groups to the application servers, make sure that all groups have enough hardware. Otherwise, separating the groups will be counterproductive.

Even if you have only one application server, you should use RFC server groups in order to limit the load generated by the mass processing (you'll find details on this topic in Section 8.3).

3. To parameterize the RFC server groups as optimally as possible, you must clarify the following points:

What system resources are available to you? What percent do you have to reserve for online users? Are there peak times when especially high numbers of users are on the system?

If there are peak times when the system is under a particularly heavy load, this makes the optimization considerably more complicated. You have two options remaining: You can guide your settings by the guaranteed available system resources; however, this would lengthen the runtime of the mass change. Alternatively, you can optimize the settings for the normal load and temporarily, or completely, stop the mass change during the peak times by stopping all, or some of, the R3A inbound queues containing the data of the mass change.

If you implemented the mobile sales scenario, the question as to the number of RFC server groups also arises:

4. Do you plan to use one RFC server group for the inbound queue processing and for the R&R, or two?

If you want to run the inbound queue processing and the R&R on two different servers, you must set up two RFC server groups.

13.1.3 Summary of the Different Considerations

During the mass processing, x work processes — or more specifically, *dialog work processes* — will work on the R3A queues, y on the CSA queues, and z on the R&R queues. The objective is to choose y and z (depending on x) so that all queues are evenly processed and no backlog results. Since you know the number of dialog work processes available in your system, you can now determine x, y, and z.

In our considerations so far, we have exclusively concentrated on the number of work processes. Unfortunately this, as we already mentioned at the start of the chapter, is not the sole limiting factor. If you provide all dialog work processes of your system to the middleware for the mass processing, it is highly probable that you will encounter a CPU bottleneck. We therefore recommend that you make only 75% of the work processes available to the middleware during the first test and observe how the system behaves, and whether you encounter CPU problems, main memory difficulties, or database problems. Irrespective of the test results, you should never make all work processes available to the RFC. Even with a purely mobile scenario, three dialog work processes should be reserved for non-RFC users. This topic is covered in detail in Section 8.3.

Note that for all of our considerations, we have assumed linear system behavior. This is a simplification of reality. In fact, it has been shown that systems, especially with large datasets, don't behave in a linear manner. A perfect example of this is that if there are numerous inbound queues, the performance of the inbound queue scheduler deteriorates considerably (for more information on this subject, see Section 8.1). For you, this means that, regardless of your planning and tests, you must monitor the system during the mass change and be able to act quickly. If you perform certain mass changes regularly, the empirical values of the first mass change will significantly reduce the workload for the next one.

13.2 Organizational Measures

Besides the technical optimization options that the CRM system offers for optimizing a mass change, there is also a series of organizational measures that you can (and should) take in advance, in order to optimally support the processing of mass changes.

Planned mass changes

In this context, we essentially need to differentiate whether the mass change is a *planned* or an *unplanned* action. A planned mass change is different from an unplanned one in that there is a lead time (which may only be short) and the approximate data volume is known. The unplanned mass changes are more dangerous for the CRM system, because they catch it off-guard. With organizational measures, you can reduce the number of unplanned mass changes and prepare the CRM system better for the planned ones.

The territory realignment of the BGS company, which was repeatedly used as an example in the previous chapters, clearly belongs to the planned mass changes category.

Unplanned mass changes are generally caused by errors or ignorance, as the following example shows.

Unplanned mass changes

> **Example**
>
> An employee starts a request in CRM to load one business partner from R/3 into CRM. Because his entry is wrong, all business partners are requested from R/3, rather than only one. The employee does not keep an eye on how his request is running, but instead turns his attention to something else. Only one hour later does he check whether the business partner has been successfully copied from R/3 into CRM and notice his mistake.

13.2.1 Information and Training

An integrated system environment where data flows automatically from one system to the next offers a wide range of advantages and possibilities, but also a few dangers. Mass changes that previously were performed successfully and without any problems in a standalone system can suddenly affect the linked systems. Of course, this doesn't mean that these changes can no longer be carried out; however, it is very important that employees are aware of this fact and that there is close coordination between the system and process managers.

If a CRM system is implemented and connected to an R/3 system, it does not suffice to train only those employees who will be responsible for the CRM in the future. You should also analyze all system wide business processes and inform the departments and employees whose future work will also have an impact on the CRM (and vice versa). In most cases, there will be no reason to change their way of working. Still, what is vital is to identify the few cases where work in the backend system can have serious effects on the linked CRM system. For these situations, further measures should be taken, new (organizational) processes defined, or existing processes changed. Often it is enough to inform the system or process manager in advance by email or telephone so that they can take the proper measures to protect the CRM system and ensure its availability. In this way, unplanned mass changes become planned mass changes.

Informing people throughout the system

Good training initiatives and processes are needed and help to reduce the number of (human) errors, although it will still not be possible to entirely avoid them altogether. We'll discuss the options available that you can undertake for unplanned mass changes (i.e., when things go awry) in Section 13.4.

13.2.2 Final Live Test

If at all possible, a mass change should be tested in a sandbox or Q system before you run it in the production system.[1] It is not absolutely necessary to run though the whole mass change in your test from start to finish, but the dataset in the test should certainly be a two-digit percentage of the total quantity. You cannot assume that the system behavior will be linear, that is, if 1,000 orders are posted in 10 minutes, 100,000 orders will by no means be posted in 1,000 minutes.

A successful test will, first, give an impression of what to expect in terms of duration and system load during the actual mass change. Secondly, the test will identify the points in the middleware where performance problems occur. In this way, the corresponding optimizations can already be performed in advance.

13.2.3 System Preparations

Cleaning up During a mass change, the system not only creates, deletes, and updates very large volumes of user data in CRM Online and in the Consolidated Data Base (CDB), but it also creates very large numbers of BDocs and writes a lot of log files. Therefore, you should check whether enough space is available for these datasets. It wouldn't be the first time a full tablespace caused a system shutdown! Regardless of the available disk space, you should ensure that the reorganization jobs have successfully run prior to the mass change (you'll find details on this topic in Chapter 12, *Reorganization*). In particular, you should reduce the number of BDocs in the BDoc Store as much as possible. One option is to temporarily set the retention duration of the reorganization job to one day. In this way, the system will only

---

1 Here we are talking about a volume test, rather than a functional test. We also assume that there are no functional problems.

contain the BDocs from the previous day and the faulty BDocs. You must also check whether you need to rebuild the indexes.

13.2.4 Monitoring

It is vital to build in time and schedule the necessary personnel for more intensive system monitoring during a mass change. Until you have ensured that the system is processing the datasets without any problems, it must be closely monitored. Only when the system is in a steady state and the system load is not expected to increase (i.e., no additional users or data), can you reduce the intensity of the monitoring again.

13.2.5 Mobile Scenario

If you implemented CRM with the mobile scenario, the handling of mass changes is a bit more complex than it would be for pure online or Internet sales scenarios. Not only must the data be copied from R/3 into CRM and validated there, it must also be loaded into the CDB, replicated to the mobile clients, and fetched from these clients. We already described in detail the technical background and possible problems that you might encounter in the outbound queue processing, and how to avoid them, in Chapter 10, *Outbound Queues*. At this point, we would also like to add an organizational measure.

If there are large datasets in the outbound queues of the mobile clients, users (e.g., sales representatives) cannot, as otherwise happens, just collect the data on the fly in the morning, before "hitting the road." Alternatively, it is far better if they start ConnTrans the evening before and take the time to get something to eat, for example, while the data is collected and processed. Since the mobile user doesn't know how much data there is in his outbound queue, it is important that he be notified in advance (e.g., by email) of an imminent mass change. If the users are surprised by long ConnTrans times, this only leads to frustration and discontent. In particular, many users terminate ConnTrans because they interpret the unexpectedly long runtime as an error, and call the hotline.

Information

Early notification of employees also enables you to control the number of parallel ConnTrans sessions (see Chapter 10, *Outbound Queues*). You can divide the mobile client users into groups and ask the different groups to start ConnTrans at different times.

13.3 System Monitoring and Analysis Roadmap

In previous chapters, we have pointed out repeatedly how important system monitoring is to ensure the successful operation of a CRM system. Of course, this requirement also applies to a smooth, successful mass change run.

Now we will explain what you should look out for when performing a mass change, and we will provide you with an analysis roadmap for performance bottlenecks. Note that many things can cause performance bottlenecks. The analysis roadmap will focus solely on settings and optimizations in the CRM Middleware. We will not look at other error causes (database problems, incorrect parameter values in SAP Basis, wrong Customizing settings, etc.), as this would exceed the scope of this book. Furthermore, a simplified analysis roadmap cannot cover all possible details for the various situations and problems that can arise. You should regard the analysis roadmap as a guideline that supports you in monitoring the system and offers you courses of action. In our recommendations, we assume that no system shutdown has occurred so far, but rather that the system is *still* working normally. We describe indicators pointing to a possible performance problem and provide general recommendations on how you can prevent the problem from occurring in the first place, or stop it from worsening. If a performance bottleneck has already occurred, you should take immediate action. For more information on this topic, see Section 13.4.

The left column in Table 13.1 gives the transactions you should regularly call during a mass change. The middle column describes indicators that point to problems. If you identify a problem, the right-hand column suggests what action to take.

Trans-action	Indicator	Further action
SM50/ SM66	All work processes, or more and more work processes are permanently busy. Work processes spend a long time in the action "sequential read".	Analyze the work process occupancy (see Section 13.3.1)
SMQ2	There are thousands of CSA and/or R3A queues, and the number keeps growing. The number of entries in a queue is very high and keeps growing.	Analyze the queue processing (see Section 13.3.2)
SMOH-QUEUE	The number of entries in the queues keeps growing. The entries in the queues are processed slowly.	R&R optimization (see Section 13.3.3)
SMW02/ SMW02a	The number of BDocs with an error status keeps growing.	BDoc error analysis (see Section 13.3.5)
ST06	The CPU idle time is lower than 20 % (see Section 13.3.4).	Optimize the parallel processing (see Section 13.1)

Table 13.1 System Monitoring During a Mass Change

13.3.1 Analyzing the Work Process Occupancy

During your monitoring, you have noticed in Transaction SM50 or SM66 that all, or almost all, dialog work processes are busy. Since a mass change is in the process of being run, a very high system load is not surprising, and this is also reflected in the process overview. Nevertheless, in a case like this, you should check whether the system is already in an overload situation or is about to be overloaded. An initial, straightforward indication is given by the response times from the monitoring transactions you have called. If you're encountering long system response times, this indicates an overload situation. As the next step, you should check whether the CRM system is suffering from a CPU bottleneck. You'll find a detailed description in Section 13.3.4.

If all dialog work processes are occupied, there are basically two possible causes:

▶ Too many users[2] are requesting work processes.

▶ Individual work processes stay busy for a very long time; therefore, they aren't available to other users.

Too many users In the first case, the problem may be due to too many online users or to parallel processing in the CRM Middleware that is too high. Since all queues are filled during a mass processing and all schedulers try to process the entries as quickly as possible, the parallel processing is utilized to maximum capacity in all areas of the middleware. This is not the case during normal operation, or at least it only happens for a short time. If the number of CRM Online users and/or the parallel processing in CRM Middleware is set too high, it can lead to a lack of dialog work processes.

In the **User names** column in Transaction SM50, you can see which users occupy what work processes (if you have maintained logical destinations as described in Section 8.4.1). In Figure 13.2, you can see Transaction SM50 from a CRM system where six of the 13 dialog work processes are occupied by online users (user name **B***), and two by mobile client users (user name **COMMUSER**). The inbound queue scheduler (user name **R3A_INBOUND**) only occupies two work processes, and the R&R (user name **RFCUSERRR**) occupies three work processes, although the maximum parallel processing for the R&R and the inbound queue scheduler is five in each case in this system.

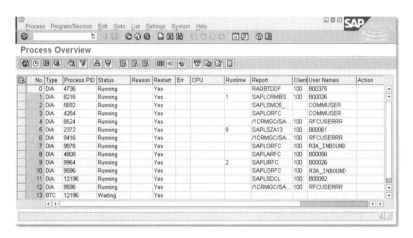

Figure 13.2 All Dialog Work Processes of the CRM System Are Occupied (Transaction SM50)

If the mass change is time-critical, you need all system resources to ensure fast processing and your day-to-day activities to allow for it,

---

2 The term "user" not only refers to persons who are using the system, but also to "internal users" such as the scheduler or the R&R service.

you can lock the CRM for online users. Alternatively, you can reduce the parallel processing in the CRM Middleware. In Section 13.1, you'll find some key considerations that will help you to optimize the parallel processing in the middleware.

Figure 13.3 shows Transaction SM50 of the same CRM system at a later point. Online and mobile client users occupy five of the 13 dialog work processes. Five work processes are occupied by R&R. As you can see in the **Time** column, the work processes have been "blocked" by R&R for some time. In the **Action** column, you can see that all five work processes are reading on the database.

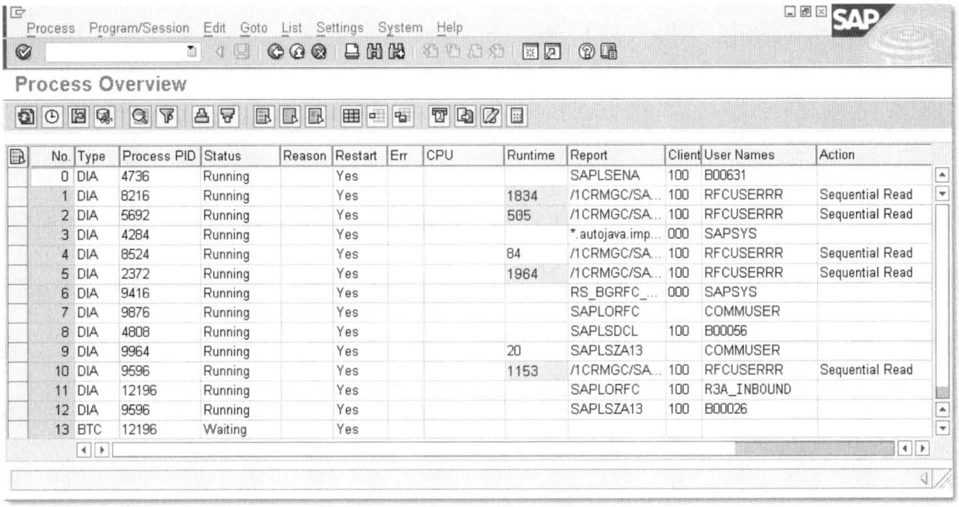

Work processes stay busy for too long

Process Program/Session Edit Goto List Settings System Help

Process Overview

No.	Type	Process PID	Status	Reason	Restart	Err	CPU	Runtime	Report	Client	User Names	Action
0	DIA	4736	Running		Yes				SAPLSENA	100	B00631	
1	DIA	8216	Running		Yes			1834	/1CRMGC/SA...	100	RFCUSERRR	Sequential Read
2	DIA	5692	Running		Yes			585	/1CRMGC/SA...	100	RFCUSERRR	Sequential Read
3	DIA	4284	Running		Yes				*.autojava.imp...	000	SAPSYS	
4	DIA	8524	Running		Yes			84	/1CRMGC/SA...	100	RFCUSERRR	Sequential Read
5	DIA	2372	Running		Yes			1964	/1CRMGC/SA...	100	RFCUSERRR	Sequential Read
6	DIA	9416	Running		Yes				RS_BGRFC_...	000	SAPSYS	
7	DIA	9876	Running		Yes				SAPLORFC		COMMUSER	
8	DIA	4808	Running		Yes				SAPLSDCL	100	B00056	
9	DIA	9964	Running		Yes			20	SAPLSZA13		COMMUSER	
10	DIA	9596	Running		Yes			1153	/1CRMGC/SA...	100	RFCUSERRR	Sequential Read
11	DIA	12196	Running		Yes				SAPLORFC	100	R3A_INBOUND	
12	DIA	9596	Running		Yes				SAPLSZA13	100	B00026	
13	BTC	12196	Waiting		Yes							

Figure 13.3 Dialog Work Processes Stay Busy for Too Long (Transaction SM50)

There are many possible causes for long reading times. Perhaps the table is very large and a huge amount of data must be read, and there are no optimal access paths on the database, statistics are missing, and indexes have degenerated, etc. The only next step you can take is to run a performance analysis of the database. If the work processes are occupied by R&R, as they are in this example, you will find details on optimization options in Chapter 9, *Replication Model and R&R*. If the work processes are occupied by mobile clients (outbound queue processing), you will find details on optimization options in Chapter 10, *Outbound Queues*.

Suboptimal coding may be another reason why work processes stay busy for a long time. This is a possible cause when data is posted in the CRM Middleware, although it's not the most likely cause, unless you're also running non-standard SAP code. The SAP code has already been tried and tested and optimized in this area. Nevertheless, you shouldn't rule out suboptimal coding as a possible cause. However, as the first step in your analysis, we recommend that you ensure that the problem is not caused by the database.

In Figure 13.4, you'll find the roadmap for the work process analysis.

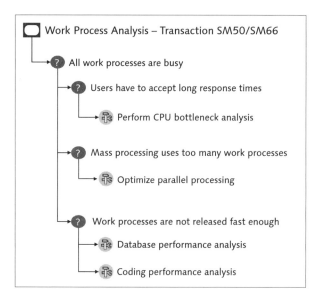

Figure 13.4 Roadmap for the Work Process Analysis

13.3.2 Analyzing the Queue Processing

Immediately after you start a mass change, it is normal for the number of inbound queues to grow. But, after a while the system should settle down and the number of R3A[3] and CSA inbound queues should remain reasonably stable. You only have to take measures if the number of queues keeps growing and becomes very large, or if the number stays so small that the data is only processed slowly and the available system resources are not being used.

---

3 In this chapter, we're assuming that the data is copied from the R/3 system to the CRM. If the data originates from a change in the CRM itself, no R3A inbound queues will be created.

Besides the number of queues, you should also monitor the number of entries in the queues. Generally, R/3 sends the data faster than it is processed by CRM. It is therefore not uncommon for the number of entries in the R3A queues to grow. Ideally, the number of entries in all R3A queues will be roughly the same, and they will be uniformly processed.[4] The number of CSA queues and the number of entries in the CSA queues should become stable, and remain stable, after some time. You will only have to intervene if individual queues are not processed, or if processing slows down or is very slow from the start.

If the number of inbound queues continually grows and reaches a value higher than 10,000, you should consider stopping the mass change and limiting the number of queues. You will find details on limiting the number in Chapter 8, *Inbound Queues*. Note that you can only change the queue name if all queues have been processed.

The number of queues increases

You can easily prevent additional CSA queues from being created by stopping the R3A queues (or deregistering them). Then, you have to wait until the CSA queues have been processed before you can limit the number of CSA queues.

It is almost impossible for you to prevent new R3A queues (in R/3) from being created. However, you can prevent the data from being copied to CRM. To do this, you must write a generic stop entry for all R3A queues into the R/3 outbound queues. In this way, you relieve the inbound processing in CRM, however this may generate a very large number of outbound queues in R/3.

If the number of inbound queues stays very small, or if only a small number of queues are processed in parallel, it is possible that not all available system resources are being used. Consequently, the mass processing would take longer than necessary. Nevertheless, before you increase the number of queues or the level of parallel processing, you should ensure that you still have enough system resources available. First, check in Transaction SM50 whether the system still has enough free dialog work processes. Then, use Transaction ST06 to check the utilization of the CPUs (you'll find details on this in Section 13.3.4). If the check verifies that you do have sufficient resources available, you can increase the number of queues (see

The number of queues remains very small

---

4   See Chapter 8, *Inbound Queues*.

Chapter 8, *Inbound Queues*). Note that a parallel processing that is too high will have the same effect as one that is too low. Both extend the duration of the mass processing.

Inbound queue processing stops
If all inbound queues are not being processed or are no longer being processed, first check the status of the inbound queue scheduler in Transaction SMQR. If the scheduler has the status *INACTIVE*, activate it. To do this, choose **Edit • Activate scheduler in the menu**. If the problem is not solved by the restart, you must run an error analysis.

If only a few inbound queues are not being processed, check in Transaction SMQR whether the queues are registered (**Type** "R"). If the queues are not registered, you should clarify who deregistered the queries and why, and then register them again. Once the queues are registered, start Transaction SMQ2, mark the affected queues, and select **Edit • Display Selection**. Check the status of the queues. If the status indicates an error, you must perform an error analysis. You'll find details on the queue scheduler and on registering queues in Section 2.3.2.

Dependencies between CSA queues
If the status of the queue is *waiting*, this can mean that there are dependencies between the queues, that is, the queue is not processed until another queue has been processed. In the **Wait for queue** column, you can see what queue has to be processed first (Chapter 8, *Inbound Queues*, describes this CRM Middleware behavior).

Dependencies between the inbound queues significantly slow down the processing speed. First, only fewer queues can be processed in parallel; secondly, the scheduler needs longer to determine what queue can be processed. Unfortunately, there is no easy way to optimize performance problems caused by dependencies.

One option is to increase the number of CSA queues or to cancel the limitation altogether. Note that the queues must be completely processed beforehand. If you stop the limitation altogether, you may need to keep stopping the R3A queues manually to prevent too many CSA queues from being created. This technique requires that the CRM system is closely and continuously monitored.

In Figure 13.5 and Figure 13.6, you'll find the analysis roadmaps for the queue processing.

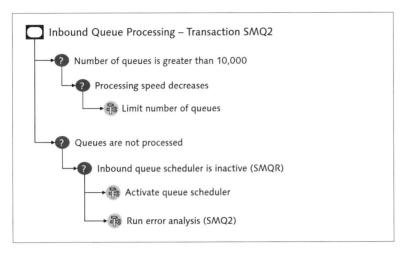

Figure 13.5 Roadmap for Analyzing the Inbound Queue Processing

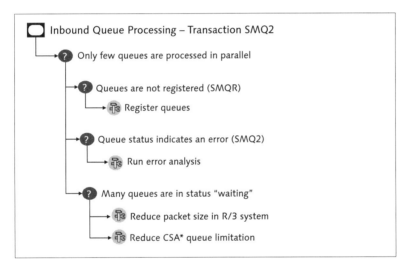

Figure 13.6 Roadmap for Analyzing the Inbound Queue Processing

13.3.3 R&R Optimization

It is normal if the number of entries in the REALIGN queue and EXTRACT queue increases during a mass change. There are many CSA queues that are processed in parallel, but the datasets are only written into one REALIGN queue. In particular, new REALIGN and EXTRACT queue entries are generated from the processing of a REALIGN queue entry.

Growth of the R&R Queues

If a realignment is performed for an object, the dependent objects are determined and then placed in the REALIGN queue. For instance, if a business partner is followed by activities and orders, the processing of a business partner can cause the REALIGN queue to grow by umpteen new entries. You'll find a detailed description of when specific data is written into the R&R queues in Chapter 2, *Inbound Processing and Validation*. But, although this is "normal" growth of the R&R queues, very large R&R queues can also be caused by parallel processing that is set too low or the very slow processing of individual entries.

Experience also shows that sometimes you just think that the R&R queues are being processed slowly, when, in fact, the individual entries are being processed very quickly. It is just that almost the same exact number of new entries is being written into the queues very quickly too. If you just look at the number of queue entries, you won't immediately notice the difference between slow processing and fast processing in conjunction with large numbers of new entries. To ensure that the entries are really being processed slowly, you can look at the response times in the workload statistics (you'll find details in Section 8.4.2). Alternatively, you can open the detail view of the affected R&R queue and use "Refresh" to see whether the foremost entries are being processed quickly, or check in Transaction SMW01 to determine how many sBDocs are generated in a certain timeframe with flow context *SO4*.

Parallel processing of the R&R queues

In Transaction SMOHQUEUE, in the **Active tasks** column, you can see how many objects are processed concurrently. In Figure 13.7, you'll notice that four entries are being processed simultaneously. To speed up the processing, you can increase the maximum number of the active tasks (you'll find a detailed description in Chapter 9, *Replication Model and R&R*). Don't forget to stop the queue and restart it once you have changed the parallel processing.

First, however, it is very important that you check whether the CRM system can cope with an increase in the parallel processing. Excessively high parallel processing at one point (e.g., R&R processing) can easily cause performance problems in other areas of the middleware (e.g., in the inbound processing).

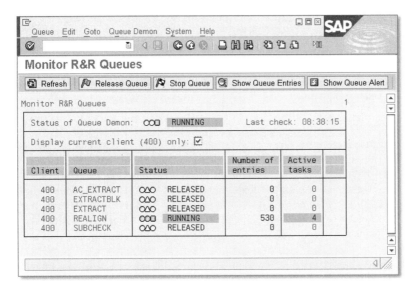

Figure 13.7 Parallel Processing in the REALIGN Queue (Transaction SMOHQUEUE)

To check whether the CRM can cope with an increase in the parallel processing, go to Transaction ST06 and determine to what extent your CPUs are already being utilized (you'll find more details in Section 13.3.4). Check in Transaction SM50/SM66 to determine whether there are still enough free dialog work processes (see also Section 13.3.1). You can also find out whether you have enough main memory available by checking the paging rates of the system in Transaction ST06.

If you're using RFC server groups, be sure to check the capacity utilization of the CPUs and the work processes on the corresponding application servers.

If you still have enough resources available on the application servers, you should also check whether the database server has capacity for additional queries (also check the CPU and memory load on the database server and the I/O values). If you have enough resources available on the application servers and all the other necessary aforementioned prerequisites, you can increase the parallel processing of the corresponding R&R queries. If you dramatically increase the parallel processing level of the REALIGN queue, you should also increase the parallel processing of the EXTRACT queue. Otherwise, the entries in the REALIGN queue will be processed quickly, but the data will pile up in the EXTRACT queue.

RFC server groups When you use RFC server groups, you may also have to adjust the parameters of the RFC server group (you'll find detailed information on RFC server groups in Chapter 8, *Inbound Queues*). The following example illustrates the dependencies between the various settings.

Example

You have an application server and a database server. The RFC server group that you use for the R&R only contains the application server. This has 20 dialog work processes. The parameter **Min. no. free WPs** of the RFC server group has the value 15. The parameter **RRQUEUE_PARALLEL** in Table SMOFPARSFA has the value 3 for the REALIGN queue and the value 2 for the EXTRACT queue (i.e., the REALIGN queue is processed no more than three times in parallel and the EXTRACT queue no more than twice in parallel).

If you now double the value of the **RRQUEUE_PARALLEL** parameter for the REALIGN queue, the REALIGN queue is not processed up to six times, however, but rather will be processed no more than five times in parallel. The reason is the limitation in the RFC server group. The parameter **Min. no. free WPs** has the value 15, and since the application server has 20 dialog work processes, the R&R can only occupy a maximum of five work processes. But even if the R&R occupies all five work processes, this doesn't mean that the REALIGN queue will be processed five times in parallel. For instance, if the REALIGN and EXTRACT queue are filled, both queues share the five work processes. Because of the changed settings, the EXTRACT queue gets a maximum of two, and the REALIGN a maximum of five, work processes. The parallel processing of the REALIGN queue therefore fluctuates between three times and five times. The increase in the parallel processing of the REALIGN queue is entirely borne by the EXTRACT queue. If five work processes are working on the REALIGN queue, there are no more processes available to the EXTRACT queue.

The settings in the RFC server group and the parallel processing of the R&R should be chosen so that they are coherent. If you change the settings in the RFC server group, note the effects this has on the application server(s) and other applications or users.

If you noticed during your analysis of the system resources that the system, while not overloaded, doesn't have any more free capacity, it is not advisable to simply increase the parallel processing of the R&R queue. Nevertheless, you can reduce the parallel processing at other points in the CRM Middleware, or to temporarily stop the processing, in order to thereby obtain capacities for the R&R processing. In Section 13.1, we will discuss the dependencies between the various areas in the middleware.

If the level of parallel processing is optimally set, but the R&R queues continue to grow, you can also optimize the processing of the individual entries. A common reason for slow processing is a *degenerated index* on Table SMOHMSGQ. Table SMOHMSGQ contains all entries of the R&R queues. Since a very large number of database records are written into this table and deleted again, particularly with mass changes, the indexes SMOHMSGQ~0 and SMOHMSGQ~OPT very quickly degenerate. Chapter 9, *Replication Model and R&R*, offers you a detailed description of how to check the degree of fragmentation of indexes and rebuild them again. During mass changes, you may need to rebuild the indexes several times a day in order to obtain an optimal processing time.

Slow processing of the R&R entries

If the processing of the R&R queue entries is not accelerated by rebuilding the indexes, you must run a database performance analysis to identify and solve the problem.

In Figure 13.8, you'll find the analysis roadmap for the R&R optimization.

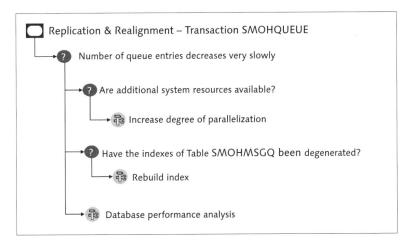

Figure 13.8 Analysis Roadmap for the R&R Optimization

13.3.4 CPU Bottleneck Analysis

In the CRM Middleware, a *CPU bottleneck* can very quickly arise as a result of the parallel processing in the various areas, which leads to corresponding performance crashes. This is especially the case if – as during a mass change – all queues are filled with data and all queues are handled with maximum parallel processing. SAP's recommendation is that the **CPU: Idle (%)** value should not be lower than 20 % on average. To check the **CPU: Idle (%)** value of the last 24 hours, open Transaction ST06 and click the **Detail analysis menu button**. In the next window, in the area **Current data for selected server** in the sub area **Previous 24 hours**, click the **CPU** button (see Figure 13.9).

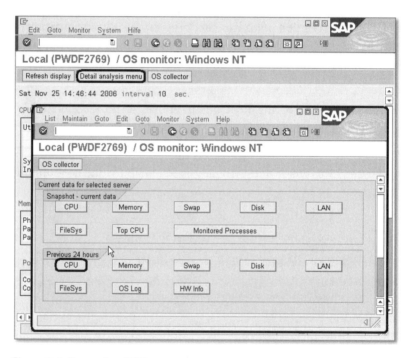

Figure 13.9 Transaction ST06

Figure 13.10 shows the CPU load of a system where a mass change was started between 6 and 7 o'clock (see column **Hour**). Until 6 o'clock, the system was almost idle (**CPU: Idle (%)** is higher than 85 %), but when the mass change was started, the system load initially increased to up to 70 % (**CPU: Idle (%)** went down to 30 %). Between 8 and 9 o'clock, the online users began to work; this further increased the system load and the **CPU: Idle (%)** value dropped to

7 %. Since this value is an average value over a period of one hour, we must assume that the actual CPU load was almost 100 % for an extended period and that performance bottlenecks arose. Counter-measures were taken between 10 and 11 o'clock, and from that point, the **CPU: Idle (%)** value swung between a value of 20 % and 25 %.

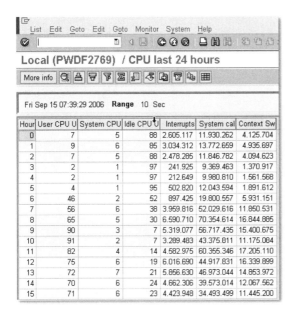

Hour	User CPU U	System CPU	Idle CPU U	Interrupts	System call	Context Sw
0	7	5	88	2.605.117	11.930.262	4.125.704
1	9	6	85	3.034.312	13.772.659	4.935.697
2	7	5	88	2.478.285	11.846.782	4.094.623
3	2	1	97	241.925	9.369.463	1.370.917
4	2	1	97	212.649	9.980.810	1.561.568
5	4	1	95	502.820	12.043.594	1.891.612
6	46	2	52	897.425	19.800.557	5.931.151
7	56	6	38	3.959.816	52.029.616	11.850.531
8	65	5	30	6.590.710	70.354.614	16.844.885
9	90	3	7	5.319.077	56.717.435	15.400.675
10	91	2	7	3.289.483	43.375.811	11.175.084
11	82	4	14	4.582.975	60.355.346	17.205.110
12	75	6	19	6.016.690	44.917.831	16.339.899
13	72	7	21	5.856.630	46.973.044	14.853.972
14	70	6	24	4.662.306	39.573.014	12.067.562
15	71	6	23	4.423.948	34.493.499	11.445.200

Figure 13.10 CPU Load Over the Last 24 Hours (Transaction ST06)

You can see the current CPU utilization in the start window of Transaction ST06 in the **CPU** area under **Utilization** (see Figure 13.11, top-left). The **Utilization** information in this transaction is only a snapshot, and in the standard setting, it is queried every 10 seconds by the OS collector. To display the most up-to-date value, click the **Refresh display** button. You should update the transaction a few times and examine the values to get an idea of the actual system load. Furthermore, just because you get a value of < 20 % once under **CPU: Idle (%)** doesn't necessarily mean you have an acute CPU bottleneck.

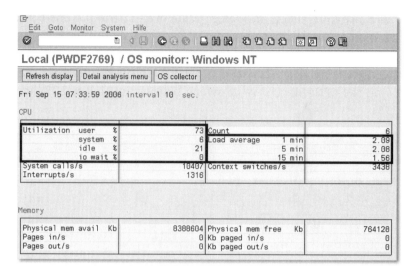

Figure 13.11 Current CPU Utilization (Transaction ST06)

Conclusions from the CPU demand of the last few minutes will give you the values **Load average 1 min, 5 min**, and **15 min** (see Figure 13.11, top-right). These values indicate how many processes (not only SAP work process) have had to wait for the CPU, on average, in the last minute, the last five minutes and the last 15 minutes.[5] In Figure 13.11, you can see that the system has the **Load average** values 2.09, 2.08, and 1.56. So in the last 15 minutes, an average of 1.56 processes have had to wait for the CPU. More processes had to wait during the last minute, namely an average of 2.09 processes. If you compare the values for the last minute with the values of the last five minutes, you can see that the wait time has increased moderately. This means that the CPU load in the last 15 minutes has increased, and continues to increase. Conversely, if the **Load average** value for the last minute is lower than the values for the last five or 15 minutes, this means that the CPU load has gone down in the last minute.

If you monitor the **Load average** values and the current **CPU: Idle (%)** value over a certain period (and factor in the **CPU: Idle (%)** value for the last 24 hours), you'll get an idea of the current utilization and whether it's rising, falling, or remaining constant, and also approxi-

---

5 Every second the system checks how many processes are in the "Ready" status (i.e., how many processes are waiting to be assigned processor time). Based on these numbers, the three average values are then calculated.

mately how high it is. If the **CPU: Idle (%)** value is below 20% and constant or around 20% and falling, you will need to take action.

Note that the CRM system may not necessarily be causing the CPU bottleneck. Other programs running on the server can generate the load that is crippling the CRM system. The information in Transaction ST06 relates to the server and not to an SAP instance.

Figure 13.12 displays the analysis roadmap for a CPU bottleneck. In this roadmap, we assume that the CRM system is causing the CPU bottleneck.

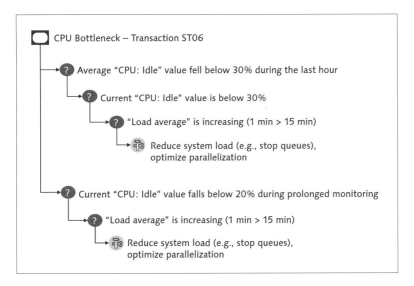

Figure 13.12 Roadmap for CPU Bottleneck Analysis

13.3.5 BDoc Error Analysis

If you monitor your CRM system regularly, during or after a mass change there should be no or few BDocs in an error or intermediate status.[6] Nevertheless, we recommend that you determine in Transaction SMW02 (or SMW02A) whether this is really the case during mass changes. Restrict the selection criteria in the field **BDoc Status** in Transaction SMW02 to the value "E*" (*Error*) and choose the start date/time of the mass change as your **Send date** and **Send time**, so that only the faulty BDocs are displayed. Aside from the faulty

---

6 As mentioned earlier, a successful functional test is a prerequisite for a successful mass change.

BDocs, you should also check how many BDocs are in the "I*" status (*Intermediate*). During a mass change, the number of BDocs in the *Intermediate* status is usually higher than it is in normal operation. But even during mass changes, the number should be constant to a certain degree. The BDocs, in particular, may not occupy the status "I*" beyond a certain period of time. If they do, you should run an error analysis.

If there is a fundamental problem (e.g., missing or faulty Customizing in the CRM system), you will be bombarded with hundreds or thousands of BDocs, with an error status that must be analyzed and processed. Depending on the error, the work involved may be considerable. Moreover, errors can quickly trigger follow-on errors. For instance, if business partners and business partner relationships are loaded from R/3 into CRM, the business partner relationship can only be successfully updated if the business partner has been successfully created (i.e., each BUPA_MAIN BDoc (business partner) in an error status can potentially cause a BUPA_REL BDoc (business partner relationship) in an error status).

If you discover a large number of faulty BDocs during a mass change, you should stop the mass change by stopping the corresponding R3A inbound queues and analyzing the errors. There are three possible cases after the error analysis:

1. You can ignore the error (for now) and continue with the mass change.

2. You can solve the error immediately and then continue with the mass change.

3. Because the data cannot be validated, it must be loaded again.

Case 3 is the most disastrous of all. The mass change was triggered in R/3 and ran successfully in R/3 or is still running. The data is written into the inbound queues of the CRM and is not processed or cannot be successfully processed. If you release the inbound queues again, the mass change does run, but you get thousands of faulty BDocs (and thus inconsistencies with R/3). If you delete the corresponding inbound queues, you also generate inconsistencies with R/3. In particular, it is possible that you may also delete data records that were not sent as part of the mass change to CRM, but instead were generated during everyday operations and are in the R3A inbound queues, dispersed among the data of the mass change. We cannot generally say which variant is better. In any case, you must eliminate the inconsistency with R/3. You may be able to request the data from R/3, re-run the mass change in R/3, or restart the BDocs again after making the necessary corrections.

Nevertheless, the best thing to do is not to allow this scenario to happen in the first place, and to test the processing of the mass change adequately beforehand.

13.4 Immediate Actions When Things Really Go Wrong

There is a range of problems that can arise during a mass change. Some of these problems are so critical that they can cause a complete system shutdown, or come close to a complete shutdown. We have selected the problems we have encountered most frequently during our work. We will describe these scenarios for you in the following sections and explain what actions you can take to stabilize the CRM system again.

13.4.1 A Performance Bottleneck Has Occurred in the CRM

When a performance bottleneck occurs, the first immediate action you can take is to completely or partially stop the processing of the mass change. You do this by stopping parts of the queue processing in the CRM Middleware. To quickly stop the entire mass change, you must stop the corresponding R3A inbound queues, CSA queues, and the R&R queues (see Figure 13.13). If you stop only the R3A inbound queues, this will also stop the mass change, but not immediately. It can still take a while until the CSA and R&R queues have been processed, and during this time, the load may remain at a very high level.

You can stop the processing of R3A and CSA queues by selecting a queue in Transaction SMQ2 and clicking the button with the glasses symbol (see the circled icon in Figure 13.14). In the next window, click the **Immediately** button and in the dialog box, enter the name of the queue or the queue group that you want to stop and confirm your entry (see Figure 13.14).

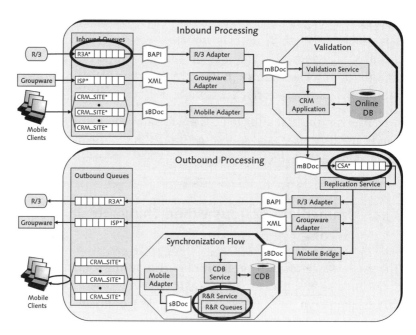

Figure 13.13 Queues for Stopping the Mass Change

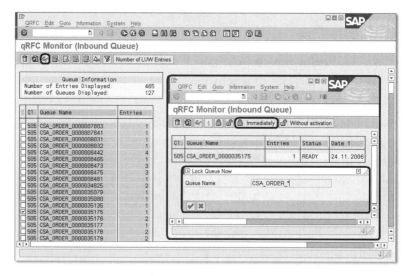

Figure 13.14 Stopping Inbound Queues (Transaction SMQ2)

If you want to stop entire queue groups, you can also deregister these in Transaction SMQR. To do this, in Transaction SMQR, click the **Deregistration** button, enter the name of the queue group in the dialog box, and confirm your entry (see Figure 13.15).

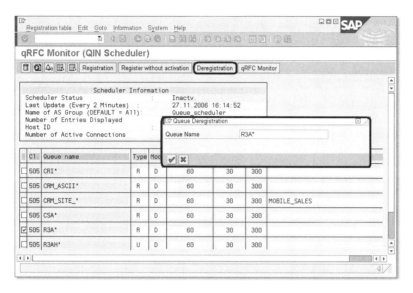

Figure 13.15 Deregistering Queues (Transaction SMQR)

Often all you need to do to relieve the load on the CRM system is to stop or slow down parts of the mass processing. The success of doing this will depend on what and how many inbound queues you stop and how the parallel processing of your system is set. The following example shows how you can control the load in the system by stopping and starting inbound queues.

Relieving the CRM system

> **Example**
>
> Data is loaded from an R/3 system with a package size of 500 into a CRM system with 50 dialog work processes. For the object that is changed, the R3A inbound queues are limited to five, and the CSA queues to 1,000. Due to the settings in the RFC server group, the inbound queue scheduler can occupy a maximum of 30 dialog work processes. For the mass change, this means that no more than five work processes can be occupied for processing the R3A inbound queues and no more than 25 for processing the CSA queues. Needless to say, the number reduces if R3A and CSA queues are created that have nothing to do with the mass change, but must nevertheless be processed by CRM. Based on the parameter settings, the R&R can be processed no more than five times in parallel.

The five R3A queues contain a few thousand entries awaiting their processing, but, on average, there are fewer than 100 CSA queues each only containing one entry. This is because the processing of the 500-sized blocks in the R3A queues takes longer than processing a CSA queue entry and the CSA queues are processed with a much higher level of parallel processing. The R&R queues contain several thousand entries. The CRM system processes the data with no problem, until the number of online users increases and a CPU bottleneck occurs. The CSA queues can no longer be updated as fast, and a number of them (i.e., the number of entries in the 1,000 queues) grows. As an immediate action, the five R3A inbound queues (containing the mass data) are stopped. This does increase the number of entries in the R3A queues, but no more CSA queues are generated. After a few minutes, the CSA queues are processed and the CPU bottleneck is resolved. Instead of changing the parameter settings in the CRM system, two of the five R3A inbound queues are restarted. Fewer CSA queues are created, so that the CRM system, despite the higher load caused by the online users, can process all of the queues at roughly the same speed as that at which they are created. If the load reduces again in the CRM system, more of the five R3A inbound queues can be started. If the load increases again, all five R3A inbound queues can be stopped. In this way, you can ensure that the data "flows" evenly through the CRM Middleware.

However, if a large number of CSA queues has already been created during the mass change, or if the CSA queues contain many entries, then stopping the R3A inbound queues might not bring any short-term relief. The following example illustrates just such a case.

Example

A mass change is executed in a CRM system with two application servers, each with 30 dialog work processes. Together, the REALIGN and EXTRACT queues of the R&R can be processed 10 times in parallel. The R&R and inbound queue processing are assigned to two different RFC server groups. The RFC server group for the inbound processing can occupy up to 20 work processes. The RFC server group of the R&R can occupy no more than 10 dialog work processes.

The number of R3A queues and CSA queues is limited to 100 in each case. Due to the high system utilization, the 100 CSA queues now contain over 10,000 entries, and the R&R queues contain over 20,000 entries. If all R3A inbound queues are stopped in this system, initially this only causes the existing CSA queues to be handled with a higher parallel processing level. The system load will decline, at the earliest, if the number of CSA queues falls below 18. But, if the REALIGN and EXTRACT queue are stopped in the system, this instantly reduces the system load because the application server is freed from the RFC load.

These two examples illustrate that there is no simple, universal rule for what queues you should stop. It always depends on the situation and the system. What is important is that you understand the interplay and the dependencies in the CRM Middleware, so you can respond optimally.

13.4.2 Performance Collapse During Inbound Queue Processing

Too many inbound queues

Several thousand inbound entries have appeared in the CRM system. The number keeps growing, and the performance of the inbound queue processing has collapsed. The cause for the deterioration in performance is probably the behavior of the inbound queue scheduler, which is described in detail in Chapter 8, *Inbound Queues* (i.e., the inbound queue scheduler's performance deteriorates considerably if there are a very large number of inbound queues). As an immediate response, you should prevent the number of inbound queues from continuing to grow at this rate. As long as the mass processing is running in R/3, there is no real way for you to prevent the number of R3A queues from continuing to increase (see Section 13.3.2). You can only prevent even more CSA queues from being created by stopping or deregistering the R3A queues (see Section 13.4.1). Now that the queues have been generated, they have to be processed. If there is a very high number of inbound queues, the performance of the inbound queue scheduler may be so poor that it is better not to use it and instead to start queues manually, in small groups. To do this, deregister the inbound queues (see Chapter 2, *Inbound Processing and Validation*). Then start a small group of queues by clicking the **Select Generic** button in Transaction SMQ2 and specifying the name of the queue group that you want to activate in the dialog box. Then, click the **Show Selected** button (see Figure 13.16).

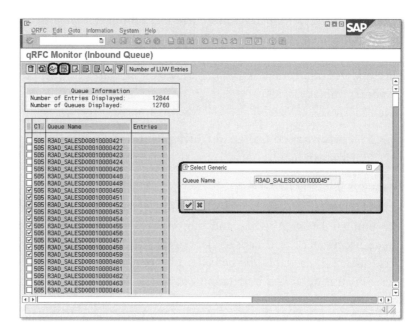

Figure 13.16 Manually Starting Inbound Queues (Transaction SMQ2)

In the new window, select the menu path **Edit • Generic queue • Acti-vate**. In the dialog box that appears, enter the name of the queue group and confirm your entry.

While this method does take time, it is sometimes faster than waiting until the scheduler has completed the job.

If the inbound queues have been processed, you should limit the number of these queues (see Chapter 8, *Inbound Queues*) and check the parallel processing setting in the middleware (see Section 13.1).

Very Large Inbound Queues

In your CRM system, you see a series of inbound queues, most of which have only a few entries; however, a few of the inbound queues generated by the mass change have many entries. If you observe how the inbound queues are processed, you'll notice that the performance of the inbound queue scheduler is good and that the system is working on the queues with maximum parallel process-ing. The only problem here is that the system is not permanently working on the large queues. Still, this would be necessary in order to complete the mass change.

To ensure that the system works longer on a queue, you can increase the **MAXTIME** parameter from 60 (standard value) to 600 (you'll find details on this in Chapter 2, *Inbound Processing and Validation*). To do this, open Transaction SMQR, select the queue whose parameter you want to change, click the **Registration** button, and enter the new value in the **MAXTIME** field (see Figure 13.17).

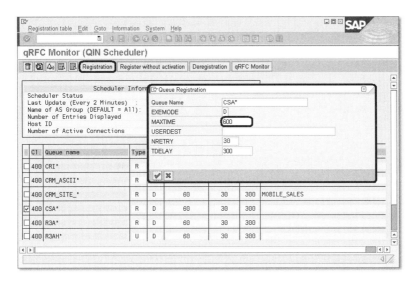

Figure 13.17 Changing the MAXTIME Parameter (Transaction SMQR)

13.4.3 Performance Collapse During Outbound Queue Processing – "ConnTrans Takes Forever!"

If several million entries have been written into the outbound queues as part of your mass change, it isn't surprising if writing into the outbound queues becomes slower, the performance of the outbound processing collapses, and it takes a very long time until ConnTrans has received the data from the server. We have described this phenomenon extensively in Chapter 10, *Outbound Queues*.

If not all data of the mass processing has been processed yet, as an immediate response, you should first stop the EXTRACT queue of the R&R. To do this, select the EXTRACT queue in Transaction SMOH-QUEUE and click the **Stop Queue** button (see Figure 13.18).

If no realignment is triggered by the data of the mass change (i.e., it isn't processed in the R&R queues), you should also stop or deregister the corresponding CSA queues (see Section 13.4.1). In this way,

353

you can prevent even more data from being written into the out-bound queues.

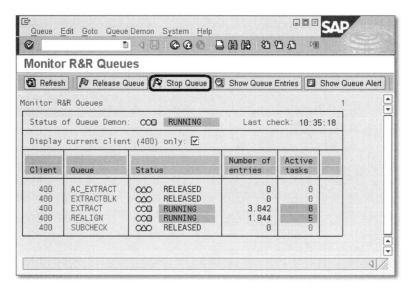

Figure 13.18 Stopping R&R Queues (Transaction SMOHQUEUE)

You must next reduce the number of entries in the outbound queues to a normal level. Unfortunately, there is no simple and fast solution for this. Essentially you have only two options.

Retrieving data via ConnTrans

The first solution is to collect the data via ConnTrans, even if it takes a very long time, possibly many hours. To not overload the CRM server, you should limit the number of mobile clients that collect their data in parallel. If possible, the mobile clients should dial in via LAN or DSL and not by modem. Modem connections are slow and keep getting interrupted. If the mobile client is connected in the LAN or by DSL, the user can start ConnTrans in the evening and just let it run overnight. As the number of entries in the outbound queues goes down, performance improves, and the ConnTrans times begin to normalize again. Nevertheless, the individual mobile clients have to collect very large amounts of data, which means that ConnTrans takes much longer than it would during normal operation, even if the system performance is normal.

Deleting data

The second solution is to delete the data in the outbound queues.

If you delete entire queues, you must then run an initial load for all affected mobile clients, because you have deleted not only the data for the mass change, but also the data that has been placed in the outbound queues during normal operation. You can delete individual or multiple queues using the RSTRFCQD report (see Figure 13.19). As the selection criterion, just enter the **Queue Name** (you can also use wildcards).

Leave the **Transaction ID** field empty. If you enter the value "*" in the field, all entries are deleted in all outbound queues.

You can use the **Package** parameter to define the package size by which a COMMIT WORK is executed.

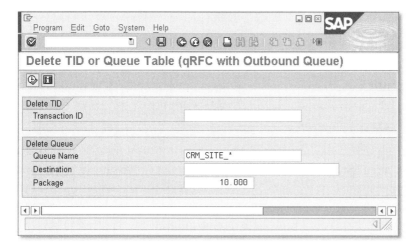

Figure 13.19 Deletion Report RSTRFCQD

It is better to delete only those entries that the mass change has created from the outbound queues. SAP Note 760113 describes the RSTRFCQDS report with which you can delete LUWs with a certain function module for various destinations from a queue (see Figure 13.20).

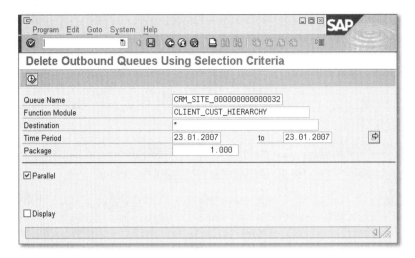

Figure 13.20 Deletion Report RSTRFCQDS

You also have the option of restricting the period during which the LUWs were written into the outbound queue, and of defining the package size by which the COMMIT WORK is executed, using the **Package** parameter.

The easiest way to find the name of the function module is to select a queue in Transaction SMQ1 and display it. In the window that opens, select the queue again and display it. A window opens, displaying the first and last eight LUWs of the outbound queue (see Figure 13.21). You'll find the name of the function module in the column of the same name.

Unfortunately, you can't use a generic name as the **Queue Name** in deletion report RSTRFCQDS; instead, you have to enter the complete, qualified name of the outbound queue. The report is therefore only suitable to a very limited extent for deleting LUWs in scores, if not hundreds, of outbound queues.

If you delete entries from the outbound queues, data inconsistencies occur. To correct the data inconsistency, you *must* start an AC extract for the deleted object type for all affected sites.

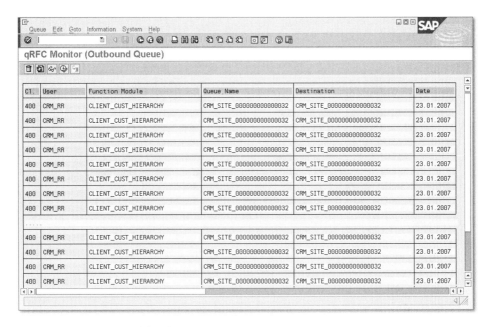

Figure 13.21 Function Module of an LUW (Transaction SMQ1)

The repeated adding and deleting of data records in the tables of the outbound queues rapidly leads to a high degeneration of the indexes. This has a negative impact on the performance of ConnTrans and the deletion report. Therefore, we recommend that you check the defragmentation of the indexes and rebuild them if necessary. These involve the following tables:

Degeneration of indexes

- ▸ TRFCQOUT
- ▸ ARFCSSTATE
- ▸ ARFCSDATA
- ▸ QREFTID

Once you have deleted the data from the outbound queues, you must decide how you want to continue with the mass processing, if this has not yet finished. Chapter 10, *Outbound Queues*, describes various ways for preventing a large number of entries from being written into the outbound queues. Alternatively, you can simply restart the queues again and use the deletion report. Still, you should do your utmost to prevent the number of entries in the outbound queues from becoming too big, because the performance of the deletion report also depends on the number of entries in the queues.

Once the mass change has been fully processed, you must, as already mentioned, fix the data inconsistency that has resulted. Before you start an AC extract, you need to check the packing factor in Table SMOFPARSFA and increase it if necessary (for more information on this subject, see Chapter 10, *Outbound Queues*). You must also determine how high the parallel processing of the AC_EXTRACT queue is set to, and adjust the value accordingly.

13.4.4 The CommStation Occupies All Work Processes

When the mobile clients collect their messages after a mass change, ConnTrans takes longer than normal because of the large volumes of data that must be collected. It is therefore not uncommon for the number of parallel ConnTrans sessions to be higher than normal, and for more work processes to be occupied by the CommStation (see Chapter 10, *Outbound Queues*). By setting up a logon group, you can prevent the CommStation from occupying all work processes of the CRM system, and you can do this simply by *reserving* an application server for the CommStation.

So far, this book has described what SAP CRM Middleware looks like today and how it can be optimized. In this chapter, we'll discuss potential improvements that could be implemented in the near future.

14 A Look Ahead

SAP is always working on improvements for its current products to better meet the various customer requirements. In the following sections, we'll describe anticipated improvements that are likely to be implemented in the areas of maintainability and performance, and introduce new developments in SAP NetWeaver that may be relevant to SAP CRM Middleware as well. Because the stability of solutions that are already being widely used in production systems must always take precedence over the potential side-effects of advanced developments, it is still uncertain whether the potential improvements discussed in this chapter (i.e., those that are primarily intended for customers with high data volumes) will be implemented in the CRM system. Although not all the details of intended optimizations have been defined yet, and it still isn't clear how they will be implemented, we believe it will be helpful to you for us to describe their basic principles to give you a look ahead into the near and more remote future of operating an SAP CRM solution. Not only are the intended enhancements supposed to be made available in future releases, but at least in part, also in SAP CRM Release 4.0 and Release 5.0. If you're interested in a project-specific pilot operation, please contact your Support representative. The Support staff can provide you with information about the current development status and availability of the different enhancements.

14.1 Improvements in R&R

As you have seen in Chapter 9, *Replication Model and R&R*, there are interdependencies between the individual Replication & Realign-

New queue model

ment (R&R) queues, which may lead to bottlenecks and must be accounted for when the queues are processed concurrently. For example, the value for parallel processing of the REALIGN queue must generally be twice as high as that of the EXTRACT queue. Regarding new features in SAP CRM, SAP intends to implement a new queue model that can be activated. If that is the case, the following queues will be available in R&R after activation:

▶ **SUBCHECK**
This queue will continue to be used only if a subscription is created or modified in the administration console.

▶ **AC_EXTRACT**
This queue will continue to be used during an AC extraction that is carried out via the administration console.

▶ **REALIGN**
This queue will continue to contain the data that is used for receiver determination, but it will be used for a smaller amount of data because parts of that data will be processed through a new queue.

▶ **DEPENDENCY**
This new queue will contain dependent objects for the data in the REALIGN queue.

▶ **EXTRACT**
As before, this queue will contain the data after the receivers have been determined.

▶ **EXTRACTBLK**
This queue will continue to be used for bulk objects.

As you can see, the only major change consists of the implementation of a new queue. What will the benefits of this be?

Advantages As you've seen in Chapter 3, *Outbound Processing*, and Chapter 9, *Replication Model and R&R*, once the data has been written into the REALIGN queue, the system determines dependent data, for instance, via interlinkages. In the old model, the complete replication service, including receiver determination, must be carried out for this data (i.e., the dependent data is also written into the REALIGN queue). However, as the name *dependent data* suggests, this data is directly related to the outbound data; in other words, it is sent to the same receivers as the original data. For this reason, it isn't necessary to run another complete receiver determination process for this data in the REALIGN queue. This aspect is taken into consideration by the new DEPENDENCY queue (see Figure 14.1). The new queue is responsible for determining the receivers of dependent data while taking into account existing dependencies. As a result, the quantity of data written into the REALIGN queue is smaller and the queue can be processed faster. In this way, during mass changes, data created by other tasks will be forwarded faster into the outbound queue, instead of having the new, important data reside in the REALIGN queue for an extraordinarily long period of time. Furthermore, the load that is placed on the hardware resources will be reduced, because fewer processing steps need to be carried out in R&R.

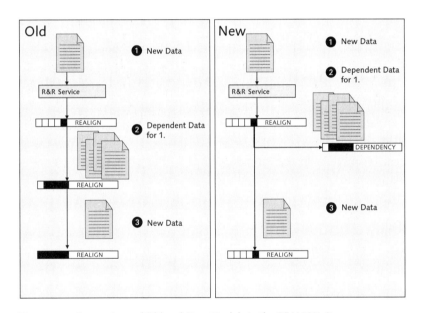

Figure 14.1 Comparison of Old and New Models in the REALIGN Queue

14.1.1 Effects on the Parallelization Process Caused by the New Framework

As described in Section 9.3, not all the R&R queues can be processed in parallel. The new queue framework enables you to parallelize all queues without any restriction. In order to configure parallel processing, the following abbreviations are available in the PARNAME2 field of Table SMOFPARSFA for the RRS_COMMON key (PARS-

Configuring parallelization

FAKEY field) and parameter name RRQUEUE_PARALLEL (PAR-NAME field):

- SU for the subcheck queue
- RE for the realignment queue
- RD for the dependency queue
- EB for the extract bulk queue
- EX for the extract queue
- AC for the AC_Extract queue

As before, you can specify the maximum number of processes to be used for the parallel processing of the respective queue in the PARVAL1 field. In general, the number of processes used should be less than 10, but again you should consider the current purpose of the SAP CRM system and, if necessary, parallelize a bigger number of processes, provided the system resources allow for that. Once you have switched your system to the new queue framework, we recommend that you set up parallel processing for the new dependency queue (RD) in addition to the existing parallelizations. As a general ballpark figure, you should start with making five parallel processes available to all queues; however, this depends on the available system resources and the intended usage of the CRM system (see Section 9.3).

14.1.2 Processing Queue Entries in Blocks

Under certain circumstances, the new queue framework can process the queue entries in *blocks*. In this context, a block may only contain data of one object type, as is the case in AC extracts as well. Since it often happens that different object types are mixed within the queues, the configured block size cannot always be fully utilized. You can configure a block-based processing of queues by using new entries in the central Middleware maintenance table SMOFPARSFA. You can store these entries for the RRS_COMMON key (PARSFAKEY field). If no individual parameters are maintained, the default setting will be used, which depends on the respective queue. If additional tasks occur during the processing of a block (such as the determination of dependent data in the dependency queue), these tasks are also forwarded in aggregated form to the subsequent services. This means that if you configure an individual block size for the REALIGN queue (e.g., for mass changes to be carried out), this block size may also reduce the number of subsequent orders in downstream queues.

As you have seen in Chapter 9, *Replication Model and R&R*, and Chapter 10, *Outbound Queues*, the calculation and distribution of dependent data can result in an extremely high number of queue entries. For this reason, we will describe further improvements at this point, which are caused by a block-based processing of the DEPENDENCY queue. For this queue, you can define the block sizes for the calculation by using two parameters in Table SMOFPARSFA for the RRS_COMMON key: a read access parameter and a write access parameter. You can enter the block size for the dependency calculation for both the read and write access in the PARVAL1 field. In addition, another object-specific entry in the PARNAME2 field might be made possible in the future. This field will then enable you to specify the BDoc type for which you want to define an exception.

DEPENDENCY queue

The read access parameter defines the number of parent entries that are supposed to be read in a block of the dependency queue, whereas the write access parameter specifies the number of dependent entries that are supposed to be rewritten into the queue for further processing once a parent block has been processed. Thus, if you enter a value in the SMOFPARSFA entries via PARNAME2, the specified type refers to the type of the parent object in the case of a read access, whereas in a write access, it refers to the type of the dependent object.

> **Example**
>
> At the BGS company, the activities depend on the customers. To calculate this dependency, the service department is provided with a list of customer-site assignments, based on which it calculates a list of activity-site assignments. In the event of a distribution-relevant mass change of the complete customer base, the list would contain 500,000 entries, because each of the 50 field sales representatives is assigned 100 customers via the ZIP code. The question as to how many customer-site assignments are included in one internal processing block is answered by the read access parameter. If the block size configured for this parameter was 5,000, the list would be processed in 100 blocks, consisting of 5,000 entries each, instead of a step-by-step processing of 500,000 individual entries. Now, let's suppose that 10 activities exist for each customer. This means that the first processing block has 50,000 dependent entries.

> These dependent entries are then forwarded to subsequent processes in blocks whose size is specified in the write access parameter. For example, if the block size were set to 10,000, five blocks containing 10,000 each would have to be processed.

Packet size

The new queue framework considers the maximum packet size not only in AC extracts, but also in all new R&R processes that involve a block-based extraction of data. For example, if a dependency calculation leads you to conclude that 100 instances must be sent to the same site, the system will no longer dispatch 100 individual messages (as it used to do); instead, it will dispatch two blocks of 50 messages each (in the default setting). Even the extractions carried out by the data collector (see Chapter 9, *Replication Model and R&R*) take into account this packet size. This automatic creation of blocks will certainly solve some of the problems described in Section 10.2 and subsequent sections.

14.2   BDoc Merge

The BDoc merge function is an improvement in the mobile client's framework, not within the CRM Middleware itself. But, because it has a direct affect on reducing the load for the Middleware, we included this topic in this book.

Generating multiple sBDocs on the client

In the current design of the mobile client application, a synchronization BDoc (sBDoc) is generated every time the user saves a new data status. In particular, this happens whenever the user changes to a new tile set. This means that a particularly large number of sBDocs is generated when a user edits an object in multiple steps. Then, all these individual sBDocs containing different delta information about the same object instance are transferred to the CRM Server and must be processed in CRM Middleware, although, strictly speaking, one sBDoc containing the final status would suffice.

If the end user creates an opportunity in the mobile sales application, he would typically start by entering the header information. Then, he must go to a different tile set in order to store information about other colleagues involved and save the current status. During this change to the different tile set, the system creates the first sBDoc of the type, OPPORTUNITY_WRITE. Then the user wants to add product-related information to this opportunity, which might be of interest to the customer. To do that, he accesses another tile set, and once again, an sBDoc is generated when the data is saved. Finally, the user saves the opportunity, and the system generates a final BDoc.

Thus, a total of three sBDocs of the OPPORTUNITY_WRITE type are generated in this example instead of only one sBDoc. Consequently, the load increase on the CRM Server is significant, because the flow processing must be carried out for each BDoc. If the data was already aggregated on the client, the load could be reduced by approximately two thirds. The planned new function will now enable the combination of multiple sBDoc messages in the BDoc layer of the mobile client into a single message, which will then be the only sBDoc message to be sent. Of course, combination is only possible under certain circumstances (e.g., the sBDocs in the memory must have the same root GUID), so that an improvement by two thirds is a rather theoretical value. Nevertheless, we can expect a significant reduction in the number of sBDocs.

In addition to that, the number of BDocs generated on the CRM Server is also "too high." In the current design, two BDoc messages are returned to the sender of the message: a confirmation that the data has been processed accurately and the same message again as a result of the R&R process. Because the mobile client that had originally sent the message is usually also a valid receiver of the message content, the message will be sent by the R&R process to this mobile client, along with all the other recipients. In this context, SAP plans to implement a way to dispatch only the confirmation based on the sBDoc type via a Customizing entry.

Generating too many BDocs on the server

14.3 Changes in the Administration Console

If a large number of sites and different subscriptions must be maintained, the administration console can quickly become unclear and confusing, so that changes that affect the selection of available objects can be very time-consuming. For this reason, SAP is planning several functional enhancements in this area so as to reduce the necessary maintenance work. For example, with regard to object mappings or the selection of sites in the administration console, it has been very difficult up until now to find the required objects in the

Maintenance efforts

list on the left-hand side of the console. To make this process more efficient, the administration console will probably be complemented with additional filters that allow you to restrict the hit list by using specific criteria. For example, regarding the object type, *site*, it will then be possible to filter subscriptions by subscription values when you assign subscriptions.

Bulk activation and deactivation

It is already possible to activate and deactivate mobile clients (or rather the respective sites) in bulks via reports (see Chapter 9, *Replication Model and R&R*). This function will be better integrated into the administration console and complemented with additional filter options in order to enable the improved compilation of site lists for a block-based site deactivation. These deactivation processes will be logged, along with time and user data, to make it easier to reactivate the respective sites in a single step at a later stage (see Figure 14.2).

Deactivating replication objects

Whereas up until now, it has only been possible to deactivate sites either entirely or not at all, it may sometimes be necessary to deactivate only certain replication objects of a site. For this reason, SAP will probably provide a function that enables you to temporarily stop the distribution of specific object types, while all other object types will continue to be replicated. If the download of such a "deactivated" object type is reactivated, extracts will be triggered for the object type in question (as is the case in a standard deactivation of a site), should changes have occurred during the period in which the object type was deactivated (see Chapter 9, *Replication Model and R&R*).

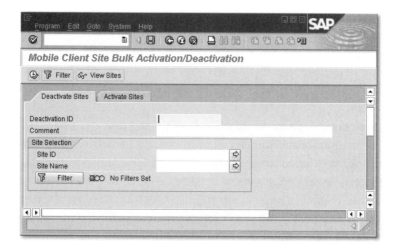

Figure 14.2 Filter for Deactivating Mobile Client Sites

14.4 bgRFC

As described in Chapter 10, *Outbound Queues*, performance problems may occur in *queued Remote Function Calls* (qRFC) if a large number of entries exist in the outbound queues. To lessen the likelihood of this happening in the runtime behavior, SAP developed the *background RFC* (bgRFC), which should be based on the same protocol as the qRFC. The modified design ensures that mass data, which contains strong sequence dependencies, can be processed more efficiently. It also ensures that each entry is processed exactly once (i.e., *transactional RFC*, tRFC), or exactly once in the correct order.

Both the bgRFC and the classic qRFC will be available in SAP NetWeaver in the future. Note, however, that the two processes cannot be combined. Therefore, there must be a way to distinguish which process is used and when. Regarding outbound scenarios, starting with SAP NetWeaver 7.0 (formerly known as SAP NetWeaver 2004s), it will be possible to store the information according to which process is used in the destination section. However, this means that all transactions that use qRFCs must either be switched to the new bgRFC process or continue to use the old process.

In the classic qRFC model, dependencies between individual queue entries are not determined until the data is actually processed. In order to determine these dependencies, the outbound scheduler starts a destination scheduler for each destination. This destination scheduler processes the data for a specific destination. However, the destination schedulers are only active on the destinations for a certain period of time to ensure the equal distribution of processes among all destinations. For this reason, the destination scheduler has to determine the sequence of the processes prior to each destination processing, because new dependencies may have been created during the period in which a destination has been processed. But, the determination of dependencies can be very time-consuming, particularly if the outbound queues contain large numbers of entries, which may lead to a decrease of the data throughput (see Chapter 10, *Outbound Queues*). The new bgRFC can determine the dependencies already when the data is stored. This means that the dependencies need to be determined only once, and it is easier for the queue scheduler to find the data to be sent. This new design involves a cer-

Determining
dependencies

tain shift of the workload away from the processing of queues towards the writing of queue entries; but the additional effort involved in the storage of data is more or less compensated by efficient algorithms and further optimizations in the database design.

For each client, several outbound schedulers are started for the bgRFC, which jointly carry out the tasks to be done. In addition, the new RFC schedulers will be better able to respond to the load on the destination systems since the information required for an efficient load distribution will be updated more frequently. Like the improvements of the actual CRM Middleware described in Sections 14.1 and 14.2, the improvements introduced by the new design will primarily take effect under conditions of high load, with many dependent entries per destination. This is because SAP didn't intend to improve the processing of individual entries, but rather wanted to establish a linear scalability for processing RFC data.

Switching the SAP CRM Middleware from one RFC to another would entail a great deal of work and represents a fundamental change. For this reason, it is not yet clear when and whether CRM Middleware will actually use the bgRFC.

Our brief Middleware overview once again provides the most important terms, components, and processes, as they exist in SAP CRM Middleware.

A   SAP CRM Middleware at a Glance

In an integrated system landscape, data is exchanged between different systems, particularly between the CRM system and other systems. SAP CRM Middleware connects the CRM application with other systems, such as an R/3 system, a Groupware server, and mobile clients. CRM Middleware ensures that data, which is entered or modified in the CRM system, gets replicated to all interested systems and that data, which originates from the other systems, is received and updated in the CRM system.

A.1   The Flow

The flow of messages through the CRM system is referred to as the *flow*. Controlling the flow is a central task of the CRM Server. In this context, we must distinguish between two types of flow:

Message flow

▶ The *messaging flow* is an infrastructure for the transfer of data to the CRM application and for processing data that originates from the CRM application.

▶ The *synchronization flow* is an infrastructure that's used for the exchange of messages between the CRM Server, mobile devices, mobile clients, and Groupware servers.

The different data formats of these two types of message flow are converted into each other via mapping functions.

A.2 Inbound and Outbound Processing

The flow is divided into two major parts (see Figure A.1):

▶ **Inbound Processing**
In inbound processing, data is processed that is sent from other systems to the CRM Server.

▶ **Outbound Processing**
In outbound processing, data is processed that is sent from the CRM Server to other systems.

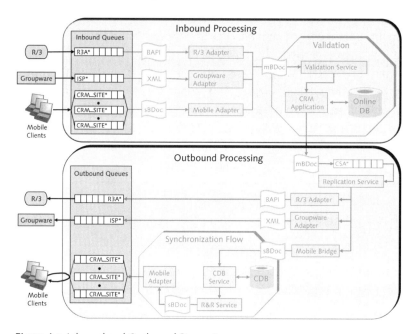

Figure A.1 Inbound and Outbound Processing

Using queues — The use of *queues* in inbound and outbound processing ensures that different steps are isolated from each other:

1. *Inbound queues* collect the data that is sent from other systems to the CRM Server. This way, the processing of data that originates from other systems is decoupled from the inbound processing, which is carried out in the CRM Server.

2. *CSA queues* collect the data that is replicated to interested systems once inbound processing has finished. This way, inbound processing is separated from outbound processing.

3. *Outbound queues* collect the data that is sent from the CRM Server to other systems. This way, the processing of data that originates from the CRM Server is decoupled from the data processing process carried out in other systems.

Inbound queues and CSA queues are based on inbound qRFC, while outbound queues are based on outbound qRFC with receiver list.

A.3   BDocs

Within SAP CRM Middleware, data is transported in *BDocs* (*Business Documents*), which are containers for business-related data (see Figure A.2). We distinguish between different types of BDocs:

▸ *mBDocs* (*messaging BDocs*) are used to transport data in the messaging flow.

▸ *sBDocs* (*synchronization BDocs*) are used to transport data in the synchronization flow.

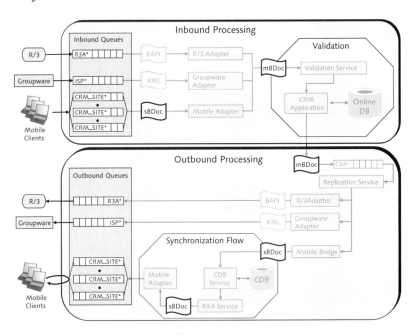

Figure A.2 BDocs in SAP CRM Middleware

A.4   Adapters and Services

BDocs are processed by *adapters* and *services* (see Figure A.3). The following adapters and services are available in inbound processing:

- ▶ Inbound adapters convert data from the inbound queues into mBDocs and make these mBDocs available to the flow.

- ▶ Validation services check whether data that is sent from other systems to the CRM Server meets the requirements of the respective CRM application and whether the data can be stored in the online database of the CRM Server.

The following adapters and services are available in outbound processing:

- ▶ The replication service determines the receivers of an mBDoc and makes the data available to the respective outbound adapters.

- ▶ Mobile bridges are services that map an mBDoc to one or several sBDocs.

- ▶ CDB services are responsible for updating the *consolidated database (CDB)*, which contains all data that can be sent to mobile clients.

- ▶ The R&R service determines the mobile clients that are supposed to receive an sBDoc, and makes the data available to the mobile outbound adapter.

- ▶ Outbound adapters receive data from the flow, convert this data into a different format, if necessary, and then write it into outbound queues so that it can be sent to other systems.

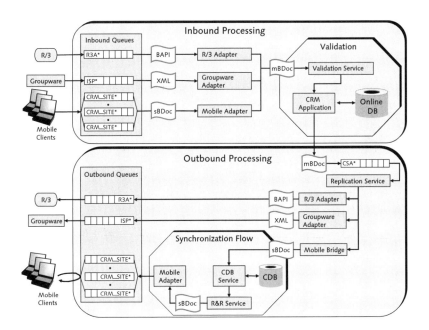

B   Glossary

.NET   Platform developed by Microsoft with the objective to develop programs that are independent of the system they are running on and of the programming language.

.NET Connector   Successor to the DCOM Connector, based on .NET.

ABAP   Advanced Business Application Programming. Programming language developed and frequently used by SAP.

AC extract   An AC extract reads data from the CDB and writes this data into an outbound queue. The AC extract can be started in the administration console.

Adapter   In SAP CRM, adapters are responsible for assigning and converting data.

Adapter object   Adapter objects define how business objects and business data are supposed to be exchanged via adapters by linking the BDoc type, flow context, filters, and function modules with each other. The block size parameter in the adapter object defines the number of BDocs that can be concurrently processed through one BAPI.

Administration console   The administration console is the primary tool for maintaining SAP CRM Middleware. The administration console can be used to edit sites, publications, replication objects, and subscriptions.

aRFC   Asynchronous RFC

BAPI   Business Application Programming Interface. BAPIs are specific RFC-enabled function modules with defined and guaranteed properties.

BAPIMTCS   Transfer structure between R/3 and CRM

BDoc   Business Document. A BDoc is a document that contains information about changes to a business object. BDocs are used to exchange and process data in a CRM solution. There are different classes of BDocs available.

BDoc Modeler   The BDoc Modeler allows users to create and modify BDoc definitions.

BDoc instance   A *BDoc instance* is an actual representation of a BDoc type. The BDoc instance contains the field values.

BDoc class   The SAP CRM system contains two classes of BDocs: *synchronization BDocs* (sBDocs) and *messaging BDocs* (mBDocs). sBDocs are exchanged with mobile clients, for example, via the synchronization layer. mBDocs were introduced in SAP CRM Release 3.0 and are exchanged through the messaging layer.

BDoc message   See *BDoc*

BDoc status   Status of a BDoc. The following statuses are possible:

- I01 – received (intermediate status)
- I02 – written to qRFC queue
- I03 – after qRFC step
- T01 – temporary lack of resources in application layer
- F01 – rejected (processing completed)
- F02 – confirmed (processing completed)
- F03 – set to "processed" (processing completed)
- F04 – confirmed (processed by all receivers)
- F05 – information (no processing)
- E01 – technical error (incomplete)
- E02 – partly sent
- E03 – cannot read BDoc from DB
- E04 – BDoc validation error
- O01 – send to receiver

BDoc type The BDoc type describes the structure of a business object. Business objects contain all relevant fields that describe an object, such as a business partner.

BTE Business Transaction Event. Business transaction events are an enhancement technology based on so-called *publish* & *subscribe* interfaces.

Bulk replication The bulk replication is the simplest replication model in SAP CRM. In a bulk replication, objects are replicated to the receivers without any filtering of their contents and only on the basis of the BDoc type.

CDB Consolidated Data Base. The CDB contains all data that can be replicated to the mobile clients.

Code page A code page represents the mapping of a character set to bit strings. The most commonly known code pages are Latin 1, which contains all characters of the Western European languages, and Unicode, which can represent all characters used in all languages of the world.

CommStation Communication station. The CommStation is based on the DCOM Connector or the .NET Connector. It receives data from the mobile clients. The DCOM Connector converts the data before it is sent to the CRM Server (and vice versa).

Communication monitor The communication monitor is used to monitor the data exchange between the CommStation and the CRM Server. It provides details about individual sessions, as well as overviews of statistical data.

CRM Customer Relationship Management. A concept that describes the maintenance of all aspects of customer relationships. SAP's CRM system, for example, provides various functions such as Mobile Sales, Internet Sales, and a Call Center, which can access a single, central customer view.

DCOM Distributed Component Object Model. A protocol defined by Microsoft that is used for the communication of different programs through a network.

DCOM Connector The DCOM Connector is a component of the CommStation. It works as an interface between the Microsoft world and the ABAP world by translating *Remote Function Calls* (RFCs) into DCOM components and vice versa.

DDIC The Data Dictionary is the central metadata repository of SAP NetWeaver Application Server.

Delta load Transfer of data changes (delta) between, for example, CRM and R/3 or CRM and mobile clients; not all values of an object instance are transferred in a delta load, but only those that have been modified. If possible, the delta load is activated automatically after an initial load.

Download Transfer of data from the backend into the CRM system, or from the CRM system into the mobile clients.

Extract 1: Name of a queue in R&R: EXTRACT queue. 2: Process of extracting data.

ERP Enterprise Resource Planning. ERP describes the planning of resources of an enterprise in order to use the resources as efficiently as possible in business processes. Today, ERP is usually carried out in an ERP system such as SAP R/3.

Filter Option to reduce the scope of data distribution between the systems of a CRM solution in the Middleware on the basis of specific application data.

Flow definition The flow definition controls the route of individual BDocs through the Middleware. Flow definitions can be displayed and edited via Transaction SMO8FD.

Flow context The flow context defines a sequence of services that are carried out during the processing of a BDoc message.

GWA_01 Special variant of the Groupware adapter, which exchanges data only with the public folder of the Groupware solution. In contrast to GWA_02, GWA_01 uses mBDocs.

GWA_02 Special variant of the Groupware adapter, which exchanges data also with private folders of the Groupware solution. In contrast to GWA_01, GWA_02 uses sBDocs.

GUID Globally Unique Identifier. Automatically generated, globally unique ID of an object.

ICalendar Commonly used format for exchanging calendar and date information through the Internet.

Inbound adapter The inbound adapter reads data from the inbound queues and generates mBDocs from this data.

Inbound processing In inbound processing, inbound data is converted into mBDocs and updated in the online database.

Inbound queue See *Queue*

Initial load Initial import of data. In this context, a distinction is made between loading data from the backend to the CRM Server, loading data from the CRM online database to the CDB, and the initial loading of data into the mobile clients.

Intelligent replication Selective distribution of BDocs to selected receivers based on defined criteria. In this context, a distinction must be made between a single intelligent replication with mBDocs and an intelligent replication with sBDocs. A single intelligent replication can only occur on the basis of the application-dependent address part (envelope) of the mBDoc, whereas in the case of sBDocs, the receivers can be selected by accessing the entire content.

Interlinkage Free links between different intelligently replicated

BDocs. Interlinkages are very flexible; however, they bear the risk of being recursively linked.

ISP Internal SyncPoint. Combination of MapBox, Groupware adapter, and the general messaging interface of the Middleware.

Java Connector (JCo) The Java Connector establishes the connection between ABAP and Java programs on SAP NetWeaver Application Server.

Lookup tables Lookup tables are used in R&R and contain information as to which object instances were or are supposed to be replicated to which sites.

LUW Logical Unit of Work. A logically indivisible sequence of database operations that should either be processed altogether or not at all.

mBDoc Messaging BDoc. See *BDoc class*

Middleware portal Commonly used short name for *CRM Middleware Monitoring Cockpit.* The Middleware portal provides status information and can be used for navigation purposes in SAP CRM Middleware. The Middleware portal enables users to access important monitoring and administration transactions in SAP CRM Middleware.

Mobile bridge The mobile bridge converts mBDocs into sBDocs.

Mobile client 1: A PC (notebook or desktop PC) on which the CRM Field Sales or Field Service application is installed. 2: Specific site type in the administration console that is used for the MSA and MSE scenarios (or FSA and FSE scenarios respectively).

Outbound adapter The outbound adapter converts data from the mBDoc format into a format that corresponds to the respective receiver of the message.

Outbound processing In outbound processing, BDoc messages are transferred to the outbound adapter or synchronization flow and then written to the outbound queues once the receivers have been determined.

Outbound queue See *Queue*

PLIF Payload Interface. Provides the technical options for exchanging data with external systems in a Groupware integration scenario.

Publication A publication is used to provide one or several replication objects for subscription.

qRFC RFC with a queue ("queued" RFC). The queued RFC is an enhancement of the tRFC, which, in addition to the transactionally correct processing, ensures that the data is processed in the sequence in which it was written to the queue.

Queue Business data that is requested via the qRFC method is supposed to be processed sequentially, that is, in the order in which the requests were received. To ensure that this requirement is met, queues are generated to store the data temporarily and to process it in sequence. Queues exist for inbound and outbound data.

Queue monitor The queue monitor enables users to monitor RFC queues. The CRM system contains different monitors: the inbound monitor (Transaction SMQ1) for monitoring inbound queues, the outbound monitor (Transaction SMQ2) for monitoring outbound queues, and the R&R monitor for monitoring the R&R.

Replication & Realignment
Receiver determination and replication of data to the receivers that have been determined. Replication & Realignment is also referred to as R&R.

Replication object   A replication object specifies BDoc types according to their replication type, based on which the BDoc type is exchanged.

Request   Explicit request in the CRM system for data from another system.

RFC   Remote Function Call. RFCs are used to execute code from a computer (client) on another machine (server). The function calls can be *synchronous* (sRFC) or *asynchronous* (aRFC). Enhancements of RFCs, which are used in the CRM environment, are *queued* RFCs (qRFC) and *transactional* RFCs (tRFC).

R&R   See *Replication & Realignment*

RFC Software Development Kit (SDK)   The SAP RFC SDK enables users to communicate with an SAP system from within their own, external applications through an RFC connection. The current version is available for download from SAP Service Marketplace.

SAP NetWeaver Application Server   Successor to the SAP R/3 Basis system. SAP NetWeaver Application Server provides both an ABAP and a Java runtime environment. For a certain period of time, it was referred to as SAP Web Application Server (Web AS).

sBDoc   Synchronization BDoc. See *BDoc class*

Scheduler   The CRM system contains two basic schedulers: the outbound scheduler and the inbound scheduler. The inbound scheduler must be configured on the basis of queue names. It controls the processing of inbound queues. The configuration of the outbound scheduler is based on the logical destination. The outbound scheduler is responsible for sending the LUWs in the outbound queues.

Service   1: From the Middleware perspective: A module of SAP CRM Middleware that processes BDoc messages. A combination of multiple services defines the flow context. 2: From the application perspective (mobile service or CRM online): A service for the customer.

Single intelligent replication   See *Intelligent replication*

Site   CRM Middleware term for the receiver or sender of data. Each site is assigned to a specific site type (e.g., GWA_01 or mobile client), which defines specific properties of the site.

Statistics   The statistics about the size and indexes of database tables is used by the *cost-based optimizers* (CBO) of database systems to identify the ideal execution path. Old and inaccurate statistics are a frequent cause of performance degradation in the area of SAP CRM Middleware.

Subscription   A subscription is used to control the distribution of data based on a publication. Only receivers (sites) that have subscribed to the relevant subscription will receive the corresponding data records.

Transaction 1: A sequence of operations that should either be carried out completely or not at all. 2: Commonly used term in the SAP environment for starting program flows via a transaction code.

tRFC Transactional RFC. If transactional RFC calls are used, a transaction ID ensures that the data is processed exactly once. The advantage of a tRFC is that it ensures transactional security and that duplicate updates of data in the server system are avoided. The important aspect about tRFCs is that the data doesn't need to be processed sequentially.

Upload Transfer of data from the mobile clients to the CRM Server and from the CRM system to the backend.

Validation The validation process checks the data to be saved for validity and accuracy based on the application logic.

vCard Standard for electronic business cards that can be edited by common Groupware solutions.

Web AS See *SAP NetWeaver Application Server*

XML Extensible Markup Language. XML is a subset of the SGML standard and has established itself as a standard for the structured description of information. You can find the current XML specification on the website of the World Wide Web Consortium (W3C) at *www.w3.org/XML*.

C Transactions and Menu Paths

Transaction Code	Short Description
	Menu Path
FIBF	Edit BTEs
R3AC1	(Adapter Settings for) Business Objects
	Architecture and Technology • Middleware • Data Exchange • Object Management
R3AC3	(Adapter Settings for) Customizing Objects
	Architecture and Technology • Middleware • Data Exchange • Object Management
R3AC5	(Adapter Settings for) Condition Objects
	Architecture and Technology • Middleware • Data Exchange • Object Management
R3AC6	Define Middleware Parameters
	Architecture and Technology • Middleware • Administration
R3AM1	Monitor Objects
	Architecture and Technology • Middleware • Monitoring • Data Exchange
R3AR3	Monitor Requests
	Architecture and Technology • Middleware • Monitoring • Data Exchange
R3AR4	Start Requests
	Architecture and Technology • Middleware • Data Exchange • Synchronization
R3AS	Start (Initial Load)
	Architecture and Technology • Middleware • Data Exchange • Initial Load
RZ12	RFC Server Group Maintenance
SBDM	BDoc Modeler
	Architecture and Technology • Middleware • Development • Meta Object Modeling

Transaction Code	Short Description
	Menu Path
SDIMA	Data Integrity Manager
	Architecture and Technology • Middleware • Data Exchange • Synchronization
SE16	Data Browser
	Architecture and Technology • ABAP Workbench • Overview
SE38	ABAP Editor
	Architecture and Technology • ABAP Workbench • Development
SM50	Process Overview
	Architecture and Technology • System Administration • Monitor • System Monitoring
SM66	Global Process Overview
	Architecture and Technology • System Administration • Monitor • Performance • Exceptions/Users • Active Users
SM59	RFC Destinations
	Architecture and Technology • System Administration • Administration • Network
SMO8FD	Display and Check Flow Definitions
	Architecture and Technology • Middleware • Message Flow
SMOEAC	Administration Console
	Architecture and Technology • Middleware • Administration
SMOECK	Check Replication Relevant Objects
	Architecture and Technology • Middleware • Development • Checks
SMOHQUEUE	Monitor R&R Queue
	Architecture and Technology • Middleware • Monitoring • Queues
SMQ1	Display Outbound RFC Queues
	Architecture and Technology • Middleware • Monitoring • Queues
SMQ2	Display Inbound RFC Queues
	Architecture and Technology • Middleware • Monitoring • Queues
SMQR	Register / Deregister inbound Queues
	Architecture and Technology • Middleware • Administration
SMQS	Register / Deregister Outbound Queues

Transaction Code	Short Description
	Menu Path
SMW01	Display BDoc Messages
	Architecture and Technology • Middleware • Monitoring • Message Flow
SMW02	Display BDoc Message Summary
	Architecture and Technology • Middleware • Monitoring • Message Flow
SMW02a	BDoc Message Error Analysis
	Architecture and Technology • Middleware • Monitoring • Message Flow
SMW03	Display Unprocessed BDoc Messages Summary
	Architecture and Technology • Middleware • Monitoring • Message Flow
SMW3FDBDOC	Define BDoc Type Specific Flow
	Architecture and Technology • Middleware • Development • Message Flow
SMW3FDCUST	Define Customer-Specific Flow
	Architecture and Technology • Middleware • Development • Message Flow
SMW3FDIF	Define BDoc Type Specific Flow Attributes
	Architecture and Technology • Middleware • Development • Message Flow
SMW3WD	Detect Aborted BDoc Messages
	Architecture and Technology • Middleware • Message Flow
SMWMCOMM	Communication Monitor
	Architecture and Technology • Middleware • Monitoring • Mobile Client
SMWMFLOW	Display Message Flow Statistics
	Architecture and Technology • Middleware • Monitoring • Message Flow
SMWMQUEUES	Display Mobile Site Queue Information
	Architecture and Technology • Middleware • Monitoring • Queues
SMWMSCHED-ULER	Display qRFC Scheduler Information
	Architecture and Technology • Middleware • Monitoring • Queues

Transaction Code	Short Description
	Menu Path
SMWP	Monitoring Cockpit
	Architecture and Technology • Middleware • Monitoring • Central Monitoring
SMWT	Display Middleware Trace
	Architecture and Technology • Middleware • Monitoring • Message Flow
SMWTAD	Set up Middleware Trace
	Architecture and Technology • Middleware • Monitoring • Message Flow
ST06	OS Monitor

D Coding Examples for Chapter 6

This appendix contains commented coding examples for exchanging custom data, as described in Chapter 6, *Exchanging Customer-Specific Data*. These examples (exchange of book data between SAP R/3 and SAP CRM) are only used to illustrate what has been described in Chapter 6. However, you can adapt them to your specific requirements and use them as templates for your own coding.

D.1 Extracting the Book Data from the R/3 System

```
FUNCTION ZBUCH_EXTRACT.
*"----------------------------------------------------
*"*"Locale interface:
*"  IMPORTING
*"    VALUE(I_OBJ_NAME) LIKE  BAPICRMOBJ-OBJ_NAME
*"    VALUE(I_BAPICRMDH1) LIKE BAPICRMDH1 STRUCTURE
*"      BAPICRMDH1
*"  EXPORTING
*"      VALUE(E_STATUS) LIKE  BAPICRMEXP-STATUS_EXT
*"  TABLES
*"      TI_TABLES STRUCTURE  CRMTABLES
*"      TI_RELATION STRUCTURE  CRMRELA OPTIONAL
*"      TI_RANGE STRUCTURE  CRMSELSTR OPTIONAL
*"----------------------------------------------------

* Declaration of required internal tables
* Internal table LT_CONDITION for storing the
* WHERE clause for a dynamic SELECT statement:
  DATA LT_CONDITION LIKE MCONDITION OCCURS 0
    WITH HEADER LINE.

* Internal table LT_ZBUCH for temporary storage of
* the result of the dynamic SELECT statement:
  DATA LT_ZBUCH LIKE ZBUCH OCCURS 0 WITH HEADER LINE.

* Internal table LT_BAPIMTCS for converting the
* result set:
```

```
DATA LT_BAPIMTCS LIKE BAPIMTCS OCCURS 0
   WITH HEADER LINE.
DATA LT_MESSAGES LIKE BAPICRMMSG OCCURS 0
   WITH HEADER LINE.

* Variables
DATA LV_LOAD_HEADER LIKE BAPICRMDH2 VALUE IS INITIAL.
DATA LV_BLOCKNO LIKE BAPICRMDH2-BLOCKNO
   VALUE IS INITIAL.
DATA LV_RECORDNO LIKE BAPICRMDH2-RECORDNO
   VALUE IS INITIAL.
DATA LAST_AUTHOR LIKE ZBUCH-AUTOR VALUE IS INITIAL.
DATA LV_RECS_FOUND LIKE SY-DBCNT VALUE IS INITIAL.
DATA LV_LASTBLOCK TYPE C VALUE IS INITIAL.
DATA LV_FORCE_ERROR TYPE C VALUE IS INITIAL.
DATA LV_USE_CRMMWTST LIKE CRM_PARA-XFELD
   VALUE IS INITIAL.

* Check filter conditions contained in
*  TI_RANGE for logical correctness
REFRESH LT_CONDITION.
LOOP AT TI_RANGE.
  IF TI_RANGE-TABLE <> 'ZBUCH'.
    MESSAGE E048(C_) WITH TI_RANGE-TABLE.
  ENDIF.
ENDLOOP.

* Structure of WHERE clause for dynamic SELECT
CALL FUNCTION 'CRS_CREATE_WHERE_CONDITION'
   TABLES
      ti_range = ti_range
      to_cond  = lt_condition.

* Populate header structure
CALL FUNCTION 'CRS_FILL_CRMDH2_FROM_DH1'
   EXPORTING
      I_BAPICRMDH1 = I_BAPICRMDH1
      I_LASTBLOCK  = ' '
      I_BLOCKNO    = LV_BLOCKNO
      I_RECORDNO   = LV_RECORDNO
      I_UPLOADSTAT = 'S'
   IMPORTING
      E_BAPICRMDH2 = LV_LOAD_HEADER.

* Read data from database
```

```
* The data is read in blocks based on the block size
* set in the adapter. The last value
* must be stored internally.
  CLEAR LAST_AUTHOR.
  DO. "for all blocks
   LV_LOAD_HEADER-BLOCKNO = LV_LOAD_HEADER-BLOCKNO + 1.
    SELECT * FROM ZBUCH
       UP TO I_BAPICRMDH1-BLOCKSIZE ROWS
       INTO TABLE LT_ZBUCH
       WHERE ( AUTOR > LAST_AUTHOR )
       AND (LT_CONDITION) ORDER BY PRIMARY KEY.
       IF SY-DBCNT LT I_BAPICRMDH1-BLOCKSIZE.
         LV_LOAD_HEADER-LASTBLOCK = 'X'.
         LV_RECS_FOUND = SY-DBCNT.
       ELSE.
         LV_RECS_FOUND = I_BAPICRMDH1-BLOCKSIZE.
       ENDIF.
       READ TABLE LT_ZBUCH INDEX LV_RECS_FOUND.
       MOVE LT_ZBUCH-AUTOR TO LAST_AUTHOR.

* Call mapping module between data and
* BAPIMTCS container
    CALL FUNCTION 'ZMAP_ZBUCH_TO_BAPIMTCS'
       EXPORTING
         I_OBJ_NAME    = 'ZMADP_BUCH'
         I_BAPICRMDH1  = I_BAPICRMDH1
       TABLES
         TI_ZBUCH      = LT_ZBUCH
         TE_BAPIMTCS   = LT_BAPIMTCS.

* Call CRS_SEND_TO_SERVER for the actual
* download into the CRM system
    CALL FUNCTION 'CRS_SEND_TO_SERVER'
       EXPORTING
         I_OBJ_NAME       = 'ZMADP_BUCH'
         I_BAPICRMDH2     = LV_LOAD_HEADER
         I_OBJ_CLASS      = 'ZBUCH_CLASS'
       TABLES
         T_BAPISTRUCTURES = LT_BAPIMTCS
         T_MESSAGES       = LT_MESSAGES
       EXCEPTIONS
         DATA_NOT_SENT    = 1
         OTHERS           = 2.

* After each block a COMMIT WORK must be
```

```
* triggered. This triggers the actual qRFC step.
   COMMIT WORK.
   IF LV_LOAD_HEADER-LASTBLOCK = 'X'.
     EXIT.
   ENDIF.
  ENDDO.
ENDFUNCTION.
```

D.2 Mapping the Extracted Data to the BAPIMTCS Container in SAP R/3

```
FUNCTION ZMAP_ZBUCH_TO_BAPIMTCS.
*"-------------------------------------------------------
* Local interface:
* IMPORTING
*   VALUE(I_OBJ_NAME) LIKE  BAPICRMOBJ-OBJ_NAME
*   VALUE(I_BAPICRMDH1) LIKE BAPICRMDH1
*              STRUCTURE BAPICRMDH1
*"  EXPORTING
*"     REFERENCE(E_STATUS) LIKE  BAPICRMEXP-STATUS_EXT
*"  TABLES
*"      TI_ZBUCH STRUCTURE  ZBUCH
*"      TE_BAPIMTCS STRUCTURE  BAPIMTCS
*"-------------------------------------------------------

* Move to Unicode environments
* Field-symbols
field-symbols: <source> type x,
               <target> type x.

* Declaration of the variable
DATA LV_ZBUCH LIKE ZBUCH.

* Loop at table ZBUCH to populate the fields of the
* BAPIMTCS container.
LOOP AT TI_ZBUCH INTO LV_ZBUCH.
    TE_BAPIMTCS-TABNAME = 'ZBUCH'.
    TE_BAPIMTCS-SEGTYPE = 'DA'.
    TE_BAPIMTCS-OBJKEY = LV_ZBUCH-AUTOR.
    TE_BAPIMTCS-RELKEY = LV_ZBUCH-AUTOR.
    ASSIGN LV_ZBUCH TO <source> TYPE 'X'.
    ASSIGN TE_BAPIMTCS-DATA TO <target> TYPE 'X'.
    Move <source> to <target>.
```

```
      APPEND TE_BAPIMTCS.
ENDLOOP.
ENDFUNCTION.
```

D.3   Mapping in SAP CRM

```
FUNCTION ZM_MAP_BAPIMTCS_TO_ZMBDOC_BUCH.
*"----------------------------------------------------
*"*"Local interface:
*"  IMPORTING
*"     VALUE(I_OBJNAME) TYPE  SMO_OBJNAM
*"     VALUE(I_OBJCLASS) TYPE  SMO_OBJCLA
*"     VALUE(I_SENDER_SITE_TYPE) TYPE  SMW1STID
*"     VALUE(I_SENDER_SITE_ID) TYPE  SMO_SITEID
*"     VALUE(I_NO_PROCESS) TYPE  SMODLTPROC
*"  EXPORTING
*"     VALUE(HEADER) TYPE  SMW3_FHD
*"     VALUE(REF_MESSAGE) TYPE REF TO  DATA
*"     VALUE(REF_MESSAGE_EXT) TYPE REF TO  DATA
*"     VALUE(OBJECT_LINKS) TYPE  TRL_BORID
*"     VALUE(E_DO_NOT_CALL_GDH) TYPE  CRM_PARA-XFELD
*"     REFERENCE(E_FLOW_LUW_HANDLING) TYPE  XFELD
*"  TABLES
*"      TI_BAPIMTCS STRUCTURE  BAPIMTCS
*"      T_MESSAGES STRUCTURE  BAPICRMMSG
*"      TI_KEY_INFO STRUCTURE  BAPICRMKEY
*"      TI_OTHER_INFO STRUCTURE  BAPIEXTC
*"      TI_BAPIIDLIST STRUCTURE  BAPIIDLIST
*"  CHANGING
*"     VALUE(E_BAPICRMDH2) TYPE  BAPICRMDH2
*"     VALUE(ERROR_SEGMENTS) TYPE  SMW_ERRTAB
*"----------------------------------------------------
** Data declarations for BDoc and DDIC component of
** mBDoc and required references
* Classic BDoc part
  DATA message TYPE ZMBDOC_BUCH000 VALUE IS INITIAL.
  FIELD-SYMBOLS <bdoc> TYPE ZMBDOC_BUCH000 .

* Declarations for the classic (DDIC)part
  DATA message_ext TYPE ZMBUCH_EXTENSION
    VALUE IS INITIAL.
  FIELD-SYMBOLS <ddic> TYPE ZMBUCH_EXTENSION.

* Declaration for individual segments
```

```
      DATA segment_line
        type line of ZMBDOC_BUCH000-ZBUCH_ROOT.
      DATA ext_line
        type line of ZMBUCH_EXTENSION-ZMBUCH_ROOT.
      DATA transfer_structure like ZCRMBUCH.
      DATA lv_task type c.

* Create ABAP-OO references
      CREATE DATA ref_message LIKE message.
      ASSIGN ref_message->* TO <bdoc>.
      CREATE DATA ref_message_ext LIKE message_ext.
      ASSIGN ref_message_ext->* TO <ddic>.

* Move BAPIMTCS container to
* destination mBDoc ZMBDOC_BUCH
      LOOP AT TI_BAPIMTCS WHERE TABNAME = 'ZBUCH'.

* Populate classic mBDoc part as
* defined in BDoc Modeler
        MOVE TI_BAPIMTCS-DATA TO transfer_structure.

* Evaluate key information
        IF E_BAPICRMDH2-DWNLOADTYP = 'D'.
          READ TABLE TI_KEY_INFO
                WITH KEY TABNAME = 'ZBUCH'
                R3K_NAMES = 'AUTOR'
                R3K_VALUES = transfer_structure-AUTOR.
*         if sy-subrc eq 0.
*           * MOVE TI_KEY_INFO-sfa_key TO lv_sfakey.
*         endif.
        ENDIF.

* Consider the TASK field
        CASE E_BAPICRMDH2-DWNLOADTYP.
          WHEN 'I'.
            lv_task = 'I'.
          WHEN 'D'.
            lv_task = E_BAPICRMDH2-delta_op.
        ENDCASE.
        MOVE transfer_structure-autor
          TO segment_line-autor.

        APPEND segment_line to <bdoc>-zbuch_root.

* Populate the extension part
```

```
      ext_line-data-autor = transfer_structure-autor.
      ext_line-data-buchtitel =
          transfer_structure-buchtitel.
      ext_line-datax-autor = 'X'.
      ext_line-datax-buchtitel = 'X'.
      ext_line-control-task = e_bapicrmdh2-delta_op.
      APPEND ext_line to <ddic>-zmbuch_root.
    ENDLOOP.
    CALL METHOD CL_SMW_MFLOW=>SET_HEADER_FIELDS
      EXPORTING
        IN_BDOC_TYPE = 'ZMBDOC_BUCH'
      IMPORTING
        OUT_HEADER   = header.

ENDFUNCTION.
```

D.4   Validating Received Book Data in SAP CRM

```
FUNCTION ZMBUCH_VALIDATION.
*"----------------------------------------------------
*"*"Local interface:
*"  IMPORTING
*"     VALUE(OPTIONS) TYPE  SMW3FOPT OPTIONAL
*"  EXPORTING
*"     REFERENCE(STATUS) TYPE  SMWVALSTAT
*"  CHANGING
*"     REFERENCE(TRANSACTION_MESSAGE)
*"        TYPE  ZMBDOC_BUCH000
*"     REFERENCE(MESSAGE_EXT) TYPE  ZMBUCH_EXTENSION
*"     REFERENCE(ERROR_SEGMENTS)
*"        TYPE  SMW_ERRTAB OPTIONAL
*"     REFERENCE(OBJECT_LINES) TYPE  TRL_BORID OPTIONAL
*"     REFERENCE(HEADER) TYPE  SMW3_FHD
*"  EXCEPTIONS
*"     TECHNICAL_ERROR
*"----------------------------------------------------
DATA lt_messages TYPE TABLE OF bapicrmmsg.
DATA lt_zbuch_insert TYPE zcrmbuch OCCURS 0.
DATA lt_zbuch_update TYPE zcrmbuch OCCURS 0.
DATA lt_zbuch_delete TYPE zcrmbuch OCCURS 0.
DATA lv_zbuch TYPE zcrmbuch VALUE IS INITIAL.
DATA lv_zbuch_seg TYPE zmbuch_root.

* Transfer the data of the extension part into internal
```

```
* tables depending on TASK
LOOP AT message_ext-zmbuch_root INTO lv_zbuch_seg.
  CLEAR lv_zbuch.
  MOVE-CORRESPONDING lv_zbuch_seg-data TO lv_zbuch.
  CASE lv_zbuch_seg-control-task.
   WHEN 'U'. "Update existing entries
     APPEND lv_zbuch to lt_zbuch_update.
   WHEN 'I'. "Insert new entries
     APPEND lv_zbuch to lt_zbuch_insert.
   WHEN 'D'. "Delete entries
     APPEND lv_zbuch TO lt_zbuch_delete.
  ENDCASE.
ENDLOOP.

* Update database table from
* internal ABAP tables
UPDATE ZCRMBUCH FROM TABLE lt_zbuch_update.
INSERT ZCRMBUCH FROM TABLE lt_zbuch_insert.
DELETE ZCRMBUCH FROM TABLE lt_zbuch_delete.

*Return status to the flow
status = cl_smw_mflow=>c_valstat_success.

ENDFUNCTION.
```

E   Analysis Roadmaps

This appendix provides an overview of the analysis roadmaps for performance bottlenecks during a mass change described in Chapter 13, *Performing Optimized Mass Changes*.

The purpose of these roadmaps is to provide you with a procedure that enables you to monitor and, if necessary, optimize your SAP CRM Middleware during a mass change. Needless to say, the roadmaps aren't a solution to all conceivable problems; instead, they are intended to act as a kind of orientation guide.

E.1   Checklist

The left-hand column of Table E.1 lists the transactions that you should call regularly for monitoring purposes during the course of a mass change. The center column describes indicators of possible problems. Should one of these indicators occur in your system, the right-hand column tells you which analysis roadmap to use.

Trans-action	Indicator	Further Action
SM50/ SM66	All work processes or a constantly increasing number of work processes are permanently busy. Work processes remain in action "sequential read" for a long period of time.	Analyze work process utilization Ø Figure E.1, *Work Process Analysis*
SMQ2	There are thousands of CSA and/or R3A queues and the number is constantly increasing. The number of entries in a queue is very high and is continually increasing.	Analyze queue processing Ø Figure E.2, *Inbound Queue Processing I*, and Figure E.3, *Inbound Queue Processing II*

Table E.1 During a Mass Change

Trans-action	Indicator	Further Action
SMOH-QUEUE	The number of entries in queues is continually increasing. The queue entries are processed slowly.	R&R optimization → Figure E.4, *Replication & Realignment*
SMW02/ SMW02a	The number of BDocs showing an error status is continually increasing.	BDoc error analysis
ST06	The CPU idle time is below 20 %.	Optimize parallelization → Figure E.5, *CPU Bottleneck*

Table E.1 During a Mass Change (cont.)

E.2   Analysis Roadmaps

The icons used in the flow diagrams have the following meanings:

▶ **Monitor icon**
  Analysis action — start the specified transaction.

▶ **Question mark**
  Point of decision — if you answer "Yes" to the question in this line, then follow the indented path.

▶ **Tool icon**
  Final point of analysis — carry out the action specified.

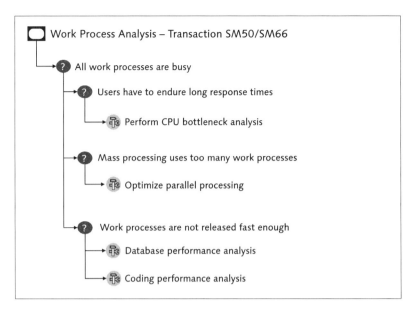

Figure E.1 Work Process Analysis

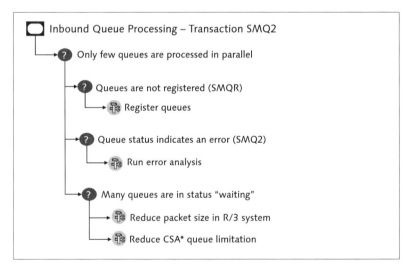

Figure E.2 Inbound Queue Processing I

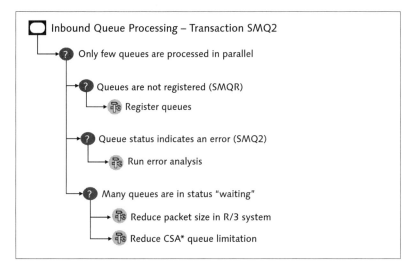

Figure E.3 Inbound Queue Processing II

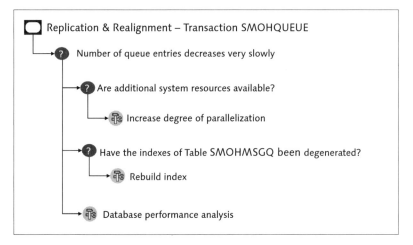

Figure E.4 Replication & Realignment

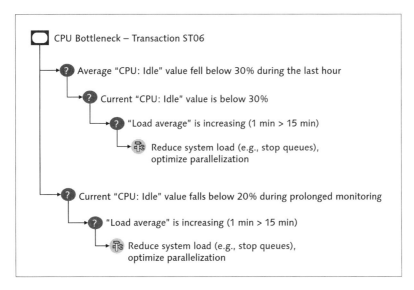

Figure E.5 CPU Bottleneck

F Authors

Juliane Bode studied Information Technology at the Technical University of Braunschweig, Germany. She worked for three years in software development before moving to SAP in the year 2000, where she initially worked as a Business Development Architect on strategic CRM development projects. Since 2004, she has worked as a De-Escalation Architect in the Center of Expertise (CoE) for CRM in Active Global Support. Her main responsibility is to support critical customer projects, both on-site and remotely. The technical focus of her work is CRM Middleware.

Stephan Golze studied Information Technology at the Technical University of Karlsruhe, Germany. After completing his studies, he worked as an E-Commerce Consultant at various firms over a period of eight years. In 2001, he moved to SAP to work in the Center of Expertise (CoE) for CRM in Active Global Support. Besides the ongoing development of various services, the focus of his work was and is to deliver analysis and optimization services to customers, both on-site and remotely. Stephan has also been active as a De-Escalation Architect in highly critical customer situations. He now heads up the CRM Middleware and Mobile Sales team in the regional CoE for Europe, Africa, and the Middle East.

Dr. Thomas Schröder studied Physics and Chemistry, and graduated with a doctorate in Physics from the Max Planck Institute for Flow Research (now the Max Planck Institute for Dynamics and Self-Organization) and the University of Göttingen, Germany. He joined SAP in 1999 after working for some years in research projects in various international institutions. At SAP, he first worked in Active Global Support in the Regional Support Center Europe for the SD area, before moving to the Center of Expertise (CoE) in 2003, where he took on responsibility for the CRM Middleware and Mobile Sales area. In this capacity, he worked on a broad range of integration problems in a variety of customer projects, both on-site and remotely, in the area of messages. He is now a Service Architect and is head of the Business Process Integration team in the Global CoE.

Index

.NET Connector 45

A

AC extract 119, 281
  bulk extract 283
  unfiltered extract 283
AC_EXTRACT queue 111
Adapter 63
Adapter framework 63
Adapter object 64
  activating and deactivating 68
  assignment to a BDoc type 65
  block size 65
  business object 64
  condition object 64
  customizing object 64
  filter settings 72
  initial flow context 69
  mapping module CRM → R/3 73
  object class 67
  parent objects 73
  tables/structures 70
Administration console 31, 90
  improvements 365
  wizard 98
Analysis roadmap
  CPU bottleneck analysis 345, 397
  inbound queue processing 336, 337, 395
  R&R optimization 341
  work process analysis 334, 395
ARFCRDATA, Table 47, 50
ARFCRSTATE, Table 46, 47
ARFCSDATA, Table 46, 47, 49
ARFCSSTATE, Table 46, 47

B

Background RFC 367
BAPI structure 25
BAPIMTCS 171
BDoc 37, 38
  assignment of segment and database 143
  class 135

error status 148
final Status 149
instance 140
interim status 148
release 146
robust data storage 152
sendbits 147
standard field 147
static WHERE clause 144
status 147
task type 147
type 140
BDoc instance 40, 140
BDoc link
  adjacent functionality 316
  avoiding 315
  reorganization 314
BDoc merge 364
BDoc message 39
BDoc Modeler 140
BDoc release, WHERE clause 146
BDoc statistics, reorganization 309
BDoc store 75, 79
BDoc type 26, 39
  lock 146
bgRFC → see Background RFC 367
Block size 278
Bulk extract 283
Bulk message 123
Business document 38
Business object, adapter object 64

C

CDB 31, 107
CDB service 31, 107, 108
Checkbox structure 175
Classic part→ see mBDoc 137
Communication monitor, reorganization 310
Condition object, adapter object 64
Confirmation message 122
ConnTrans 32, 74
  transfer duration 272
Consolidated database → see CDB 31
CP_CODEPAGE 302

Creating a database table 172
Creating an object class 181
CRM_MAX_QUEUE_NUMBER_DELT
  A, parameter 204, 207
CRMPAROLTP, Table
  CRM_XML_BACKGROUND_PROCES
    SING_ON 299
CRMPAROLTP, table
  number of inbound queues 204
CRMQNAMES, Tabelle
  FLDOFFSET, Feld 202
CRMQNAMES, Table 61, 204
  LENGTH, field 202
CRMRFCPAR, Table
  XML control 297
CRMSUBTAB, Table 67, 171
CRS_FIRST_DOWNLOAD_TRIGGER
  171
CSA queue 29, 101
Current state message 122
Customizing object, adapter object
  64

D

Data collector 253, 281, 295
  reorganization 312
Data Integrity Manager 134
Data transfer
  delta 63
  initial 63
DB statistics 261
DBSTATC, Table 262
Default pool 276
Deletion message 123
  avoiding 247
Delta data transfer 63
Destination
  excluding 127
  parameters 127
  registering and deregistering 127
DIMa → see Data Integrity Manager
  134
Disk subsystem 274
Distribution
  bulk 238
  intelligent 237
  intelligent, switching to bulk 242
  intelligent, without filter criteria 241

Distribution model 31
Dynamic mapping 76

E

Error Handler 78, 81, 82
EXEMODE, Parameter 54
Extended Markup Language → see
  XML 297
Extension part→ see mBDoc 137
EXTRACT queue 111
EXTRACTBLK queue 111
Extractor 171

F

Flow 37, 40
  context 40, 179
  definition 42

G

Generated mobile inbound adapter
  74
Generic mobile inbound adapter 74
GNRWB, Transaction 304
Groupware adapter
  GWA_01 156
  GWA_02 156
Groupware connector → see Groupware integration 158
Groupware integration
  analysis 164
  client-client scenario 155
  data queue, primary 160
  data queue, secondary 160
  folder, private 156
  folder, public 156
  groupware adapter 156
  groupware connector 158
  groupware connector proxy 158
  MapBox 157
  MapBox, log files 164
  MapBox, RFC destination 158
  MBMANDTSTORE, table 162
  overview 155
  payload interface 158
  server-server scenario 155
  system queues 160, 164

trace of internal SyncPoint   165
trace of payload interface   166
userlist.xml   162
GWI → see Groupware integration
  155

H

Hardware Bottleneck   209

I

Inbound adapter   26, 37, 63, 69
Inbound processing   37
  data from R/3   27
  mobile client data   35
Inbound queue   26, 33, 37, 44, 48
  dependencies   231
  deregistering   54
  details   59
  entries   60
  of mobile client   32
  overview   56
  parameters   54
  reduce number of queues   200
  registering   52
  slow processing   199
  status   58
Inbound queue name
  data from mobile clients   61
  data from SAP R/3   61
  for CSA queues   101
Inbound queue scheduler   45, 51
  activating   52
  performance   199
  status   51
Inbound scheduler   51
Index fragmentation   262
Index quality   262
Initial data transfer   63
Initial load   183
Integration model
  message exchange   136
  synchronization   136
Interlinkage   98, 248

J

Java Connector (JCo)   45

K

KEEP pool   276
Kernel application statistics   220

L

Logical Unit of Work   47
Lookup table   31, 90, 252
LUW   47

M

MapBox → see Groupware integration
  157
Mapping   75
  BAPI container in mBDoc   180
  dynamic   76
  mBDoc to sBDoc   31
  static   75, 139
Mapping function module   26
Mapping method   34
Mass change   188
  planned   326
  unplanned   326, 327
MAX_PACKAGE_SIZE, parameter
  278
MAXTIME, Parameter   54, 353
mBDoc   26, 38, 135
  classic part   137
  creating the classic part   177
  creating the extension part   174
  extension part   137
MBMANDTSTORE, table   162
Message flow statistics   224
  kernel application statistics   220
  Middleware message flow statistics
    221
  switching on/off   220
Messaging BDoc → see mBDoc   26, 38
Messaging flow   101
Middleware message flow statistics
  221
Middleware trace   228
  displaying a trace   229
  Reorganization   309
  setting trace levels   228
Mobile adapter   107
Mobile application BDoc   136

Mobile bridge   30, 90, 102, 104
Mobile inbound adapter   34
  generated   74
  generic   74
Mobile outbound adapter   31, 122

N

Naming for queues
  advantages/disadvantages   206
Neighbour functionality   315
NRETRY, Parameter   54

O

Online database   26, 37
Outbound adapters   69, 90, 102, 104
Outbound processing   89
  for mobile clients   32
  for R/3   29
Outbound qRFC with recipient list
  269
  benefits   270
Outbound queue   29, 31, 48, 89, 124
  displaying an overview   128
  displaying details   130
  displaying entries   131
  in R/3   25
  of mobile client   33
  status   129
Outbound queue name
  additonal ones   134
  data to mobile clients   132
  data to R/3   132
Outbound Scheduler   125

P

Parallel processing, optimizing the
  middleware   318
Payload interface → see Groupware
  integration   158
Performance analysis   215
  SMWMFLOW   219
  SMWT   228
Publication   93

Q

QIN Scheduler → see Inbound queue
  scheduler   51
QOUT Scheduler   125
  activating   126
  status   126
QREFTID, Table   49
qRFC   45, 48, 125
  monitor for inbound queues   56
qRFC Monitor
  for Outbound Queues   128
qRFC monitor for inbound queues   45
Query BDoc → see Mobile application
  BDoc   136
Queue naming
  changing the naming for queues   201
Queue, stopping   257
Queued RFC → see qRFC   45

R

R&R   285
  definition   235
  DEPENDENCY queue   360
  distribution-relevant fields   238
  internal optimization   264
  new improvements   360
  new queue framework   360
  optimizing a mass change   267
  parallel processing of queues   361
  parallelizing queue processing   256
  processing queues in blocks   362
  queues   236
  realignment   235
  replication   235
  replication wrapper   238
R&R queue   111
  displaying   111
  starting and stopping   114
  status   113
R&R queue demon   112
  starting and stopping   113
  status   113
R&R queue framework   110
R&R service   31, 107
R/3 outbound adapter   29
R3AC1, Transaction   64, 182
R3AC3, Transaction   64, 180

R3AC5, Transaction 64

R3AC6, Transaction
    controlling the reorganization pro-
      cess 310
    queue parallelization 256

R3AM1, Transaction 183

R3AR2, Transaction
    one-time request 314

R3AS, Transaction 183

REALIGN queue 111

Realignment 31, 109

Rejection message 78, 123

Remote Function Call → see RFC 45

Reorganization
    BDoc links 314
    BDoc messages 308
    BDoc statistics 309
    data collector 312
    key generation 309
    middleware trace 309
    of data for sites that cannot be activa-
      ted 313
    request 314
    SAP_MW_REORG, variant 308
    SMO6_REORG 308
    SMO6_REORG2 308
    SMW3* tables 308
    standard variant 308
    statistics of the CommStation sessions
      310
    subscription agent 313

Replication 31, 108, 114
    bulk 115
    intelligent 116

Replication & Realignment 287

Replication & Realignment → see R&R

Replication & Realignment service →
    see R&R service 31

Replication model 90
    optimization 239, 248
    optimizing interlinkages 248
    optimizing the bulk publications 240

Replication object 90

Replication object type 91, 92
    bulk 96
    Dependent 97
    Intelligent 96
    Simple Bulk (MESG) 95
    Simple Intelligent (MESG) 96
    Simple Intelligent (SYNC) 96

Replication service 29, 102
    mBDoc 103
    sBDoc 114

Replication wrapper
    mBDoc 103
    sBDoc 114

RFC 45

RFC libraries 45

RFC server group 209, 257
    assign 213
    create 210
    optimal number 325
    parameters 211
    profile parameters 212

RFC Software Development Kit 45

RSANAORA, Report 263

RSRLDREL, program 314

RSTRFCQD, Report 355

RSTRFCQDS, Report 355

RZ12, Transaction 210

S

SBDM, Transaction 74, 77, 140, 177

sBDoc 30, 38, 135
    block size 278
    structure 136

Scheduler, tRFC 46

SDIMA, Transaction 134

SDK, (RFC) Software Development Kit
    45

SE11, Transaction 172

Segment, field assignment 136

Service, generating 182

Setting up a logical destination 216

Site 93
    deactivating 244
    mass deactivation 246

Site type 94
    site decativation not supported 313

Sizing 277

SM50, Transaction
    occupancy of the work processes 332

SM59, Transaction 54, 126
    setting up a logical destination 216

SMO 275

SMO8FD, Transaction 42, 79

SMO9_KYTBL, Table
    reorganization 309

SMOE_BULK_SITE_ACTIVATION,
   Report 285
SMOEAC, Transaction 61, 90, 132
   AC extract 281
   XML optimization 303
SMOECK, Transaction 241
SMOEGENDET, Table 100
SMOEGENHEA, Table 100
SMOEGENLOG, Table
   reorganization 313
SMOEJOBID, Table
   reorganization 310
SMOFFILTAB, Table 72
SMOFINICON, Table 69
SMOFOBJCLA, Table 68
SMOFOBJECT, Table 64, 65, 68
SMOFOBJPAR, Table 73
SMOFPARSFA, Table 301, 310
   deactivating mBDoc links 315
   processing R&R queues in bloks 362
SMOFPARSFA, table
   block size 278
SMOFQFIND, Table 204
SMOFQNAMES, Table 132
SMOFSUBTAB, Table 73
SMOFUPLMAP, Table 73
SMOGGEN, Transaction 182, 244
SMOHILTP, Table 99
SMOHJOBQ, Table 259
SMOHLUBULK, Table 96, 238
SMOHMSGQ, Table 111, 259
   optimizing the access path 259
SMOHMSGST, Table 259
SMOHPUBL, Table 93
SMOHQTAB, Table 61, 132
SMOHQUEUE, Transaction 111, 113,
   114, 236, 243
   AC extract 282
   block size 278
   Stop queue 353
SMOHREPOBJ, Table 92
SMOHSGQST, Table 111
SMOHSITEID, Table 94
SMOHSITEQ, Table 111, 259
SMOHSUBSCR, Table 95
SMOHSUBSIT, Table 95
SMOJDC, Transaction 255
SMOJDCPROC, Table
   reorganization 312
SMQ1, Transaction 128

SMQ2, Transaction 56
SMQR, Transaction 51
   changing RFC server group 213
   MAXTIME 353
   setting up a logical destination 216
SMQS, Transaction 125
SMW01, Transaction 83, 316
   jumping to the Middleware trace
      231
SMW01, transaction
   DEBUGMODE 152
SMW1SPRVDR, Table 313
SMW3*, Table
   reorganization 308
SMW3BDOCIF, Table 43, 79, 179
SMW3FDBDOC, Table 44, 105
SMW3FDBDOC, Transaction 44, 105
SMW3FDCUST, Table 44
SMW3FDCUST, Transaction 44
SMW3FDIF, Transaction 44, 76, 79,
   179
SMW3FDSTD, Table 44
SMW3FDSTD, Transaction 44
SMWMCOMM, Transaction 310
SMWMFLOW, Transaction 219
   message flow statistics 224
   workload statistics 221
SMWMSESSHT, Table 310
SMWMSESSIN, Table 310
SMWT, Transaction 229, 309
SMWT_TRC, Table
   reorganization 309
SMWTAD, Transaction 228
SPRO, Transaction 82
ST03N, Transaction 309, 310
ST06, Transaction
   Idle time 342
   Load average 344
Static mapping 75
Storage Area Network 274
Storage quality 276
SUBCHECK queue 111
Subscription 94
   changing the assignment of sites 120
Subscription agent 99
   reorganization 313
Subscription generators 99
Synchronization 63
Synchronization BDoc → see sBDoc
   38

Synchronization flow   90, 107
System landscape   187
  heterogeneous   297
  homogeneous   297
  inhomogeneous   297
System monitoring   330
System Optimization Services   275

T

TDELAY, Parameter   54
TID   47
Transaction Identifier   47
Transactional Remote Function Call →
  see tRFC   45
Transactional RFC → see tRFC
tRFC   45, 46
TRFCQDATA, Table   50
TRFCQIN, Table   50
TRFCQOUT, Table   49, 50
TRFCQSTATE, Table   50
TRFCRSTATE, Table   50
TRFCSDATA, Table   50
TRFCSSTATE, Table   50
TSMW3_STAT, table   147

U

Upload   63
USERDEST, Parameter   54

V

Validation   37, 79, 179
  data from R/3   27
  mobile client data   35
Validation service   26, 79

W

WHERE clause→ see BDoc   144
Wizard   98
Workload statistics   221
  switching on/off   220

X

XML   297

between CRM Server and a mobile client   300
between R/3 and CRM   297
code page conversion   300
data exchange between R/3 and CRM   297
data exchange with mobile clients   300
decoupling the application from the conversion   299
performance increase for mobile client data exchange   300
restrictions regarding optimization   305
synchronous RFC   298

Z

ZAP message   123, 284

Detailed methodology for developing and implementing functional and load tests

Functionality and implementation of eCATT, SAP Solution Manager, SAP Test Data Migration Server, and more

367 pp., 2007, 69,95 Euro / US$ 69,95
ISBN 978-1-59229-127-4

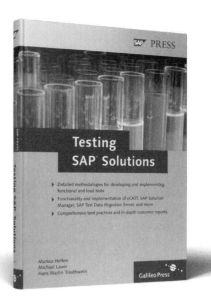

Testing SAP Solutions

www.sap-press.com

Markus Helfen, Michael Lauer,
Hans Martin Trauthwein

Testing SAP Solutions

This book provides you with comprehensive coverage of all testing requirements and techniques necessary for implementing, upgrading or operating SAP solutions. Readers get an overview of all existing tools, their functionalities, and best practices for utilization. The authors focus mainly on SAP Solution Manager, Test Workbench and eCATT, and their use in functional and load tests is highlighted in detail.

>> www.sap-press.de/1408

Interested in reading more?

Please visit our Web site for all
new book releases from SAP PRESS.

www.sap-press.com